An Official Cambridge IELTS Course

UPDATED
DIGITAL PACK

GW00771020

MINDSET
FOR IELTS

STUDENT'S BOOK
WITH DIGITAL PACK
Level 2

MAP OF THE BOOK

MEET THE AUTHORS

With a thorough understanding of the essential skills required to succeed in the IELTS test, let our team of experts guide you on your IELTS journey.

Greg Archer

Greg Archer is an experienced, DELTA-qualified teacher and teacher trainer who began teaching *IELTS* at International House in London, where he trained and qualified as an *IELTS* Examiner in both Writing and Speaking. After moving to Cambridge in 2013, he has been working at an international college, at various times managing the English Language department, developing appropriate courses to run alongside A Level and GCSE study, and primarily teaching *IELTS* and English for Academic Purposes classes to students whose ambition is to enter a UK or English-speaking university.

Lucy Passmore

Lucy began teaching English in 2002 in the UK and Spain, where she prepared young learners for Cambridge English exams. She has been a tutor of English for Academic Purposes since 2008, and has taught on *IELTS* preparation courses in addition to preparing international students to start degree courses at Brunel University and King's College London. Lucy is currently based at King's College London, where she teaches on foundation programmes for international students, provides in-sessional support in academic writing for current students and contributes to materials and course design.

The *Mindset for IELTS* authors have extensive experience teaching in the UK and globally. They have helped prepare students for the *IELTS* test from all over the world, including:

China, UK, Pakistan, Middle East, Republic of Korea, Italy, Indonesia, Sri Lanka, Kazakhstan, Greece, Russia, Spain

Peter Crosthwaite

Peter has worked in the TESOL and applied linguistics fields for 13 years. His previous experience includes writing and consultancy work with various publishers, two sessions as Director of Studies for language schools in the UK, over six years' experience in the Korean EFL context, and teaching and supervision experience at the University of Cambridge. He worked as an Assistant Professor at the Centre for Applied English Studies (CAES), University of Hong Kong, where he is the coordinator of the MA Applied Linguistics (MAAL) and the MA TESOL. He is currently working at the School of Languages and Cultures at the University of Queensland. He has worked on *IELTS* test preparation, publishing and materials development for over 10 years, with 4 years of experience as a qualified *IELTS* Examiner.

Natasha De Souza

Natasha has been involved in the ELT industry for 15 years – as a teacher, Director of Studies, Examiner and an Examinations Officer. She started teaching *IELTS* in 2006, when she worked on a University Pathway and Foundation Programme for a language school in Cambridge. More recently, as a Director of Studies and an Examinations Officer, she was responsible for giving guidance to students and teachers on how the *IELTS* test works and how best to prepare for it.

Jishan Uddin

Jishan has been an EFL teacher since 2001. He has taught on a range of courses in the UK and Spain, including general English, exam preparation and English for Academic Purposes (EAP) courses and is currently an EAP lecturer and academic module leader at King's College, London. He has extensive experience teaching *IELTS* preparation classes to students from around the world, particularly China, the Middle East and Kazakhstan. He also has experience in designing resources for language skills development as well as exam preparation and administration.

Susan Hutchison

Susan Hutchison has been an ESOL teacher and examiner for more than 30 years. She has taught overseas in Italy, Hungary and Russia. She now lives and works in Edinburgh, Scotland as an ESOL teacher in an independent school for girls. She has co-authored a number of course books, preparation and practice materials for both Cambridge English Language Assessment and *IELTS*. She has also developed online and interactive *IELTS* practice materials for the British Council.

Marc Loewenthal

Marc has been teaching for 35 years, mostly in the UK but also abroad in Greece, Russia, Middle East, Indonesia and Pakistan. He has taught in the public sector since 1990, mostly in further education and adult education, and more recently on pre-sessional EAP university courses. He has been a Speaking and Writing Examiner for over 25 years and has expert knowledge of *IELTS* requirements for university admission.

Claire Wijayatilake

Claire has been teaching English since 1988. She spent much of her career in Sri Lanka, including 16 years at British Council, Colombo. She became an *IELTS* Examiner in 1990 and examined regularly in Colombo and Malé, Maldives for almost 20 years. She worked as the *IELTS* Examiner Trainer for Sri Lanka, recruiting, training and monitoring examiners. She then moved into training and school leadership, serving as Teacher Trainer and Principal at various international schools. She returned to the UK in 2013 and worked for Middlesex University, where she started her materials writing career. She is currently a Visiting Lecturer at Westminster University, which allows her time to write. She has a PhD in Applied Linguistics and English Language Teaching from the University of Warwick.

HOW DOES MINDSET FOR IELTS WORK?

AVAILABLE AT FOUR LEVELS

FOUNDATION LEVEL	LEVEL 1 Target Band 5.5	LEVEL 2 Target Band 6.5	LEVEL 3 Target Band 7.5

CORE MATERIAL

- Student's Book (print and digital).
- Digital workbook that gives focused exam practice on all four skills: Reading, Writing, Listening and Speaking.

ADDITIONAL MATERIAL

- The online workbook can be used to reinforce knowledge in the classroom and improve IELTS skills as homework or during the lesson.
- The end of unit tests will help your teacher check your language development.
- The Practice Tests will help your teacher assess where you are in relation to the IELTS test.

TAILORED TO SUIT YOUR NEEDS

Mindset for IELTS gives teachers the ultimate flexibility to tailor courses to suit their context and the needs of their students.

GIVES TEACHERS CHOICE

- Course design means teachers can focus on either the skills or the topics that their students need the most help with.

CAMBRIDGE CORPUS-INFORMED

- Corpus-informed digital workbook helps students avoid common mistakes.

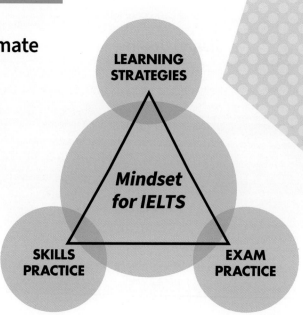

COURSE CONFIGURATIONS

The *Mindset for IELTS* course comprises 4 key components:

CORE TOPICS & SKILLS	**Student's Book (print and digital)** 8 topic-based units, organised by skill, provide 60-90 hours of teaching per level (levels 1, 2 and 3)
TESTS/ONLINE ASSESSMENT	Access to Cambridge English IELTS Academic practice tests online
DIGITAL WORKBOOK	8 hours of practice per skill, per level: • Speaking • Writing • Reading • Listening
EBOOK	• Ebook gives you all of the material in the Student's Book in a digital format

01▶ SKILLS MODULES

Practice per skill, including Reading, Writing, Listening, Speaking.

RECEPTIVE SKILLS Focus on sub-skill	PRINT	ONLINE
	Reading Listening	Different topic

PRODUCTIVE SKILLS Focus on active production	PRINT	ONLINE
	Writing Speak	Same topic

READING

IN THIS UNIT YOU WILL LEARN HOW TO

- skim a text quickly to understand the general idea
- scan a text for specific information to answer short-answer questions
- use skimming and scanning to locate the answer quickly
- understand and produce paraphrasing
- use the present continuous and present simple correctly.

LEAD-IN

01 A common topic in the exam is 'home'. Put these words under the correct heading in the table.

apartment	beach	bungalow	castle	ceiling	cellar	remote island
city centre	countryside	dining room	floor	garage	stone	glamorous
leather	mountains	mansion	marble	modern	simple	skyscraper
spacious	staircase	traditional	wood	window	gym	

Location	Building type	Style	Rooms	Parts of a room	Materials
	apartment				

02 In pairs, use the vocabulary from exercise 1 to help you describe your dream home.

My dream house would be on the beach near the sea. It would be a simple bungalow with wooden floors. It would have a large dining room ...

SKIMMING AND SCANNING

⊙ Skimming and scanning are important reading techniques which are very useful in IELTS. As time is limited in the exam, skimming and scanning help you to find the answers you need quickly.

You **skim** a text quickly to understand the **general idea**.

You **scan** a text quickly in order to find **specific information**.

03 ▸ **For each activity, decide whether you would use skimming or scanning.**

1 looking up a word in the dictionary *scanning*
2 browsing the internet for the latest news stories
3 choosing a book from a library or bookshop
4 finding a particular news story in a newspaper
5 finding the price of a product in a catalogue
6 looking through a magazine for an interesting article

TIP 03

Try to practise these or similar activities as much as possible. The more you practise, the better you will become at each technique.

04 ▸ **The home in the photo cost about one billion dollars to build. What do you like or dislike about the design?**

05 ▸ **Skim the text to understand the main ideas.**

TIP 05

You are only reading for the **main ideas** at this stage, so remember to ignore unknown words.

A Mukesh Ambani is one of the richest men in the world, and the first man to own a private residence costing more than one billion dollars to build. The home is on Altamout Road in Mumbai, one of the most expensive addresses in the world. Named after the mythical island Antilia, the property has 27 floors.

B The interior of the home is very glamorous and each floor is made from different materials to give an individual look. Marble floors, rare wood and fine rugs are just some of the design features used to create this extravagant home. The lotus flower and the sun are common symbols used throughout. Many of the rooms have floor-to-ceiling glass windows, offering spectacular views of Mumbai and the Arabian Sea.

C The skyscraper has a multi-storey garage with space for 168 cars. Alternatively, there are also three helipads on the roof of the building. The lobby has numerous reception areas and nine lifts. There are also several floors for dining, vast libraries and a health spa, including a gym, several swimming pools and yoga facilities. There is even an 'ice-room' which creates man-made snow, a Hindu prayer room and several floors of gardens.

D The Ambani residence is clearly designed to entertain guests. It has a theatre which seats 50, several guest bedrooms and a grand ballroom filled with chandeliers.

E The living quarters are on the top floors, because the family wanted as much sunlight as possible. The 400,000 ft^2 residence requires 600 staff, but all three Ambani children are required to clean their own rooms when they are at home.

F Several experts have criticised the architecture of this very expensive home, comparing it to an 'unstable pile of books'. Mrs Ambani, however, describes her home as 'an elevated house on top of a garden' and 'a modern home with an Indian heart'.

*helipad - *a place where a single helicopter can take off and land*

06 ▷ **Answer these questions.**

1 When you were skim reading the text, which of these types of word did you focus on: prepositions, articles, names, verbs, adjectives, numbers?

2 Discuss with a partner what you remember about the text.

3 What overall title would you give the text?

4 Put the information in the order in which it appears in the passage.

a where the family live ☐

b opinions on the house ☐

c the materials used for the interior ☐

d the cost and address of the house ☐

e the facilities in the house ☐

f the owner of the house ☐

g information about the theatre and ballroom ☐

07 ▷ **Now scan the text for the information to answer these questions.**

1 Who owns the property?

2 How many floors does it have?

3 What are the floors made out of?

4 What are the common symbols used throughout the house?

5 How many cars does the garage have space for?

6 How many employees work in the home?

TIP **07**

In many of the IELTS reading tasks, the answers appear in the same order as the text.

PARAPHRASING

08 ▷ **These statements paraphrase each of the paragraphs in the text. Match each statement, 1–6, with the correct paragraph, A–F.**

1 The house has many desirable facilities and outside spaces. Guests can either drive or fly to the home.

2 The family live on the top floor because they want exposure to sunlight. ☐

3 Mrs Ambani and the architecture experts have different opinions about the house. ☐

4 Antilia is situated in Mumbai and owned by Mukesh Ambani. ☐

5 The appearance inside the house is very extravagant and expensive materials have been used. The house also has magnificent views of the city. ☐

6 The home is fully equipped to make visitors feel welcome. ☐

◎ 'Paraphrasing' is another important technique to understand and use in the exam. Paraphrasing is when you repeat something using different words, often in a simpler and shorter form that makes the original meaning clearer.

09 ▷ **The key to paraphrasing is understanding synonyms and words or phrases with a similar meaning. Match these words and expressions.**

1 desirable facilities   a guests

2 outside spaces   b Mumbai

3 inside   c expensive

4 extravagant   d rare wood and fine rugs

5 city   e health spa and libraries

6 visitors   f gardens

7 equipped to make visitors feel welcome   g interior

8 expensive materials   h designed to entertain guests

SHORT-ANSWER QUESTIONS

Questions which require an answer of just a few words, like those in exercise 7, are a common feature of the exam. These are known as *short-answer* questions and they ask about factual details.

TIP 10 · 11
The answers for short-answer questions come in the same order as they appear in the text.

10 Choose NO MORE THAN THREE WORDS AND/OR A NUMBER from the passage for each answer.

1 How many lifts does the home have?
2 What can you find in the ice-room?
3 What do the Ambani children have to do when at home?

TIP 10 · 11
Remember to check that your sentences are **grammatically correct** when you have chosen an answer.

COMPLETING SENTENCES

11 Complete the sentences. Choose NO MORE THAN THREE WORDS AND/OR A NUMBER from the passage for each answer.

1 The name Antilia comes from a _____ .
2 There are many facilities to accommodate a large number of _____ .
3 Opinions on the _____ of the house vary.

A similar type of task, which also requires an answer of only a few words, is the 'sentence completion task'. The sentences paraphrase words and ideas from the text.

GRAMMAR FOCUS: PRESENT SIMPLE/PRESENT CONTINUOUS

12 A 'mindmap' is a type of diagram with lines and circles for organising information so that it is easier to remember. Put these words and phrases with the appropriate tense in the mindmap.

~~temporary~~   repeated actions   general facts   opinions
an action which is not complete   happening at the time of speaking

Present continuous

_____temporary_____   _____   _____   _____

Present simple

13 Using the rules in the mindmap, correct these sentences where necessary.

1 Mukesh Ambani is living in Mumbai.
2 Mrs Ambani is believing that her home has an Indian heart.
3 The family live on the top floor because they want as much exposure to sunlight as possible.
4 When the children are at home, they are cleaning their own rooms.
5 Mrs Ambani entertains her guests in the ballroom at the moment.

14 ▸ Complete the sentences using the word in brackets and the correct form of the present continuous or the present simple.

1 Currently, my mum _____ (work) in the study.
2 I _____ (rent) in the city centre for now.
3 I _____ (think) that buying a new house now would be a very good idea.
4 What is that going to be? They _____ (build) a new accommodation block for students.
5 Every day his mum _____ (clean) the house.

EXAM SKILLS

15 ▸ Using the approach below, read the text and answer the questions which follow.

Locating the answer: one approach

• Read the questions first, so they are in your mind when you read the text.
• Make sure you have understood the question correctly – underlining key words could help.
• Skim read the text for the main ideas. This will help you to have a rough idea of where to locate your answers on a second read-through.

Choose NO MORE THAN THREE WORDS AND/OR A NUMBER from the passage for each answer.

1 What job did William Hearst do?
2 Who helped Hearst design the Castle?
3 How much did Hearst spend on art during his lifetime?
4 How many times was the Neptune pool rebuilt before Hearst was happy with it?
5 What were visitors to the Castle required to do every evening?
6 Which state now owns the mansion?

Complete the sentences. Write NO MORE THAN TWO WORDS AND/OR A NUMBER from the passage for each answer.

7 As a child, Hearst enjoyed his holidays to _____ .
8 Hearst inherited the land from his _____ .
9 Builders spent _____ creating the magnificent Neptune Pool.
10 Hearst took animals from _____ for his private zoo.
11 Although the zoo is now closed, _____ still walk about the hillside.
12 The family donated the property because of _____ .

TIP 15

Time yourself: try to do this task as quickly as possible to practise locating information quickly for the exam.

HEARST CASTLE

HOME **ABOUT** PHOTOS BOOKING

A William Randolph Hearst was a successful American newspaper publisher who received over 1,000 km^2 of land when his mother died in 1919. Initially, he had planned to build just a small bungalow, so he hired Julia Morgan, the first female architect in California. Together, however, they designed a magnificent castle which cost 10 million dollars and took 28 years to build. The property, named *La Cuesta Encantada* (The Enchanted Mountain), has 56 bedrooms, 61 bathrooms, 19 sitting rooms and about 52,000 m^2 of garden.

B Hearst loved travelling to Europe when he was a child and we can see this in the overall design of the house. He even included cathedral ceilings and Roman columns in his home. Hearst was also a keen art collector and, during his lifetime, spent $3.5 million on his collection, which is displayed in the rooms at Hearst Castle. Today, his collection is worth much more, with one piece alone valued at $10 million.

C One of the highlights of the estate is the Neptune Pool. It took 15 years to build and includes the front of an ancient Roman temple. It is on top of a hill and has wonderful views of the mountains, ocean and main house. The pool was rebuilt three times until he was satisfied.

D Although the inside of the house is very European, the outside is very Californian, with palm trees and water. Hearst loved trees and 70,000 were planted on the property during his lifetime. The castle was also home to the world's largest private zoo, holding animals from every continent. Although the zoo is now closed, zebras can still be seen on the hillside.

E As well as the *Casa Grande* (the main house), there are also three guest houses on the property: *Casa Del Monte*, *Casa Del Sol* and *Casa Del Mar*. Hearst entertained a great number of Hollywood stars and political leaders at the castle and many used his private airfield. Guests had to attend formal dinners every evening, but were free to do what they liked during the day. They were invited to stay as long as they wanted, but the longer they stayed, the further away they sat from Hearst at the dinner table.

F When Hearst died in 1951, his family learnt how expensive maintenance would be, and the mansion was donated to the State of California. Since then, it has been open for public tours and the site attracts millions of tourists every year. However, the Hearst family is still allowed to use it when they wish. The castle was never completed and remains unfinished.

GO ONLINE AND COMPLETE UNIT 1 READING EXERCISES 1–4

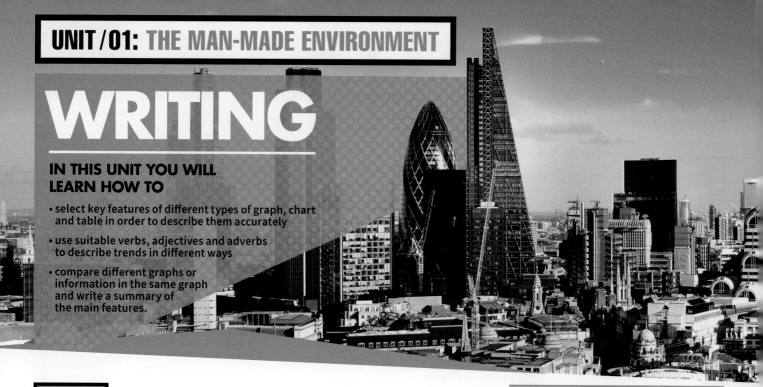

WRITING

IN THIS UNIT YOU WILL LEARN HOW TO

- select key features of different types of graph, chart and table in order to describe them accurately

- use suitable verbs, adjectives and adverbs to describe trends in different ways

- compare different graphs or information in the same graph and write a summary of the main features.

LEAD-IN

◎ In Writing Part 1, you could be given graphs/charts or tables to write about, so it is important to be very familiar with this kind of vocabulary.

01 ▷ Look at these examples of the types of diagram you might encounter in the IELTS exam. Then label the diagrams with words from the box.

row	~~line graph~~	bar chart	column	horizontal axis	key	title
bar	pie chart	segment	table	vertical axis	line	

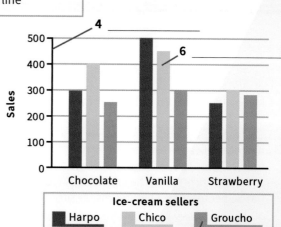

1 line graph

2 _____

3 _____

4 _____

5 _____

6 _____

7 _____

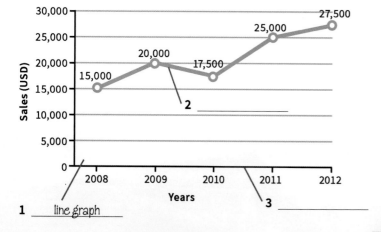

8 _____   **Favourite type of movie**

sci-fi: 4 (20%)   comedy: 4 (20%)

drama: 1 (5%)   10 _____

romance: 6 (30%)   action: 5 (25%)

9 _____   13 _____

	Keyword	Visits	Avg. Time on Site	% New Visits	Bounce Rate
1	idealist	33,103	00:10:05	19.84%	12.73%
2	idealist.org	27,105	00:11:07	21.26%	12.26%
3	volunteer	12,908	00:03:35	84.76%	53.31%
4	volunteer work	6,721	00:02:42	90.55%	59.75%
5	volunteering.org	5,363	00:03:20	86.41%	61.78%
6	non profit jobs	5,203	00:09:04	47.01%	18.68%
7	www.idealist.org	4,733	00:10:45	15.63%	12.57%
8	volunteering	3,645	00:03:15	87.46%	56.24%
9	idealist.com	3,341	00:10:39	31.94%	14.43%
10	nonprofit jobs	2,865	00:08:35	37.38%	15.78%

11 _____   12 _____

SELECTING KEY FEATURES

0 2 ▷ **Study these graphs and make notes about their main features – use questions 1–12 to help you.**

1 What does the title say the graph is about?
2 What does the vertical axis describe?
3 What does the horizontal axis describe?
4 What do the columns/bars represent?
5 Which are the tallest and shortest bars?
6 How do the bars compare to one another?

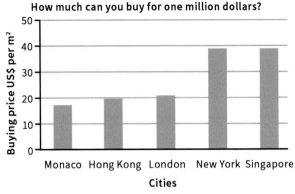

World's most expensive cities (2015)
How much can you buy for one million dollars?

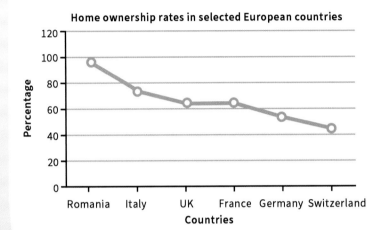

Home ownership rates in selected European countries

7 What does the title say the graph is about?
8 What does the vertical axis describe?
9 What does the horizontal axis describe?
10 What do the highest/lowest points of the line show?
11 What is the general trend of the line?
12 Are there any sharp decreases or increases?

Average house size in selected countries

- Canada
- USA
- Australia
- Hong Kong
- Japan

181 m² / 201 m² / 214 m² / 45 m² / 95 m²

13 What does the title say the pie chart is about?
14 What do the segments represent?
15 Which is the largest/smallest segment?
16 Are some segments similar in size?

Average house size in selected European countries

Country	Size
United Kingdom	76 m²
France	112 m²
Denmark	137 m²
Germany	109 m²
Italy	61 m²
Spain	97 m²
Greece	126 m²

17 What does the title say about the table?
18 How many columns are there? What do they represent?
19 Which country has the biggest average house size?
20 Which country has the smallest average house size?
21 Which countries have a similar average house size?

0 3 ▷ The sample answer describes the pie chart and table in exercise 2.

Rewrite the sample answer, correcting any errors in data.

 It is very important that the information you provide in your answer accurately reflects the information given in the text.

SAMPLE ANSWER

The pie chart and table provide information about the average house size worldwide. According to the pie chart, the Australians have the most space with the average house size being 214 m². This is perhaps because it is such a large country. The second largest houses are in Canada with the average size being 201 m². The country with the smallest houses is Hong Kong, with residences being an average of just 45 m².

In comparison, the table illustrates the average house size in all European countries. The United Kingdom and Italy have the smallest houses and Denmark and Greece have the largest. The average house size in Denmark is 137 m².

In conclusion, when comparing the two graphs, it is easily apparent that houses in Europe are much smaller than in non-European countries.

Overall, Australia has the biggest houses and Italy has the smallest. This is most probably due to the size of each country.

1 _____
2 _____
3 _____
4 _____
5 _____
6 _____

0 4 ▷ Did the writer make any other errors, not related to data? If so, what were they?

DESCRIBING TRENDS

0 5 ▷ Complete the words with the missing letters. Can you think of any more words for each category?

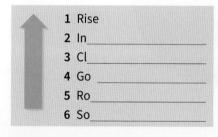

1 Rise
2 In_____
3 Cl_____
4 Go _____
5 Ro_____
6 So_____

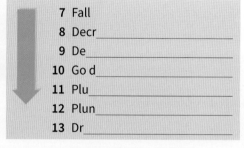

7 Fall
8 Decr_____
9 De_____
10 Go d_____
11 Plu_____
12 Plun_____
13 Dr_____

14 Maintain
15 Remain
16 Stay

0 6 ▷ Answer these questions.

1 Which of the verbs in the boxes are used to describe a sudden increase?
2 Which of the verbs in the boxes are used to describe a sudden decrease?

0 7 ▷ When using these verbs, it is important that you also consider the tense used. Look at this example.

The number of young people buying property plummet last year.   ✗
The number of young people buying property *plummeted* last year.   ✔

Complete the sentences using the verb in brackets in the correct tense. There may be more than one correct form of the verb.

1 Last year house prices _____ **(rise)** by 5%.
2 Monaco's property market _____ **(remain)** stable.
3 The line graph illustrates that since 2010 home ownership _____ **(decrease)**.
4 House prices _____ **(go up)** next year.
5 In Ireland, property prices _____ **(rocket)** substantially this year.

USEFUL ADVERBS AND ADJECTIVES

Once you know the common verbs used to describe charts and graphs, it is important to add adverbs and adjectives to your sentences in order to demonstrate your range of vocabulary.

USEFUL ADJECTIVES

Adjectives can be used to demonstrate your range of vocabulary. **Adjectives** describe **nouns** and usually come **before** the noun.

Note: these verbs are also commonly used as nouns.

to rise / a rise	to fall / a fall	to decrease / a decrease
to increase / an increase	to drop / a drop	to dip / a dip
to decline / a decline	to peak / a peak	

0 8 ▷ Complete the table with the adjectives from the box.

slight	modest	significant	dramatic
stable	steady*	substantial	unchanged*

TIP 08
Make sure you know how to spell these adjectives correctly as it is common for students to make errors with these.

*These adjectives usually go after the noun.

Big change	Small change	Gradual or no change

09▶ Complete the sentences using adjectives from the box in exercise 8 and following the prompts in the brackets. More than one answer may be possible.

1 Over the last year, Hong Kong has experienced a _____ (**big**) rise in house prices.

2 There has been a _____ (**gradual**) increase in the number of young people buying houses.

3 The rental market has seen a _____ (**small**) decrease over the last six months.

4 The graph illustrates that the rental market is _____ (**no change**) at the moment.

USEFUL ADVERBS

◎ Adverbs describe **how** something happens and usually follow a verb.
For example:

1 *Last year house prices rose* **significantly**.
2 *Last year house prices rose* **slightly**.
3 *Last year house prices rose* **steadily**.

10▶ Match sentences 1–3 with graphs A–C.

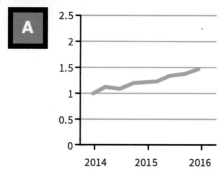
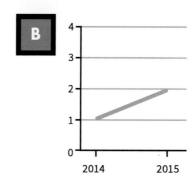
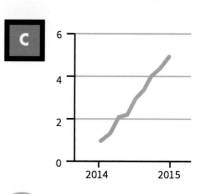

11▶ Complete the table using the adverbs from the box.

| considerably | consistently | sharply | gradually | moderately |
| substantially | dramatically | slowly | rapidly | |

TIP 11

Make sure you know how to spell these adverbs correctly as it is common for students to make errors with them.

Big change	Small change	Gradual change	Quick change
significantly	slightly	steadily	quickly
considerably			

12▶ Complete the sentences using the adverbs from exercise 11 and following the prompts in the brackets. More than one answer may be possible.

1 Home ownership has decreased _____ (**big**) over the last five years.

2 Property prices have increased _____ (**small**) over the last six months.

3 The property market is growing _____ (**gradual**) in this area.

4 Interest rates have increased _____ (**quick**) recently.

PART 1: DESCRIBING TRENDS

1 3 ▷ Look at the trends illustrated by the graphs and charts.
Discuss them with a partner using the language you have learnt in this lesson.

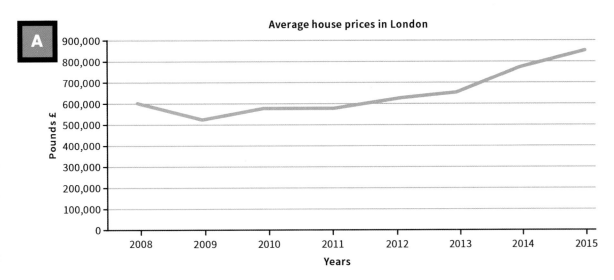

1 4 ▷ Match descriptions 1–3 with the graphs and charts A–C, then complete the first gap in each sentence with the correct country name.

1 Since 2008, house prices in _____ have ___*fluctuated*___ heavily. In 2008 prices _____ to just over 40% and then _____ to –40%.

2 Since 2008, house price increases in _____ have _____ under 11% each year. In 2008 prices reached a _____ , with a _____ of just over 10%.

3 Since 2010, house prices in _____ have _____ . In 2009, prices _____ , by almost £100,000, but _____ again rapidly in 2010 to approximately £600,000.

1 5 ▷ Complete the sentences in exercise 14 using the words and phrases in the box.

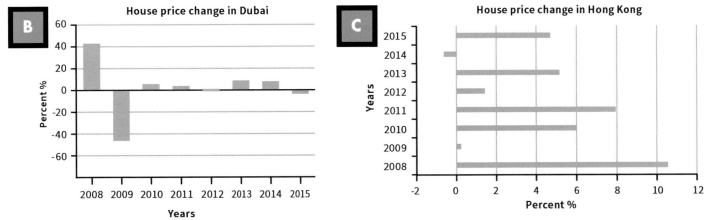

decreased substantially	increased steadily	remained	peak	rise
plummeted dramatically	went up	~~fluctuated~~	went up	

16 ▶ Use the information and language from this lesson to answer this Writing Part 1 task. You should spend about 20 minutes on this task.

The chart below gives information about how people aged 25–34 are housed in the UK.

Summarise the information by selecting and reporting on the main features, and make comparisons where relevant.

Write at least 150 words.

TIP 16

Do not give your opinion, just the **facts**.

TIP 16

Remember to include an introduction and conclusion in your answer.

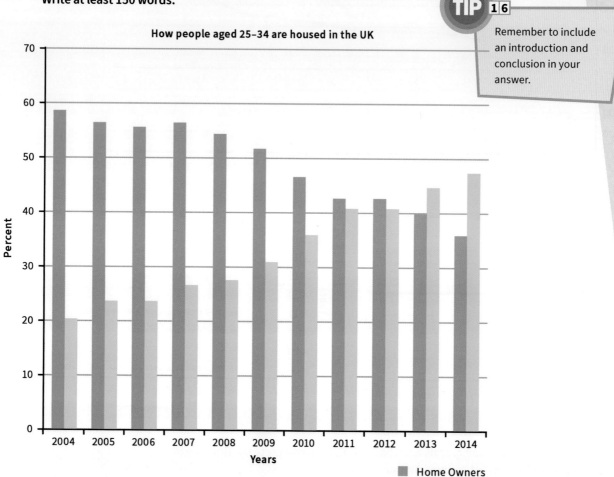

How people aged 25–34 are housed in the UK

Legend:
- Home Owners
- Renters

GO ONLINE AND COMPLETE UNIT 1 WRITING EXERCISES 1-5

LISTENING

IN THIS UNIT YOU WILL LEARN HOW TO

- predict the type of information required for short-answer questions
- listen for specific information (e.g. complex numbers, difficult spellings) and write it down correctly
- listen to understand context
- answer multiple-choice questions correctly by eliminating distractors.

LEAD-IN

01 ▶
02

Listen to an estate agent describing the three properties in the pictures and write the correct number in each box.

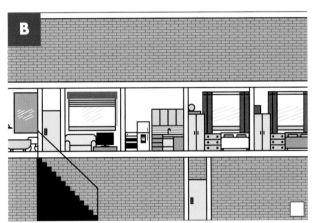

02 ▶

Listen again and note down the words which helped you find the answers.

LISTENING FOR SPECIFIC INFORMATION

03 ▶
🎧 03

Look at these notes and think about the kind of information that you will need for each gap, e.g. an address or telephone number. Then listen to the recording and complete the notes with NO MORE THAN TWO WORDS AND/OR A NUMBER.

TIP 03

In the Listening test, you will be given the context of the listening and you will have some time to look at the questions before you listen.

Address of property 1 _____

Number of bedrooms 2 _____

Number of lounges 3 _____

Access to the 4 _____ through sun-room door

Kitchen: fully-fitted, includes 5 _____ and 6 _____

Appointment time: 7 _____

Estate agent's name: Peter 8 _____

Estate agent's number: 9 _____

04 ▶
🎧 04

In the Listening test you may be asked to write down numbers, such as prices and phone numbers. Listen to these short conversations and write down the numbers in each.

1 £ _____

2 _____ km

3 _____

4 _____ m x _____ m

5 _____

05 ▶
🎧 05

In this exercise, you will hear some complex numbers, including a price and measurements. Listen to the estate agent and client and complete the information sheet.

Property for sale	
Price	1 £ _____
Room sizes	Kitchen: 3.10 x 2.25 m
	Lounge 1: 2 _____ m
	Lounge 2: 6.50 x 4.25 m
	Front garden: 10 x 8 m
	Rear garden: 3 _____ m, patio, lawn and flower beds
	Bedroom 1: 4 _____ m
	Bedroom 2: 5 _____ m
	Bedroom 3: 3.25 x 2.5 m

Listen to the final conversation between the estate agent and client and answer these questions.

1 What information does the estate agent need?
2 How will the client get the money to pay for the house?
3 How long does the estate agent think it will take to sell the house?
4 The most important thing for the client is

A to stay a little longer where she is living now.
B to help her husband travel to work more easily.
C to move in before the end of the school holiday.

DEALING WITH DISTRACTORS

 Look at this example and listen to part of the recording again.

The en-suite bathroom will be useful because
A it has a shower unit.
B it has a big bath.
C it helps everyone in the mornings.

Answer C is correct. A is true, but it is not the reason why it will be useful for the woman and her family. B is not true, because the other bathroom has a bath. C is correct because the speaker says that it will be useful when they all get up to get ready for school or work – and that happens in the morning.

 In multiple-choice questions in the Listening test, there is one correct answer and two wrong answers. The wrong answers are called 'distractors'. They are designed to seem correct. For example, they use the same words as the recording, but with a different meaning. You have to make sure that the correct answer has the same meaning as the recording.

[EXAM SKILLS]

 Listen to the final conversation again and choose the correct letter, A, B or C.

1 At the moment, Caroline lives in
  A Prendergast Road.
  B Lanchester Road.
  C Riverside Road.
2 Caroline wants to make a first offer of
  A £300,000.
  B £350,000.
  C £340,000.
3 Caroline and her family
  A have sold their house.
  B are selling their house now.
  C will sell their house in two months' time.
4 It may take longer to sell the house if
  A the bank does not check the house quickly.
  B there are plans to do some building near the house.
  C her husband has problems at work.
5 If the sellers do not accept her first offer, Caroline will need to
  A increase her offer.
  B come to an agreement in a week.
  C contact her bank and ask for more money.

TIP 08
Remember that you need to focus on the **meaning** of the distractors.

TIP 08
To arrive at the correct answer, listen for **synonyms** and **similar expressions**, or for the same ideas expressed in a different way to the recording.

GO ONLINE AND COMPLETE UNIT 1 LISTENING EXERCISES 1–4

SPEAKING

IN THIS UNIT YOU WILL LEARN HOW TO

- speak about various aspects of where you live for Speaking Part 1
- respond to *wh-*, *would* and *Yes/No* questions about where you live
- prepare more information for common Speaking Part 1 topics
- use syllable stress in words correctly.

LEAD-IN

01▷ In Part 1 of the Speaking test, you may be asked about your home town. Organise the words into things you like in your home town, things you don't like and things you would like to have, if they are not already in your home town.

architecture	monuments	mountains	museums
parks	restaurants	rivers/lakes	shopping malls
weather	theatres	the sea	sports centres

Things I like	Things I don't like	Things I wish I had in my home town

02 Listen to an extract from Speaking Part 1 and answer these questions. Discuss your answers with a partner.

TIP 02

The *Why?* question usually comes last, and might be more difficult to answer. Try to explain clearly, but don't go into too much detail at this stage.

1 How many questions did the examiner ask?
2 What kind of questions did the examiner ask? What were the question words?
3 What two topics did the examiner cover?
4 Approximately how long did the student speak for each question? How many sentences did they use?

RESPONDING TO *WH-* QUESTIONS

 03 Listen again to the recording from exercise 2. Note down useful language the student uses.

◉ Most Speaking Part 1 questions are *Wh-* questions. These include *What?*, *Who?*, *When?*, *Where?* and *Why?*

Home   Shopping
_____   _____
_____   _____

 04 With a partner, ask and answer these questions.

Your home town
1 Where do you come from?
2 What is the weather like in your home town?
3 When is the best time of year to visit your home town?
4 Why do you like/not like your home town?

Your accommodation
1 Where are you living now?
2 Who else do you live with?
3 What is your favourite room in your home?
4 Why do you like/not like the place where you live?

05 Some questions ask you to think about something you *might* do, using 'would'. Ask and answer these questions with a partner.

1 Would you recommend your house/apartment to another person?
2 Would you move house if you had the chance?
3 Would you like to buy a house in your home town one day?
4 Would you like to live by yourself or with family/friends?

These words are useful when talking about your home town.
Write four sentences about each, using prompts 1–4.

 There are a number of possible topics you might be asked about in Speaking Part 1, such as the news, entertainment or sport. To prepare for this, you need to know some basic information about each topic.

culture	historical	monument	museums	nightlife
parks	restaurants	shopping	weather	

1 People in my home town usually/don't often ___go out at night___ because
_____ .

2 My favourite thing about my home town is _____the culture_____ because
_____ .

3 A famous ____historical place____ in my home town is _____ .

4 I like / don't like _the weather in my home town_ because _____ .

RESPONDING TO *YES/NO* QUESTIONS

 Match questions 1–6 with answers a–f.

1 Do you live near the sea?
2 Is there anything you don't like about where you live?
3 Is your house in the city or the countryside?
4 Do you live in a house or an apartment?
5 Is there anything special you can do in your home town?
6 Are there any interesting places to visit in your home town?

Other types of question ask for a *Yes/No* response. These questions usually start with *Do(es)* or *Is/Are*.

TIP 07

It is not enough to just say *Yes/No*. Try to add at least two sentences with extra information, explaining your answer.

a We live in the suburbs, just outside the city, about 20 minutes' drive by car.

b Yes, we live on the coast, and we can see the beach from our window – it's pretty nice.

c Not really, I think my home town is a little boring. We mostly take a train to Shanghai when we want to do something.

d Yes, the weather there is pretty terrible. We only get about six weeks of summer, and it's very cold most of the time.

e Yes, there are many monuments and museums to see – we have a lot of culture and history.

f We currently live in a small apartment on the 33rd floor. My last house was much bigger …

0 8 Ask and answer these questions about your home town/accommodation.

Your home town
1 Do you live in the city or the countryside?
2 Do you live near the sea?
3 Is there anything special that people do in your home town?
4 Are there any interesting places to visit in your home town?

Your accommodation
5 Do you live in a house or an apartment?
6 Is your house in the city or the countryside?
7 Do other people live with you?
8 Is there anything you don't like about where you live?

09▶ Try to write FOUR questions (either *Wh-?* or *Yes/No* questions) for each topic in the mindmap. Ask and answer questions with a partner.

◎ You may be asked about a topic you know well, but the exact question could be unfamiliar. It can be useful to make your own questions for a topic to explore new ideas you have not thought about before.

Weather

Do you like the weather in your home town?
When was the last time it was really cold in your home town?
Does it ever snow in your home town?
When is the best time of year to visit your home town?

Shopping

_____
_____
_____

Culture

_____
_____
_____

Monuments

_____
_____
_____

Restaurants

_____
_____
_____

Nightlife

_____
_____
_____

Museums

_____
_____
_____

Parks

_____
_____
_____

10▶ Add TWO more topics to the mindmap.

11▶ Listen to the sentences. Underline the *stressed* syllable in the words.

09

Right now, I am living in an ap<u>art</u>ment with my friends.

1 a / <u>part</u> / ment
2 ac / comm / o / da / tion
3 ar / chi / tec / ture
4 con / struc / tion

5 es / ca / la / tors
6 in / ha / bi / tants
7 mon / u / ment
8 mu / se / um

9 res / i / den / tial
10 sta / di / um
11 coun / try / side
12 en / vi / ron / ment

13 ge / og / ra / phy
14 re / gion / al
15 temp / er / a / ture
16 sce / ne / ry

12▶ Listen to the words again and repeat them with the correct syllable stress.

10

EXAM SKILLS

13▶ Answer these questions about accommodation and your home town.
Reply with THREE SENTENCES ONLY for each question.

1 Where do you come from?
2 Are there any special places that tourists visit in your home town?
3 When is the best time of year to visit your home town?
4 Why do you like / don't you like your home town?
5 Where are you living now – in a house or an apartment?
6 Does anyone else live with you?
7 What is your favourite room where you live?
8 Would you recommend your accommodation to another person?

**GO ONLINE AND
COMPLETE UNIT 1
SPEAKING EXERCISES 1–7**

READING

IN THIS UNIT YOU WILL LEARN HOW TO

- identify questions which ask for factual information and questions which ask for the writer's opinion
- skim and scan to arrive at the correct answers quickly
- understand the whole text to answer questions about global understanding
- use the past simple and past continuous correctly.

LEAD-IN

01 Match the names with photos 1–5.

Serena Williams	Jack Nicklaus	David Beckham
Muhammad Ali	Michael Jordan	

02 Which sport are/were these people famous for?

0 3 With a partner, try and answer the multiple-choice quiz.
What else do you know about these sports stars?

 In the Reading test you may be presented with this type of multiple-choice question. The answers, however, will all be located in the text and will **not** test your general knowledge on any subject.

SPORTING LEGENDS

1 In what year did Serena Williams first become World Number 1?
A 1995   B 2002   C 2007

2 How many major championships did Jack Nicklaus win during his career?
A 18   B 21   C 12

3 How old was Muhammad Ali when he started training?
A 21   B 12   C 8

4 How long was David Beckham captain of the England team?
A 3 years   B 10 years   C 6 years

5 How tall is Michael Jordan?
A 1.98 m   B 1.70 m   C 1.82 m

FACTS AND OPINIONS

 There are two types of question:

- those which ask for **factual information**
- those which ask for the **writer's opinion**.

0 4 Read these paragraphs and answer the questions which follow. Choose the correct letter, A, B or C.

TIP 0 4 The answers are in the same order as the text.

WHY IS THE FORMER BOXER MUHAMMAD ALI STILL CONSIDERED A LEGEND?

Although Muhammad Ali was responsible for many legendary moments in the boxing ring, there was much more to this man's appeal. Not only was he a successful athlete, but he was also well known for his strong work ethic and fearless approach to standing up for his beliefs.

Born as Cassius Clay in 1942, Muhammad Ali began training at just 12 years old and, at the age of 22, won the world heavyweight championship in 1964. It was a title he went on to win again, in 1974 and 1978. He referred to himself as 'The Greatest', and was famous for boasting about his ability to 'float like a butterfly and sting like a bee'.

1 Why does the writer think that Muhammad Ali is still considered a legend?
   A because he is a successful athlete
   B because of several factors, not just his abilities as a boxer
   C because he has great appeal

2 What name did Muhammad Ali give himself during his career?
   A Cassius Clay   B The Greatest   C The Champion

05 ▸ Now answer these questions.

1 Which question is factual and which asks for the writer's opinion?
2 Look at question 1 again. Are all the answers possible? Why did you choose one particular answer?
3 Do any of the words in the first paragraph match the words in question 1? Do matching words give you the correct answer?
4 What phrase is used to mean 'give himself the name' in the second paragraph?

APPROACHING THE QUESTION

06 ▸ Complete the flow-chart showing one approach with words from the box.

> instructions   ~~understand~~   key   questions   scan   wrong

◎ In the Reading test, the texts are much longer than in exercise 4, so it is important to develop a strategy which allows you to **get the correct answer quickly.**

| Read the 1 _____ and _____ carefully. | Read the text to 2 _understand_ the general meaning. | Read the questions again and underline 3 _____ words, e.g dates, names etc. | 4 _____ the text for the key words or synonyms. | Read around the key words in the text. | Re-read the questions and choose an answer. | Quickly check the other options are 5 _____ and make your final choices. |

07 ▸ Use this approach to answer questions about the text. Choose TWO letters, A–D.

TIP 07
It is important to read the instructions very carefully as the number of letters you need to choose can vary.

Serena Williams has dominated women's professional tennis since the late 1990s, when she and her sister, Venus, became global tennis superstars. Serena in particular has become known for her determination, powerful game and unique fashion sense.

Serena was born on 26 September 1981 in Saginaw, Michigan. When she was just a baby, her family moved to California, and it was there she started playing tennis at the age of four. She was coached by her father, Richard Williams, until she was 12. Although Mr Williams was determined that his daughters would succeed in the tennis world, he was also focused on giving them a good education.

In fact, whilst they were training to be tennis stars, he also took responsibility for their home-schooling.

Serena is so successful on the tennis court because of her rapid movement, speed of thought and powerful shots. Indeed, whilst she was playing a match in the 2013 Australian Open, Serena hit a serve* at a speed of just under 207 km per hour, the third fastest recorded among female players. This powerful serve helps put her opponents under pressure from the very start of the game.

During her career, she has won 56 singles championships, 22 doubles championships and was also a gold medallist at the 2000, 2008 and 2012 Olympics.

*to serve (v) – to hit the ball to the other player as a way of starting the game

1 According to the writer, Serena has become so famous because …
  A she is aggressive.
  B she has a strong tennis game.
  C she is very good at fashion.
  D she has self-belief.

2 During Serena's upbringing, what did her father consider to be important?
  A staying at home
  B tennis training
  C her studies
  D training her to be a star

3 Her tennis game is so successful because …
  A she thinks quickly.
  B she can hit the ball hard.
  C she is the third fastest player in the world.
  D her opponents are nervous of her.

0 8 **Answer these questions.**

1 Which questions ask you to complete the sentence and which ask you to answer the question?

2 How many synonyms from words in the text are used in the questions?

3 Do any answers match the wording in the text?

4 Are these answers the correct ones?

TIP **0 8**

Both types of question may be in the Reading test, so it is important to read the questions carefully.

GRAMMAR FOCUS: PAST SIMPLE / PAST CONTINUOUS

0 9 **Say which past tenses are used in the text.**

1 0 **Study this sentence, then answer the questions.**

… whilst she was playing a match in the 2013 Australian Open, Serena hit a serve at a speed of just under 207 km per hour …

1 Underline the two past tenses in the sentence.

2 Which actions (verbs) were happening in the past at the same time?

3 Which is the long, continued action? Which is the short, finished action?

4 Are both actions finished now?

◎ You will not be given any grammar exercises in IELTS. However, it is important that you can recognise which tenses are used and what they mean.

1 1 **Study this diagram and answer the questions which follow.**

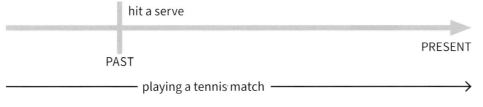

1 Are there any other examples of the past continuous in the text?

2 Complete this rule:

When we use the simple past and the past continuous in the same sentence, we use the _____ _____ to talk about the 'background action' and the _____ _____ to talk about the shorter, completed action.

1 2 **Complete the sentences by putting the verb in brackets in the correct form of the past continuous or past simple.**

1 Whilst she _____ (**play**) basketball, her phone _____ (**ring**).

2 He _____ (**fall**), while _____ (**run**) for the ball.

3 It _____ (**start**) to rain in the middle of the race.

4 It _____ (**rain**) during the race.

1 3 **Complete the sentences with your own ideas.**

1 Whilst Michael Jordan was running down the court, _____ .

2 David Beckham injured his knee whilst _____ .

3 Jack Nicklaus was taking a shot when _____ .

GLOBAL UNDERSTANDING

1 4 ▶ **This section focuses on questions which check your understanding of the text *as a whole*. Read the text and choose the correct letter, A, B or C.**

TIP 1 4

For this question type, do not choose an answer based just on one paragraph. You need to read the whole text in order to choose the correct summary.

Despite Beckham's good looks and famous marriage to Victoria Beckham, he was actually an exceptionally good footballer. His professional career began with Manchester United in 1992, at the age of 17. With United he won the Premier League title six times, the FA Cup twice and the UEFA Champions League in 1999. He later went on to play for Real Madrid and LA Galaxy.

In international football, he made his England debut in 1996 at the age of 21.

He was also made captain in 2002 and had short spells at AC Milan and Paris St Germain. His former boss, Alex Ferguson, praised David for always trying hard, playing with supreme confidence and scoring important goals.

His football career was not always easy, however. During the 1998 World Cup, in a game against Argentina, he was fouled by the player Diego Simeone. In retaliation, Beckham kicked Simeone and was given a red card. Consequently, when England went on to lose the game and go out of the World Cup, Beckham became hated by football fans and was portrayed very negatively by the media.

It took three years before Beckham was allowed to play for England again and in 2002 he redeemed himself by scoring a penalty in a 1–0 victory against Argentina.

In 2013 Beckham retired from professional football and played the last game of his 20-year career. Although he is now retired from football, reports claim that he earns more money now than he did as a successful footballer. In 2014 it was documented that he earned £50.5 million, a large portion of which came from brand endorsements for companies such as Adidas, Sky Sports and Samsung.

What is the best title for this article?

A What has Beckham achieved during his career?

B Despite all the media attention, was Beckham a good football player?

C What problems did Beckham have during his football career?

EXAM SKILLS

15 Using all the skills you have learnt in this lesson, read the text and complete the multiple-choice task which follows.

A BRIEF HISTORY OF FOOTBALL

There is no clear evidence stating where and when football was actually invented, but most historians agree that some type of ball game had been played centuries before the modern game developed in England. Football has a long and interesting history and origins of the game are present in sports played thousands of years ago in China, Egypt, Japan and Greece. Aspects of the game can be traced as early as the second and third centuries BC in China. Their game, originally named 'Tsu Chu', involved kicking a leather ball into a small hole.

The first football games played in Britain were in the 700s and the English equivalent of a football was made using an animal bladder. Games were violent and injury and death were common. Despite the violence, however, they were still very popular. The game had become so popular that in the 1300s Edward II banned the sport because people were playing football rather than practising archery. This was especially important to this king, as he was preparing to go to war with Scotland. This was to be the first of many bans imposed by the kings and queens of England.

In 1605 football became legal and once again the sport grew in popularity.

In the 1800s it became particularly common in private schools such as Eton, and it was only then that a set of rules was established. Until then, the game had continued to be violent, as it had had limited rules and no referees. Before the 1800s, for example, it was considered normal to hit players on the opposite team and to damage their possessions. In 1848, on Parker's Piece in Cambridge, these rules were developed further and a new version called the 'Cambridge Rules' was used by all schools, colleges and universities.

Though football could be considered a male sport, women also play it.

An increase in women playing the sport began during the First World War, when women did jobs traditionally done by men. Those working in places like factories regularly met to play. Unfortunately, a ban was imposed when the war ended, but it was eventually lifted in the UK in 1971. In 1991 China hosted the first Women's World Cup and in 1996 the first ever women's football event was held at the Olympics.

Choose the correct letter, A, B or C.

1 Where can the first traces of football be found?
  A Egypt
  B China
  C England

2 Why did Edward II ban football in the 1300s?
  A because it was too violent and death was common
  B because he was preparing to go to war with China
  C because people weren't practising archery

3 Before rules were established in the 1800s, which of these activities was considered normal?
  A stealing from opponents
  B destroying players' property
  C being violent towards the referee

4 Women started playing football because
  A the ban was lifted in 1971.
  B they started to work during the First World War.
  C in 1991 there was the first Women's World Cup.

GO ONLINE AND COMPLETE UNIT 2 READING EXERCISES 1–4

UNIT /02: LEISURE AND RECREATION

WRITING

IN THIS UNIT YOU WILL LEARN HOW TO

- select and compare key features of charts, graphs and tables
- structure an answer which compares information from charts, graphs and tables
- revise the form and use of comparatives.

LEAD-IN

01▷ Discuss these questions with a partner.

1 Have you ever watched the Olympic Games, either live or on television? If so, which sports did you enjoy watching the most?

2 Do you prefer the winter or summer Olympics? Give reasons for your answers.

02▷ Study the chart and graph and answer the questions which follow.

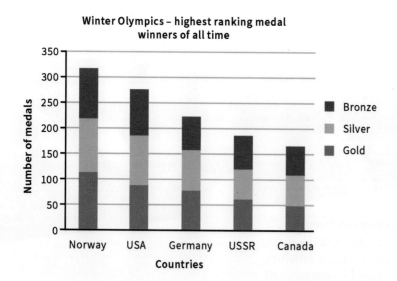

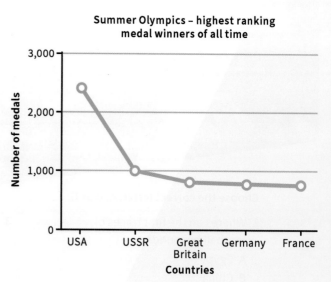

1 Which countries (or former countries) were successful in both the winter and summer Olympics?

2 Which country (or former country) won the most gold medals in the winter Olympics?

3 Which country (or former country) won the fewest medals in the summer Olympics?

03 ▶ Read this sample answer, which describes the chart and graph in exercise 2.

SAMPLE ANSWER

The bar chart shows which countries have won the most medals in the winter Olympics. It also states how many gold, silver and bronze medals each country has achieved. In contrast, the line graph shows which nations have won the most medals in the summer Olympics.

— 1 _____

Overall, the bar chart shows that in the winter Olympics, Norway has gained the most medals, winning an equal number of gold, silver and bronze medals. It has won just over three hundred medals, whereas Canada, in fifth place, has won approximately 150 medals.

— 2 _____

The results of the summer Olympics are quite different, however, with the USA having won the most medals. Overall, the USA has won just under 2,500 medals, a much higher number than the other four countries on the graph. The USSR is the second highest, winning approximately a thousand medals.

— 3 _____

To summarise, the bar chart and the graph illustrate how many medals the highest-ranking countries have won in the summer and winter Olympics. The results of each Olympics are very different, with the USA, the USSR and Germany being successful in both.

— 4 _____

04 ▶ Label the paragraphs of the sample answer 'Summary', 'Main body' or 'Introduction'.

05 ▶ Answer these questions, which deal with some minor differences between discussing one graph and comparing two or more graphs.

1 Did the writer introduce both graphs in the introduction?
2 Did the writer discuss the details (main body) of both graphs in the same paragraph or separate paragraphs?
3 Did the summary include both the bar chart and the graph or just one?

06 ▶ Complete the gaps with 'main body', 'summary' or 'introduction'.

The 1 _____ should state what the graph is about. Do not copy the wording of the question. You should paraphrase the question using synonyms, e.g. *illustrates / shows*.

The 2 _____ should discuss the general trends in the graph, supported by the relevant data, e.g. dates or numbers. Identify the most important features – do not try to include everything.

The 3 _____ should provide an overview of the key points made in the 'Main body'. Do not include new information or your own opinion.

◎ The sample answer describes a graph and a chart, as you may be asked to do in the Writing test. Although this may look difficult, the structure is similar to describing just one graph.

TIP 06
Sentences should be simple and easy to understand, not long and complicated.

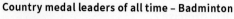

07▷ Study these two charts.

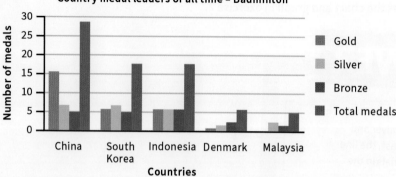

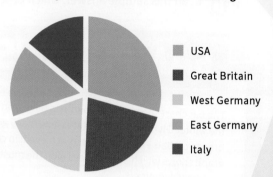

08▷ Read and order the sample answer describing the two charts.

SAMPLE ANSWER

A ☐
Looking at the bar chart it is easily apparent that China has been significantly more successful than any other country in badminton. They have achieved far more gold medals than other countries but have gained only slightly more silver and bronze medals.

B ☐
To summarise therefore, both charts illustrate the countries (or former countries) with the greatest number of medals. The bar chart indicates that China is the most successful country in badminton and the pie chart shows that the USA is the most successful in rowing.

C ☐
The bar chart illustrates the country medal leaders in badminton and also the number of gold, silver and bronze medals won by each country. The pie chart, however, shows which countries are the most successful in rowing.

D ☐
The pie chart, on the other hand, shows that the USA won the most medals in rowing. They were a little more successful than Great Britain, however. The other three countries represented won roughly the same number of medals each.

GRAMMAR FOCUS: COMPARATIVES

09▷ Read this sentence from the sample answer and underline the comparative form.

Looking at the bar chart it is easily apparent that China has been significantly more successful than any other country in badminton.

10▷ Underline all the comparative forms in the sample answer.

 Comparative forms are often needed when comparing data, either in one graph or two, so it is important to become familiar with their structure.

1 1 ▷ Complete the sentences with the correct comparative form of an adjective or adverb from the box.

| cold   far   gracefully   interesting   often   old   slow   successful   well |

1 In the triathlon he swam much _____ than he cycled.
2 In the ski-jumping event, participants were required to go much _____ than ever before.
3 Generally, countries with a _____ climate are _____ in the Winter Olympics.
4 Spectators found this ice-hockey game _____ than the last one.
5 He ran well: _____ than last year.
6 Before the Games she practised _____ than her team mates.
7 The oldest recorded male medallist was 72 years old, making him 62 years _____ than the youngest-ever medallist.
8 He accepted defeat with grace: _____ than the rest of his team.

1 2 ▷ The sample answer includes the sentence 'China has been significantly more successful than any other country in badminton.' What other modifiers are used in the answer?

In this sentence from the sample answer the word *significantly* is used to modify the comparative. In other words, to say how big or small the comparison is. Here, the word *significantly* is called a 'modifier'.

COMPARING DATA: CHOOSING THE RELEVANT INFORMATION

1 3 ▷ Study this table and graph, then answer the question which follows.

Top medal winners of all time – athletes

Athlete	Country	Sport	Total
Michael Phelps	USA	Swimming	22
Larysa Latynina	USSR	Gymnastics	18
Nikolai Andrianov	USSR	Gymnastics	15
Ole Einar Bjoerndalen	Norway	Biathlon	13
Borys Shakhlin	USSR	Gymnastics	13

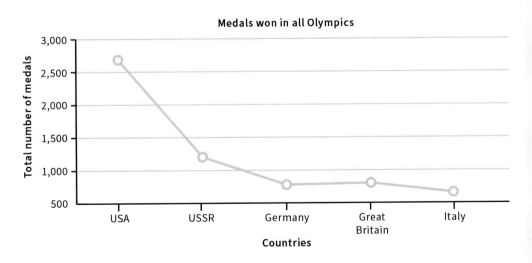

Medals won in all Olympics

Which of this information would you include in your answer?

1 The most successful athlete is Michael Phelps from the USA, who has won the most medals for swimming.

2 The chart also shows that three of the top five athletes were gymnasts from the USSR.

3 Michael Phelps won 22 medals, Larysa Latynina 18, Nikolai Andrianov 15, Ole Einar Bjoerndalen 13 and Borys Shakhlin 13.

4 The sports which the athletes achieved medals in were swimming, gymnastics and the biathlon.

5 In summary, both charts illustrate that the two most successful countries in the Olympics were the USA and the USSR.

14▶ Now, study the line graph again and write three statements similar to those in exercise 13.

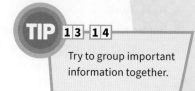

TIP 13–14

Try to group important information together.

[EXAM SKILLS]

15▶ Use the information and language from this lesson to answer this Writing Part 1 task. You should spend about 20 minutes on this task.

The chart and graph below give information about participants who have entered the Olympics since it began.

Summarise the information by selecting and reporting on the main features, and make comparisons where relevant.

Write at least 150 words.

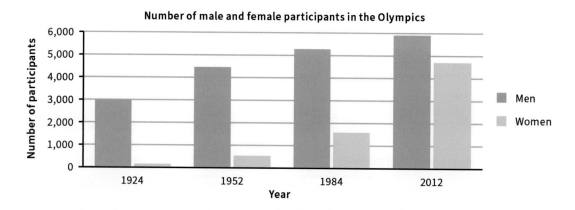

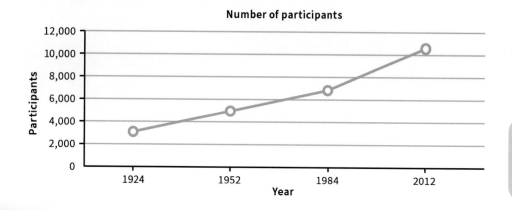

GO ONLINE AND COMPLETE UNIT 2 WRITING EXERCISES 1–4

UNIT /02: LEISURE AND RECREATION

LISTENING

IN THIS UNIT YOU WILL LEARN HOW TO

- listen to and understand directions from one place to another
- match descriptions with people, places or things
- listen for specific information and classify it in a table.

SUBURBS

INNER CITY

SEASIDE

COUNTRYSIDE

LEAD-IN

01▶ Write the correct word under each diagram to check your understanding of language connected with road travel and directions.

| bend | crossroads | flyover | junction | roundabout | traffic lights |

1

2

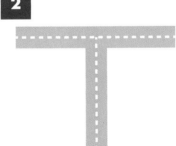

3

4

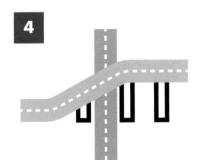

5

6

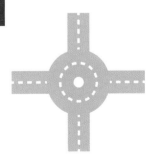

02▷ Listen to directions 1–6 and write the correct word from the box.

1 Stay in the middle lane so that you can go over the motorway. _____

2 You'll have to wait on the right till it changes for you to turn. _____

3 Go round and take the third exit on the right. _____

4 Slow down here because it goes to the left quite sharply. _____

5 When you get there, go straight across. _____

6 When you get to the end of this road, take the left turn. _____

[COMPLETION/MATCHING TASKS]

◉ Before listening to directions to complete a map, you should look at the map carefully and think about the type of information you need to identify each place on the map. When listening, you should focus on words and phrases that will help you find the information, for example *turn left* or *go straight on*. You need to follow the directions carefully and try to predict which information will come next.

03▷ Listen to the Director of Sports giving directions from one sports centre to another. Write the letters in the correct position on the map.

A roundabout **B** junction **C** traffic lights **D** crossroads **E** flyover **F** bend

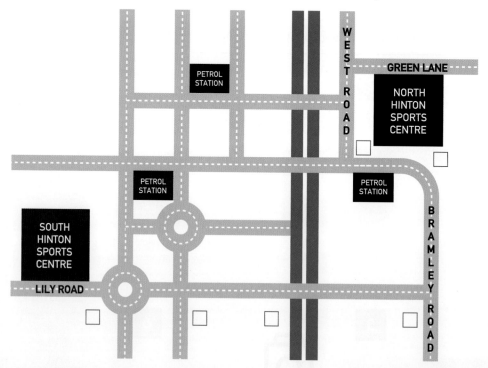

04▷ Listen to the descriptions of sports 1–5 and write the correct number next to each sport A–E.

A gymnastics ☐
B basketball ☐
C weightlifting ☐
D badminton ☐
E table tennis ☐

◉ When matching descriptions to people, places or things, you need to focus on key words and ideas which can help you decide what is being described as well as what is **not** being described. For example, if you have to choose between football and cycling, a description with key words like *goal*, *run* and *kick* is more likely to describe football, and a description with *ride*, *wheel* and *race* is more likely to describe cycling.

05 ▷ Listen to the next part of the message. The Director of Sports is giving instructions for preparing three rooms for the inter-college sports competition at the sports centre. Write the sports in the correct gap in the table. One of the sports appears twice.

| badminton | basketball | gymnastics | table tennis | weightlifting |

North Hinton Sports Centre

	Dean Room	Carsley Room	Forster Room
Sport event – morning	1 _____	2 _____	3 _____
Sport event – afternoon	4 _____	5 _____	6 _____

[EXAM SKILLS]

◉ In the Listening test you may need to complete categories in a table or set of notes which already has some of the information in place. You should look at the information in the table carefully to get a good idea of what other information is required. This will help you to focus on the missing information. For example, the word *nets* is already given under *basketball*, so you know that you will need to listen for another word connected with that category for question 2. In each case, you will hear the sport first, so you will be able focus on the missing word.

TIP 06

You need to write the same words as you hear in the recording. You will be told how many words you need to write and you will hear the words in the same order they are given in the recording script.

06 ▷ Listen to the last part of the message and complete the table with the pieces of equipment. Write ONE WORD ONLY in each gap.

Sport event	basketball	gymnastics	table tennis	badminton	weightlifting
Equipment	nets	vaulting horse	tables	1 _____	barbells
	2 _____	3 _____	nets	racquets	weights
		4 _____	5 _____	shuttlecocks	6 _____
		rings			chalk
		pommel horse			

07 ▷ The Director of Sports, Jeff, leaves another message for the three helpers, Steve, Amanda and Malik. In the message, he tells them who should be in charge of each event. Listen and write the correct organiser, A, B, C or D next to events 1–6.

A Steve

B Amanda

C Malik

D Jeff

1 badminton _____

2 gymnastics _____

3 weightlifting am _____

4 basketball _____

5 weightlifting pm _____

6 table tennis _____

GO ONLINE AND COMPLETE UNIT 2 READING EXERCISES 1–5

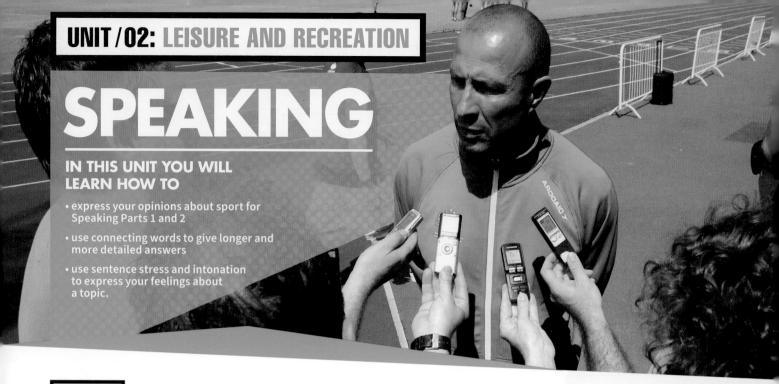

UNIT / 02: LEISURE AND RECREATION

SPEAKING

IN THIS UNIT YOU WILL LEARN HOW TO

• express your opinions about sport for Speaking Parts 1 and 2

• use connecting words to give longer and more detailed answers

• use sentence stress and intonation to express your feelings about a topic.

LEAD-IN

01 ▶ Match the photos with the activities in the box.

football	gym	hiking	surfing the internet	video games
movies	reading	swimming	karate / kickboxing	

Work with a partner to ask and answer these questions.

1 Do you like doing any of these activities in your spare time?
2 Which activities do your friends like doing?
3 Which of the activities are popular in your country?

PARAPHRASING COMMON RESPONSES

Write the phrases in the box in the correct column of the table.

I like …	I don't know if I like …	A lot of people like …
I'm not sure whether I like …	I'm not a big fan of …	I'm very keen on …
I often enjoy …	I hate …	I don't know much about …
I'm not really interested in …	I don't look forward to …	Not many people like …

TIP 03

There are many ways to say you like or do not like something. Using a variety of phrases will improve your Speaking test score.

👍	✌️	👎
I like …		

ADDING CONNECTING WORDS

04▷ Match sentence beginnings 1–4 with sentence endings a–d, using a suitable connecting word. There are several possible answers.

TIP 04

Longer sentences will show the examiner that you can use more complex grammar.

1 I love listening to K-Pop	AND	a my friends don't really like it either.
2 I sometimes enjoy mountain climbing	BUT	b I prefer staying at home.
3 I don't like spending money	SO	c it's really exciting.
4 I'm not really interested in watching football on TV	BECAUSE	d I prefer watersports.

05▷ Complete your own table using the same connecting words.

	AND	
	BUT	
	SO	
	BECAUSE	

06▷ Complete the sentences about things you do and do not like doing.

1 _____ AND _____ BUT _____
BECAUSE _____ SO _____ .

2 _____ AND _____ BUT _____
BECAUSE _____ SO _____ .

3 _____ AND _____ BUT _____
BECAUSE _____ SO _____ .

PROVIDING MORE DETAILED RESPONSES

07▷ Complete the sentences. Think of THREE reasons for your answer.

1 I like going swimming. I like it because _____ , _____
and _____ .

2 I enjoy watching football on TV. I enjoy it because _____ ,
_____ and _____ .

3 I love reading books on my sofa. I love it because _____ ,
_____ and _____ .

4 I'm a big fan of movies. This is because _____ ,
_____ and _____ .

08 ▶ Write your own ideas in the sentences.

5 I like _____ . I like it because _____ ,
   _____ and _____ .

6 I enjoy _____ . I enjoy it because _____ ,
   _____ and _____ .

7 I'm not a big fan of _____ because I _____ ,
   _____ and _____ .

8 I hate _____ because it is _____ , _____
   and _____ .

TALKING ABOUT SPORTS EVENTS

09 ▶ Ask your partner these questions about each photo.

1 Did you watch this sporting event?
2 Do you like to do this sport in your spare time?
3 Is this sport popular in your
   country/where you live?

SENTENCE STRESS AND INTONATION

10 ▶ **Listen to how the words in bold in these sentences are stressed.**

17

1 I think that **rowing** is a **great sport** if you want to stay **fit** and **healthy**.
2 I often enjoy **tennis** as it is **very competitive** and I **like** to **beat** my **friends**.

11 ▶ **Listen and underline the stressed words in these sentences.**

18

1 Ryan Giggs was a famous player for Manchester United; he played hundreds of games.
2 At London 2012, the United States was top of the medals table, followed by China, then Great Britain and Northern Ireland.
3 Last weekend, I was going to go to the gym, but I decided not to bother.
4 Michael Jordan is the number one all-time points scorer in the NBA playoffs, although Lebron James is catching up.
5 I ran in the London marathon last year. I thought I was never going to make it to the end!

12 ▶ **You can use intonation to show your feelings about a topic. Read these sentences and decide if they are positive or negative in tone.**

1 My favourite sport is hockey. It's amazing!
2 I like swimming but I wish there were more places to swim where I live.
3 I've always liked fishing but I don't have time to do it any more.
4 I'm really excited about all the new video games that will come out soon. I can't wait!

13 ▶ **Listen to the recording. The first time you hear the sentences, you will hear *flat* (no) intonation. The second time you hear them, the speaker will use correct intonation. Mark the changes in intonation with a ↗ if it rises or a ↘ if it falls.**

19

1 My favourite sport is hockey. It's amazing!

2 I like swimming, but I wish there were more places to swim where I live.

3 I've always liked fishing but I don't have time to do it any more.

4 I'm really excited about all the new video games that will come out soon.

I can't wait!

14 ▶ **Write THREE sentences about a sport you like/do not like doing/playing. With a partner, say each sentence out loud TWICE, first with *flat* (no) intonation, and then with rising and falling intonation.**

Sports I like playing

1 _____
2 _____
3 _____

Sports I don't like playing

1 _____
2 _____
3 _____

Individual **syllables** can be stressed in English words. English speakers also stress the **content words** in a sentence, and leave the **function** words (like *the*, *of*, etc.) unstressed.

1 5 ▶ Write a suitable sports verb in these sentences. More than one answer may be possible. There are more verbs than you need.

beat	train	defeat	exercise	knock out	lose (to)	play
score	shoot	tackle	support	compete	watch	win
qualify	represent (my country)					

1 I didn't think Mayweather would _____ Pacquiao in that boxing match.
2 It has always been a dream of mine to _____ at Wimbledon.
3 I try to _____ about three times a week, so that I can keep playing well.
4 I _____ Liverpool Football Club. I've been a fan for a very long time.
5 Their international football team _____ plenty of times during a game but usually _____ very few goals.

[EXAM SKILLS]

1 6 ▶ Ask and answer these Speaking Part 1 questions with a partner.

1 What do you usually do in your spare time?
2 Do you prefer doing things by yourself or with friends?
3 Is there anything special you do at the weekends?
4 Do you think you get enough free time?

1 7 ▶ Answer the prompts in this Speaking Part 2 task. Talk for at least 60 seconds. Remember to use the connecting words you studied in exercises 4–6.

Describe a sports event you watched or attended.

You should say:

- what kind of sporting event it was
- where you watched it
- how often this event takes place

and explain why you consider this sports event interesting.

GO ONLINE AND COMPLETE UNIT 2 SPEAKING EXERCISES 1–4

READING

IN THIS UNIT YOU WILL LEARN HOW TO

• match information in a question with information in a text

• skim a text to identify types of information

• recognise the passive.

LEAD-IN

01 ▷ Read these quotes, which give different opinions about how news is consumed.

A Since the birth of the internet, access to local and world news has become possible 24 hours a day, 7 days a week. This is having an increasingly negative impact on society, and consequently we have all become news addicts!

SARAH (35)

B Adults aged 60+ buy a daily newspaper as a matter of habit. Generally, they don't know how to access news online.

MATT (18)

C Youngsters these days aren't interested in the news and spend most of their time on social media sites. They don't buy a newspaper or watch a regular TV bulletin. The only news they might be interested in is entertainment news.

CHARLES (65)

D I would only use social media sites to check entertainment news. I wouldn't trust it for any serious news, such as crime or politics. For those topics, I'd only rely on television bulletins.

MARY (25)

02 ▷ Match statements 1–4 with quotes A–D.

1 Continual exposure to the news is bad for us. _____

2 As a news source, there is more confidence in television than in the internet. _____

3 Teenagers are only interested in news about actors and pop stars. _____

4 The older generation don't know how to read the news using the internet. _____

TIP 02

In the Reading test, you may be asked to match information in the question with information in the text. However, the texts will be longer (between 750 and 950 words) and you will need to match the question to a paragraph.

03 ▷ Look at the quotes again and, with a partner, discuss whether you agree or disagree with each speaker.

MATCHING INFORMATION

0 4 Skim this text to understand the general meaning of each paragraph.

A SMARTER WAY TO ACCESS THE NEWS?

A A recent report, issued by the international news agency Reuters, reveals that smartphones are quickly becoming the most popular way to access the news. Over the last year, this increase has been particularly noted in countries such as the UK, the USA and Japan. In fact, for all countries involved in the survey, usage has increased from 37% to 46%. Furthermore, 66% of smartphone users are now using the device for news on a weekly basis.

B By comparison, the number of people using tablets to access the news is decreasing in most countries. More sophisticated smartphones are reducing the need for other portable devices. The need for accessing the news on laptops and desktops has also changed. Over half (57%) still consider these devices the most important ways to access the news, but this is a decrease of 8% from last year.

C The report also revealed, however, that on average people only use a small number of trusted news sources on their phones, the average across all countries being 1.52 per person. In the UK, for example, over half of smartphone users (51%) regularly use the BBC app.

D Across all countries included in the survey, 25% stated that their smartphone was the main device used for accessing digital news, an increase of 20% since last year. This is particularly true of those aged under 35, with the figure rising to 41%. The overall trend, however, is not to use just one digital device to access the news, but rather a combination of two or three.

0 5 Which paragraphs (A–D) contain this information? You may write any letter more than once.

1 other ways news is accessed online _____
2 over half of smartphone users access news via their phones

   _____

3 the most popular way to access the news digitally is by using several methods _____
4 the younger generation are more likely to use their smartphone to access the news _____

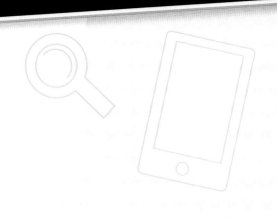

06 Look at your answers to the questions in exercise 5 and decide if these statements are True or False.

1 The answers do not follow the same order as the text.
2 The answers may not be the main idea of the paragraph.
3 Some paragraphs contain more than one answer.
4 Not all paragraphs contain an answer.
5 The questions will often use synonyms rather than wording from the text.

07 Look again at the text in exercise 4 and your answers to exercise 5. Then complete the gaps in these tables.

Words in the text		Words in the question
The overall trend		1 _____
2 _____		over half
a combination of two or three		3 _____

Words in the text	Synonyms
4 _____	a quarter of
5 _____	questionnaire
6 _____	often

IDENTIFYING DIFFERENT TYPES OF INFORMATION

08 Read extracts 1–6, taken from various news reports. Then match the extracts with a label from the box.

| account | cause and effect | description | opinion | reaction | summary |

1 Tennis fans were left shocked today, when the favourite to win the championship was defeated in the third round by an unknown player.

2 According to recent reports, the government feels it is no longer necessary to pay for school meals. Headteachers feel that this would be a disaster, however, especially given the recent progress with making dinners healthier for pupils.

3 People must be responsible for their own health, otherwise the National Health Service will no longer be able to cope. This was the warning given today by the head of the organisation.

4 Overall, last year was a very good year for the nation's economy. The unemployment rate was down, more jobs were created, and generally people felt they had more money to spend.

5 The Queen landed to a red-carpet welcome on Tuesday, as she opened her visit to the USA. She was greeted by hundreds of guests, together with the President and his family.

6 A 60-year-old man was arrested today, after he was caught stealing from his local shop. According to a witness, he was wearing black clothes and a mask during the robbery.

The matching information task can take time. To save time, one approach is to label the paragraphs before starting to answer the questions. Here are some of the types of information you may be asked to find: *a fact, a reason, a summary, a cause, an effect, a conclusion, a description, a finding.* By identifying the purpose of each paragraph, it can be easier to link the question to the relevant part of the text. For example:

The overall trend, however, is not to use just one digital device to access the news, but rather a combination of two or three – **text**

the most popular way to access the news digitally is by using several methods – **question**

Both the text and question are summarising **factual** statements.

0 9 ▷ Skim this text for the main ideas, then label each paragraph with ONE or more of the descriptions from the box.

> cause and effect   factual   opinion   problems   reason   summary

● ● ● ⟨ ⟩

Login   Sign up

| Home | About | News | Articles | Search |

HOW THE YOUNGER GENERATION CONSUMES THE NEWS

Posted September 07

A

In recent years, there has been growing concern by researchers and indeed the older generation that the younger generation are somewhat disengaged from the news, and as a result have a very narrow view of the world around them. This, however, couldn't be further from the truth, as shown by a recent study carried out by the Media Insight Project (American Press Institute & Associated Press). According to this research, 85% of youngsters say that keeping up to date with the news is important to them, and 69% receive news on a daily basis. ___opinion/factual___

B

Perhaps what some of the older generation fail to understand is that just because the younger generation does not buy a daily newspaper, it doesn't mean that they don't follow the news. Born into a digital age, or more specifically the age of the internet, the younger generation simply accesses news through the digital devices they grew up using: laptops, tablets, smartphones, etc. A recent study produced by Ofcom revealed that 60% of youngsters in the UK use the internet or apps for news, compared to just 21% of those in the older age range.

_____

C

Social media also plays an important part in consuming the news for the younger generation. It was also revealed that most youngsters actually don't seek out news from social media, but choose to follow it once they see it there. In other words, they encounter it accidentally and therefore following the news is secondary. For example, when accessing social media sites, news headlines automatically appear. These catch the user's eye and consequently the news link is clicked and followed.

_____

D

For the moment, social networks are being used selectively, however. For example, social media is used for breaking news, but is not relied on in terms of accuracy. For hard news topics, such as economics or local crime, youngsters continue to look to original sources. For accuracy and reliability, television is still the preferred choice for both generations.

_____

E

According to Alison Preston, Head of Media Literacy Research at Ofcom, motivations for following the news also vary according to the generation. In her current report on the topic, she states that, for the younger generation, news is largely about convenience and being social. For the older generation, however, motivation is greatly linked to a sense of duty and habit.

_____

F

Overall, it is fair to say that news plays an important part in all our everyday lives, regardless of generation. However, what is different amongst the generations is why and how it is accessed. _____

GRAMMAR FOCUS: THE PASSIVE

1 0 ▷ Look at extracts 1–4 from the text. Match a tense from the box with each extract.

> past simple passive   present continuous passive
> present perfect passive   present simple passive

1 … social media **is used** for breaking news … *present simple passive*
2 … it **was** also **revealed** …
3 … social networks **are being used** selectively …
4 … there **has been** growing concern by researchers …

1 1 ▸ Why has the writer chosen to use the passive rather than the active in these extracts?

1 2 ▸ Complete headlines 1–4 with the verb in brackets in one of these passive forms.

past simple	present continuous	present perfect	present simple

1 Holidays _____are ruined_____ (ruin) by air strikes.
2 The launch of London's night tube _____ (delay) until further notice.
3 The victims of the air disaster _____ (name) earlier this morning.
4 A new medicine to help fight cancer _____ (develop) in Cambridge at the moment.

1 3 ▸ Read these news headlines written in the active, then change them to the passive.

1 People blame all the wet weather on climate change.
  Climate change _____ .
2 Police found the Hollywood actor unconscious in his Manhattan apartment.
  The Hollywood actor _____ .
3 Researchers have recovered treasure from a sunken Spanish ship.
  Treasure _____ .
4 Today, the public are celebrating a royal wedding.
  A royal wedding _____ .

1 4 ▸ Answer these questions using what you have learnt in this lesson.

1 What should you read carefully before starting a matching information task?
2 Are you looking for matching words or synonyms?
3 Do the answers follow the same order as the text?
4 Can the same letter be used more than once?
5 Do all paragraphs need to be used?

EXAM SKILLS

1 5 ▸ The reading passage 'How the younger generation consumes the news' has six paragraphs A–F. Which paragraph contains the following information?

1 the reasons why the younger generation seeks news _____
2 the opinion that news is important to the younger generation _____
3 the percentage of older adults in the UK who access the news digitally

  _____

4 the idea that the younger generation largely encounters the news by chance

  _____

5 the news is of great significance to both young and old people _____
6 why the younger generation consumes the news through modern technology

  _____

> GO ONLINE AND
> COMPLETE UNIT 3
> READING EXERCISES 1 & 2

WRITING

IN THIS UNIT YOU WILL LEARN HOW TO

- use time markers and the passive to describe a process
- plan a description of a process
- interpret scientific and technical diagrams.

LEAD-IN

01 In the Writing test, you might be asked to describe a process. Look at sentences a–g describing a process for writing a local news story, then order the sentences, using the pictures to help you.

A local man risked his life today …

What? RESCUE STORY

Why? SAVE DOG

Where? LOCAL LAKE

When? THURSDAY EVENING

Local man rescues dog

Brave man saves drowning dog from lake

How to write a local newspaper story

a After that, think of a good title for your piece. ☐

b Finally, submit your article to your local newspaper via email. ☐

c Thirdly, think of a good first line: something which is attention-grabbing. ☐

d Next, write the main body of the article, answering the four 'w's: *what*, *where*, *why* and *when*. ☐

e First, think of a good idea! Choose a local and interesting news story. ☐

f Then, check your article for grammatical and spelling errors. ☐

g Secondly, accompany your story with a picture of a local person or attraction. ☐

02 ▶ In exercise 1, which words helped you choose the order?

03 ▶ Look at this table. Which set of words, 1–4, includes words to describe actions taking place at the same time?

1	First	First of all	First	To begin with
2	After	Next	Then	Secondly, Thirdly, etc.
3	Whilst	At the same time		
4	Finally			

04 ▶ Study the diagram about how a newsroom works, then read the sample answer, ignoring the gaps for the moment.

TIP 04
Do not repeat the wording in the Writing question.

Attending an event, face-to face or phone interviews, looking through archives.

TV camera crews are assigned to jobs, photo shoots are booked or graphic designers are allocated work.

Through press releases, journalists or the general public.

Raw visual footage is reviewed and edited, photographs are loaded into a computer and saved, journalists spend time finishing their stories.

Sub-editors will check stories for readability and ensure they are not libellous, while some stories can be cut, due to space or time restrictions.

SAMPLE ANSWER

The diagram illustrates how news stories are created in a newsroom.

1 _____ , news stories come into the newsroom through either journalists, press releases or members of the general public. 2 _____ , journalists are assigned to different stories. This may mean they have to attend an event, conduct interviews or search through archives.
3 _____ , images become involved in the process. This could be through television crews, graphic designers or photographers. 4 _____ , depending on the type of newsroom, visual footage is reviewed or photographs are loaded into a computer. Journalists also have time at this point to finish their stories. 5 _____ , sub-editors are used to check that stories are legally and factually correct. Also at this stage, some stories may be cut, due to space or time restrictions.

Overall, the diagram shows how news is created in five simple steps. Many people are involved in the process, from journalists to photographers.

05▷ Compare the diagram and the sample answer, then answer these questions.

    1 Is every word used in the diagram used in the sample answer?

    2 Do you need to understand every word in the diagram?

    3 Can you use nouns from the diagram in your answer?

06▷ Complete the sample answer in exercise 4, using the time markers from exercise 3. More than one answer may be possible.

PLANNING YOUR ANSWER

07▷ Spending a few minutes planning your answer will ensure it is both logical and structured. It may also help you to understand the diagram better and to choose the most significant features. Look at this example plan.

Suggested plan for describing a process

→ Introduction – The diagram explains the process of writing a news story. There are a total of seven stages in this process, each of which will be described below.

The introduction should simply state what the process is. Do not, however, copy the words used in the task instructions.

→ Main body – You need to include every stage, but not every minor detail. Many of the nouns will often be provided in the diagram, so make sure they are included in your answer.

Stage	Verbs	Nouns
1	choose	news story
2	accompany	story, picture
3	think	first line
4	write	main body, article
5	check	article, errors
6	think	title
7	submit	newspaper

→ Overview – Overall, the diagram shows how you can write a news story in just a few simple steps.

A clear overview of the diagram is essential. This can appear at either the beginning or the end of your answer.

08▷ Describe some of these processes to a partner.

boil an egg	download an app	make your favourite dish
make a cake	post a tweet	upload a video on YouTube

09▷ Write a plan for one of these processes.

GRAMMAR FOCUS: THE PASSIVE

10 ▷ When writing about a process, the passive is often used. Underline the uses of the passive in the diagram in exercise 4. Which passive tense has been used? There is also one example of a passive used with a modal verb. Can you find it?

11 ▷ Transform these active sentences into the passive.

The process of writing a local news story

1 Choose a local news story.
2 Accompany the story with a picture.
3 Think of a good first line.
4 Write the main body of the article.
5 Check the article for errors.
6 Invent a good title.
7 Submit the article to a local newspaper.

INTERPRETING SCIENTIFIC OR TECHNICAL DIAGRAMS

12 ▷ When you first read the diagram, you may not understand it. If this is the case, try and use some of these steps. Order the steps from 1 to 5.

A ☐

Circle the information in the diagram you do understand. You probably understand more than you think.

B ☐

If you are still unsure what to write, move on to Part 2 of the Writing test. This is worth more marks and it will give you longer to think about Part 1.

C ☐

Ask yourself some of these questions:
- How many stages are there?
- Are the stages in a particular order?
- Do some stages take place at the same time?

D ☐

Write a brief plan as you did in exercise 9, and include vocabulary already given. However, remember to write sentences in your own words.

E ☐ 1

Study the diagram carefully. Although the task is not testing your knowledge on the subject, your interpretation of the diagram needs to be accurate.

The type of diagrams given in this task can vary. It is common, however, to be given a process which is technical or scientific.

TIP 12

You are not expected to have any previous knowledge of the subject.

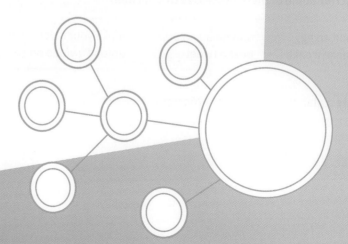

1 3 ▶ Use the useful phrases and verbs below and other language from this lesson to answer the Writing Part 1 task. You should spend about 20 minutes on this task.

Useful phrases for process tasks

The diagram / flow-chart illustrates / shows …
Each picture represents a stage in the process of …
There are … [number] stages to this process, beginning with … and ending in … .
In conclusion / To conclude, this simple process shows how …

Useful verbs for process tasks

absorb	build	link	convert	install	manufacture
attach	make	lift	provide	reflect	

The diagram illustrates the process of lithography: a method used for printing newspapers.

Summarise the information by selecting and reporting the main features and make comparisons where necessary.

Write at least 150 words.

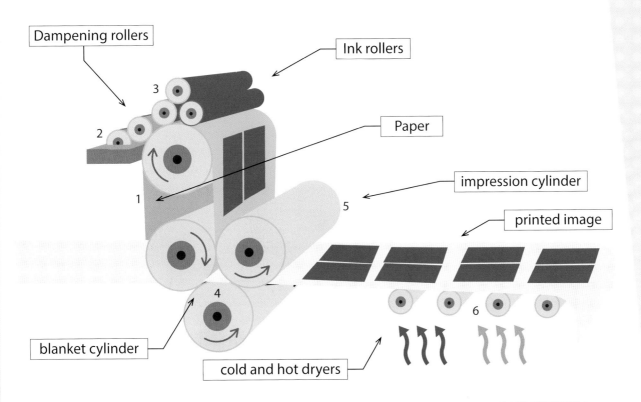

Dampening rollers

Ink rollers

Paper

impression cylinder

printed image

blanket cylinder

cold and hot dryers

GO ONLINE AND COMPLETE UNIT 3 WRITING EXERCISES 1–4

UNIT / 03: THE NEWS AND MEDIA

LISTENING

IN THIS UNIT YOU WILL LEARN HOW TO

- identify the attitudes and opinions of speakers through expressions and intonation
- recognise paraphrases of what speakers say
- understand the role of distractors when answering multiple-choice questions.

LEAD-IN

01 ▶ Listen to three short discussions, each on a particular topic. In each discussion, another topic is also referred to. Choose the main topic in each discussion.

20

1	**A** sport	**B** politics	**C** economics
2	**A** business	**B** science	**C** entertainment
3	**A** technology	**B** sport	**C** business

02▶ Look at these topics and listen to Speakers 1–3. Identify who has the positive attitude, the negative attitude and the neutral attitude. Write Speaker 1, Speaker 2 or Speaker 3.

21

TIP 02

It is important to identify each speaker and understand their **attitudes** and **opinions**. Attitude can be shown through intonation, as well as through the expressions a speaker uses.

Topic 1: Modern art
Positive: _____
Negative: _____
Neutral: _____

Topic 2: Combating climate change
Positive: _____
Negative: _____
Neutral: _____

IDENTIFYING SPEAKERS AND THEIR OPINIONS

03▶ You will hear two media studies students, Maria and Simon, discussing three space expeditions in the news with their tutor, Dr Anita Thornton. They are deciding on a study topic. Listen and identify their final choice, A, B or C.

22

A Moon expedition
B Mars expedition
C Pluto expedition

04▶ During the discussion, each of the three speakers gives their opinions on the three possibilities. Listen to the first part of the discussion again and decide what each speaker says they prefer first for each suggestion: positive, negative or neutral.

22

	Pluto expedition	Mars expedition	Moon expedition
Simon			
Maria			
Dr Thornton			

UNDERSTANDING SPEAKERS' ATTITUDES

 People often use expressions to show their attitude and opinions. Listen to six short conversations and choose Positive (A), Negative (B) or Neutral (C) for each attitude expressed by the *second* speaker.

1 A Positive   B Negative   C Neutral
2 A Positive   B Negative   C Neutral
3 A Positive   B Negative   C Neutral
4 A Positive   B Negative   C Neutral
5 A Positive   B Negative   C Neutral
6 A Positive   B Negative   C Neutral

 Listen to the conversations again and write the key words and expressions which express the speaker's attitude. Decide whether this is positive, negative or neutral.

Conversation	Key words/expressions	Positive / Negative / Neutral
1	seriously?	
2		
3		
4		
5		
6		

UNDERSTANDING THE ROLE OF DISTRACTORS

 Listen to part of the conversation again between Maria, Simon and Dr Thornton and choose the correct answer, A, B or C.

Dr Thornton thinks studying the Mars expedition is a good idea because
A she thinks the mission will be successful.
B robots and machines will be used to start a colony there.
C the students will have the chance to study it until it ends.

 Check your answer with your teacher and then answer these questions to help you find the reasons why the other two options are not correct.

1 What does Dr Thornton say is actually successful?
2 Which expedition is sending robots and machines to find a suitable place for a colony?
3 What time references do you hear?

In multiple-choice questions in the exam, there is one correct option and two wrong options. The wrong options are called 'distractors'. They are designed to be attractive, for example by talking about the correct answer but giving the incorrect information. The distractors do not answer the question.

09 Listen to a conversation between Maria, Simon and Dr Thornton one month after the start of the project and read questions 1–3. There are two options for each question: one correct answer and one distractor. For each question, choose the correct answer and think about why the distractor is wrong.

 TIP 09

When you check the answers, think carefully about why the distractors are wrong and how you can identify the correct answer.

1 Alfonso has left the Mars project because
   A he became ill while they were in Arizona.
   B he had a problem unconnected to the project.

2 If someone leaves the Mars project, the rules say that
   A a new person must take their place.
   B no new people can join at a later date.

3 Simon agrees that
   A only one person should look after the food production.
   B more than one person should look after the food production.

RECOGNISING PARAPHRASES OF WHAT PEOPLE SAY

 10 Listen to the next conversation about the project and choose the answer, A, B or C, which correctly paraphrases the information in the recording. Look at this example.

One person has most probably been physically violent because
A they do not speak very much as a rule.
B they might have difficulty being in a closed space.
C they always disliked another participant.

 The correct answer is **B**. It is mentioned that Joe is quiet, but only as an observation, not a possible reason, so A is not correct. It is also mentioned that he hit Martin, but there is nothing to say he has always disliked him. There is talk of isolation probably being the reason, which relates to being in a closed space, with no escape from the situation.

TIP 10

In multiple-choice questions in the Listening test, there are always **three** options – one correct answer and two distractors.

 11 Now listen to the next part of the conversation and choose the correct answer, A, B or C.

1 Dr Thornton's main interest is in
   A what kinds of people take part in projects like this.
   B how she can be a psychology expert on the project.
   C how people interact in long periods of isolation together.

2 Dr Thornton thinks it's good that
   A it took some time for the first serious conflict to take place.
   B problems like these happen on this type of project.
   C the project is not like a television series or soap opera.

3 Simon states that
   A Joe could cause problems for the environment of the building if he stays.
   B Joe successfully dealt with a serious environmental situation.
   C they could solve any environmental problems if Joe left.

[EXAM SKILLS]

1 2 ▶ **Listen to the final part of the conversation and choose the correct answer, A, B or C.**

28

1 Simon is going to base his main study on
   A why just over half of the participants stayed until the end of the project.
   B how to make sure that people can survive on a real trip to Mars.
   C how much the project was covered in the news media.

2 One surprising result of the project was that
   A it was reported as a major news item.
   B the participants were in danger of losing their lives.
   C information from the project will be used in a new design.

3 One thing that Dr Thornton is interested in finding out about the people in the Mars project is
   A why they had health problems.
   B how they coped physically with living close together.
   C how their physical well-being might develop in the future.

4 Maria intends to
   A make a contribution to an important scientific publication.
   B write about how well the participants performed while living in a small space.
   C focus only on the psychological issues affecting the participants.

5 In the end, the total spent on the Mars project was
   A just over the planned amount.
   B twice the planned amount.
   C just under the planned amount.

6 The person who would absolutely refuse to be a participant in a repeat project is
   A Simon.
   B Dr Thornton.
   C Maria.

GO ONLINE AND COMPLETE UNIT 3 LISTENING EXERCISES 1–3

UNIT / 03: THE NEWS AND MEDIA

SPEAKING

IN THIS UNIT YOU WILL LEARN HOW TO

• speak about the news and media for Speaking Part 1

• use adjectives and intonation to express feelings about a news story

• use paraphrase and the passive to describe an event for Speaking Part 2.

01 ▶ Ask and answer these questions with a partner.

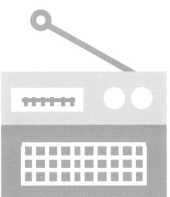

1 Where do you usually get your news?

2 Where do most people in your country get their news?

3 Do people in your country still read newspapers?

4 Are there any advantages to getting your news on the internet?

TALKING ABOUT THE MEDIA

02▷ Think of THREE advantages and THREE disadvantages of each type of media in the box. Discuss with a partner.

Newspapers	
Advantages	Disadvantages
1 _____	1 _____
2 _____	2 _____
3 _____	3 _____

The internet	
Advantages	Disadvantages
1 _____	1 _____
2 _____	2 _____
3 _____	3 _____

Radio	
Advantages	Disadvantages
1 _____	1 _____
2 _____	2 _____
3 _____	3 _____

Television	
Advantages	Disadvantages
1 _____	1 _____
2 _____	2 _____
3 _____	3 _____

EXPRESSING YOUR FEELINGS ABOUT A NEWS STORY

03▷ With a partner, describe these happy news stories, then share your story with the class. As you tell the story, try to use some or all of the adjectives from the box.

1 A person overcoming a serious health problem
2 A dog finding its owner after getting lost
3 A man being rescued from an overturned boat in the sea

brilliant	delightful	extraordinary	impressive	magnificent
marvellous	outstanding	stunning	tremendous	

It was one of the most extraordinary events I've ever seen!

04▷ With a different partner, describe these sad news stories, then share your story with the class. Use some or all of the adjectives from the box.

1 A man losing his winning lottery ticket
2 A woman breaking her leg in an accident
3 A business having to close after running out of money

absurd	bizarre	disgusting	distressing	dreadful
harmful	terrible	uncomfortable	upsetting	

It was a really bizarre thing to happen!

05 ▶ Listen to someone describe their feelings about a recent news story. For each sentence, decide whether Example A or Example B uses the correct intonation for the speaker's feelings. Practise using the correct intonation with a partner.

29

Sentence	Example A	Example B
1 When the report came in to say the mission was a success, everyone felt that we'd seen something extraordinary.	✔	✗
2 The disaster was a dreadful tragedy with a massive loss of life.		
3 I'm feeling pretty uncomfortable about the situation. I hope we can find a solution soon.		
4 The results were stunning, and the team had done a marvellous job.		
5 It was such an impressive sight and the noise that followed it was tremendous.		
6 This was such a bizarre event, and it's incredible that we haven't been able to find out what caused it.		

PARAPHRASING A NEWS STORY

06 ▶ With a partner, tell the story here in your own words (paraphrase).

FAMILY: GIRL SWEPT AWAY IN TSUNAMI TEN YEARS AGO REUNITED WITH FAMILY

A girl who was just four years old when a powerful tsunami roared into her town in Indonesia and swept her away has been reunited with her family after 10 years. The girl was returned to her family after being spotted in a crowd by her uncle. In the days following media reports of her survival, a homeless boy has also rejoined his family after he was washed out to sea at age seven with his sister.

Swap roles. Tell your partner the story here in your own words (paraphrase).

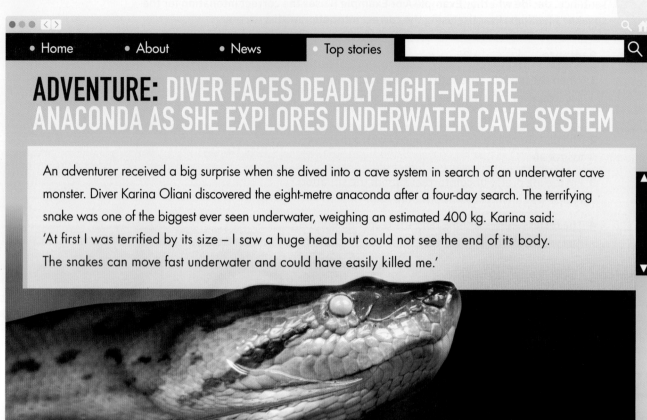

• Home   • About   • News   • Top stories

ADVENTURE: DIVER FACES DEADLY EIGHT-METRE ANACONDA AS SHE EXPLORES UNDERWATER CAVE SYSTEM

An adventurer received a big surprise when she dived into a cave system in search of an underwater cave monster. Diver Karina Oliani discovered the eight-metre anaconda after a four-day search. The terrifying snake was one of the biggest ever seen underwater, weighing an estimated 400 kg. Karina said: 'At first I was terrified by its size – I saw a huge head but could not see the end of its body. The snakes can move fast underwater and could have easily killed me.'

REPORTING A NEWS STORY

08 ▶ **Look at this picture sequence about an earthquake. Retell the story in your own words.**

09 ▶ Match these sentences with the pictures in exercise 8.

1 The earthquake destroyed a number of monuments.
2 Volunteers removed large numbers of rocks and stones to rescue people.
3 Rescuers pulled survivors from the collapsed buildings.
4 Falling buildings injured many people.
5 Helicopters arrived to take survivors to hospital.
6 The earthquake left many children homeless.
7 The earthquake struck the city at 10.00 am.

10 ▶ Change the sentences in exercise 9 from the active to the passive.

1 The earthquake destroyed a number of monuments.
 A number of monuments were destroyed (by the earthquake).

11 ▶ Practise telling the story in exercise 8 again, using the passive to describe what happened.

> **TIP 10**
>
> When reporting a news story, we use the passive to focus on **what happened** to something or someone, rather than **who** or **what** did something.

[EXAM SKILLS]

12 ▶ Ask and answer these Speaking Part 1 questions with a partner.

1 Where do you usually get your news?
2 How do most people your age get their news?
3 What kind of news are you most interested in?
4 How is getting the news today different from how we got our news in the past?

13 ▶ Answer the prompts in this Speaking Part 2 task. Talk for at least 90 seconds.

Describe a news story you read/saw.

You should say:

- what kind of news story it was
- what happened to the people in the story
- why the event was important enough to be reported on the news

and explain how you felt about the news story.

> **TIP 13**
>
> Don't forget to use the passive, and don't forget to use the expressions you learnt to talk about your feelings for the final part of the task.

GO ONLINE AND COMPLETE UNIT 3 SPEAKING EXERCISES 1–3

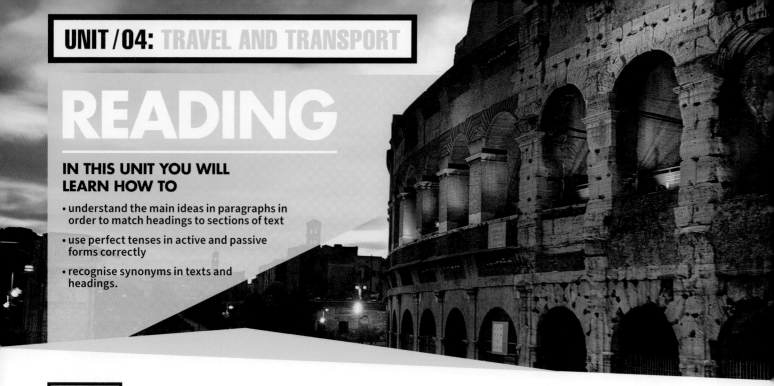

UNIT / 04: TRAVEL AND TRANSPORT

READING

IN THIS UNIT YOU WILL LEARN HOW TO

• understand the main ideas in paragraphs in order to match headings to sections of text

• use perfect tenses in active and passive forms correctly

• recognise synonyms in texts and headings.

LEAD-IN

01 A common topic in IELTS is travel and transport. With a partner, match the words and phrases 1–10 with definitions a–j. Then write FOUR sentences, each sentence using ONE word or phrase from 1–10.

1	attraction	**a**	someone who lives in the area you are talking about
2	a local	**b**	the first language that you learn when you are a child
3	cancellation	**c**	a habit or tradition
4	mother tongue	**d**	to become part of a group or society, or to help someone do this
5	custom	**e**	to make someone upset or angry
6	body language	**f**	to give all your attention to something that you are doing
7	native	**g**	relating to the people who lived in a country first, before other people took control of it
8	integrate	**h**	a place that people visit for pleasure and interest, usually while they are on holiday
9	offend	**i**	the act of stopping something that was going to happen or stopping an order for something
10	focus on	**j**	the way you move your body, showing people what you are feeling

MATCHING HEADINGS

0 2 **Skim read the article to understand the main ideas.**

◎ In the IELTS Reading test you may be asked to match a list of headings with the correct paragraph or section of the text. The headings **summarise** the **main idea** of the paragraph/section.

TRAVEL TIPS

TIP 02

You are reading only for the **main ideas** at this stage, so remember to ignore unknown words.

 A _____

In order to see all the best attractions and avoid the queues, try to get up early. Early morning is also a good time to take photographs and meet the locals.

 B _____

It is also a good idea to memorise a few useful phrases, such as 'please' and 'thank you'. You should not be worried about making mistakes, but try practising the language as much as possible. Even if your pronunciation is not perfect, locals respond better to people who make an effort.

 C _____

Travellers often face delays and cancellations, so it is important that you do not allow them to ruin your trip. Also, try not to get frustrated when you are unable to communicate with a native. Although you may be tempted to shout in your mother tongue in order to be understood, it is more polite and often more effective to simply use body language. You will have a much better trip if you are prepared for plans to change and you are able to see the funny side if things go wrong.

 D _____

Before starting your trip, find out about the people and customs of the place you are visiting. This will help you to integrate more easily and will ensure you do not do anything to offend locals. The more you know about your chosen destination, the more chance you have of gaining the most from your experience.

 E _____

Do not just socialise with other travellers, but try to start conversations with locals too. Locals are often the key to knowing the best and cheapest places to visit and eat. Furthermore, talking regularly with natives gives you a much better chance of learning the language. People enhance your travels just as much as sights do.

 F _____

In order to get a real feel for a place, spend a few hours sitting in a park or in the main square by yourself, just watching daily life happen around you. Try to absorb all the colours, smells and sounds which surround you.

◎ In order to match the headings correctly, you need to understand the main idea of the paragraph/section.

Some headings may be true of one line or phrase in the paragraph, but if the heading does not summarise **the whole section**, it is not the correct choice. For example:

Choose the most suitable heading for Paragraph A.

a Taking photographs
b Seeing the best attractions
c The best time of day to be a tourist

Only option **c** relates to information in the **whole** paragraph.

0 3 ▸ **Choose the most suitable heading for Paragraph B.**

    a Do not worry about making mistakes.

    b Make an effort with the language.

    c Your pronunciation is not important.

TIP 0 3 – 0 4

Do not just look for matching words and assume from these you have found the correct answer.

0 4 ▸ **Choose the most suitable heading for Paragraph C.**

    a Delays and cancellations

    b Be relaxed if things do not go to plan

    c Use body language

0 5 ▸ **One way to identify the main idea is to write short summaries of your own, before matching each heading. Follow steps 1–3.**

    1 Underline the key words in the text and write a summary in just a few words for each paragraph.

    2 Compare your summaries with a partner's. Are they similar?

    3 Match your summary/each paragraph with the headings in the box.

List of headings		
i	Research the culture	
ii	Use body language	
iii	Be flexible and relax	
iv	~~The best time of day to be a tourist~~	
v	Observe daily life	
vi	Take photographs	
vii	Try to speak the language	
viii	Spend time with the locals	

1 Paragraph **A**   iv
2 Paragraph **B**   ___
3 Paragraph **C**   ___
4 Paragraph **D**   ___
5 Paragraph **E**   ___
6 Paragraph **F**   ___

0 6 ▸ **Read this article, describing one of the most interesting train journeys in the world, to get a general idea of what it is about.**

The TRANS-SIBERIAN RAILWAY

A _____

The Trans-Siberian Railway has been described by some as the most memorable journey on Earth. Measuring nearly 9,300 km, it is the longest railway line in the world and takes approximately a week to complete. It is one incredible train journey from Red Square to the Great Wall, taking in Siberia, Mongolia, the Gobi Desert and arriving in the great city of Beijing. The journey has captured the imagination of travellers from far and wide since construction began in 1891.

B _____

Although officials have been building this line since 1891, it is still being expanded today. The original Trans-Siberian Railway was built from Moscow to Vladivostok on the orders of Tsar Alexander III. Building the line was not an easy task as there were only a few qualified engineers and the difficult climate often slowed progress. A lack of workmen meant that soldiers and convicts had to be conscripted to help. Up to 90,000 men were employed in its construction.

C
_____

From the moment building began, the project faced many difficulties. Even though it was considered a technological marvel at the time, there were arguments about the quality of work. Rails were considered too light and bridges not strong enough. Many claimed convicts had sabotaged the line. Furthermore, the project also caused serious problems for the Russian economy.

D
_____

Despite criticisms, however, the railway more than paid for itself in the twentieth century. The Siberian economy exploded when 2.5 million poor people moved there from European Russia between 1895 and 1916. The region quickly became famous for producing bread and butter. Without the Trans-Siberian Railway, Siberia's industrial revolution would not have happened.

E
_____

Today, this service is used by both tourists and workers. Running at an average speed of 60 km/h, it is not designed for anyone in a hurry. Nor are the trains particularly glamorous. The trip could never be described as dull, however, with breathtaking views from the carriage window and the opportunity to talk to fellow passengers.

F
_____

Although the trip certainly attracts many foreign tourists, today it gets most of its use from domestic passengers. It is responsible for 30% of Russian exports and carries more than 250,000 containers a year.

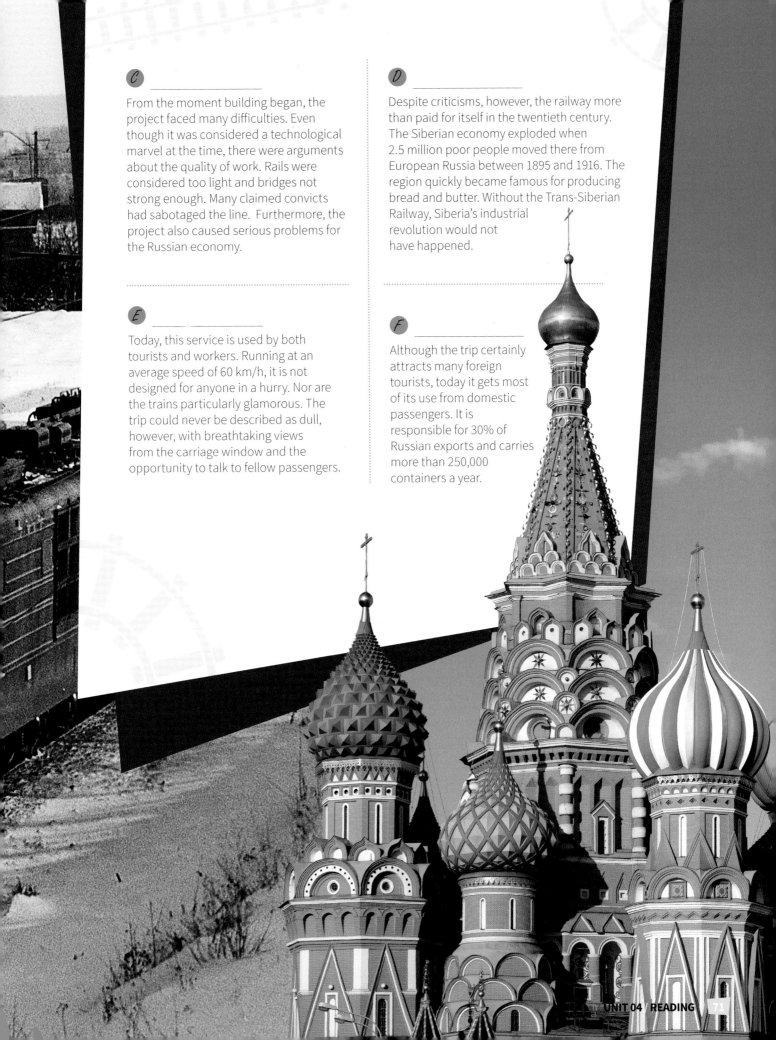

GRAMMAR FOCUS: PRESENT CONTINUOUS, PRESENT PERFECT SIMPLE, PRESENT PERFECT CONTINUOUS AND PAST SIMPLE

0 7 ▷ **Study sentences a–c, taken from the text, and answer the questions which follow.**

   a The journey has captured the imagination of travellers from far and wide since construction began in 1891.

   b From the moment building began, the project faced many difficulties.

   c Although officials have been building this line since 1891, it is still being expanded today.

   1 What tenses are used in the sentences?

   2 How are these tenses formed?

0 8 ▷ **Match sentences a–c from exercise 7 with definitions 1–3.**

   1 An action which took place in the past, and is now finished. _____

   2 An action which took place in the past, and still has a connection to the present.

   _____

   3 A continuous action which took place in the past, and still has a connection to the present. _____

0 9 ▷ **Complete the sentences with the verb in brackets in the correct form of either the present perfect simple, past simple or present perfect continuous.**

   1 I'm so tired. I _____ (**travel**) all day.

   2 I _____ (**get up**) early this morning to avoid the crowds.

   3 I'm so annoyed that my flight _____ (**cancel**).

   4 My back is red, I _____ (**sunbathe**) too much.

   5 I am very well travelled, I _____ (**visit**) many countries.

   6 Last year, I _____ (**go**) on my first-ever cruise.

RECOGNISING SYNONYMS

1 0 ▷ **Match words and phrases 1–7 with the correct synonym a–g.**

1 construction	**a** effect
2 convicts	**b** migrate
3 arguments	**c** controversy
4 move to a new area	**d** transformation
5 revolution	**e** items sold abroad
6 exports	**f** building
7 impact	**g** prisoners

 Recognising **synonyms** is an important skill for this type of question (and many of the other tasks in the Reading test). The words used in the headings are very often synonyms of words used in the text.

1 1 ▶ Put the words in 1–4 in the correct order.

1 do / twice / not / the / same / heading / use
2 of / track / keep / time
3 paragraph / read / first / shortest / the
4 understand / ignore / words / do / not / you

Use this advice to complete exercise 12.

EXAM SKILLS

1 2 ▶ The reading passage 'Trans-Siberian Railway' has six paragraphs, A–F. Choose the correct heading for paragraphs A–F from the list of headings. Write the correct number, i–ix, in the boxes provided.

List of headings

i   The impact the railway line had on Siberia
ii   The reasons why peasants migrated to Siberia
iii The construction of the line
iv   The speed and style of the train
v   The controversy which surrounded the building of the line
vi   The attraction of the Trans-Siberian Railway
vii The role of prisoners and soldiers in the building of the project
viii The length of time it took to build the line
ix   The role the line has in the local economy

1 Paragraph A ☐
2 Paragraph B ☐
3 Paragraph C ☐
4 Paragraph D ☐
5 Paragraph E ☐
6 Paragraph F ☐

TIP 1 2
Be careful! There are more headings than paragraphs.

TIP 1 2
Matching-heading questions always come before the text in the exam.

GO ONLINE AND COMPLETE UNIT 4 READING EXERCISES 1–3

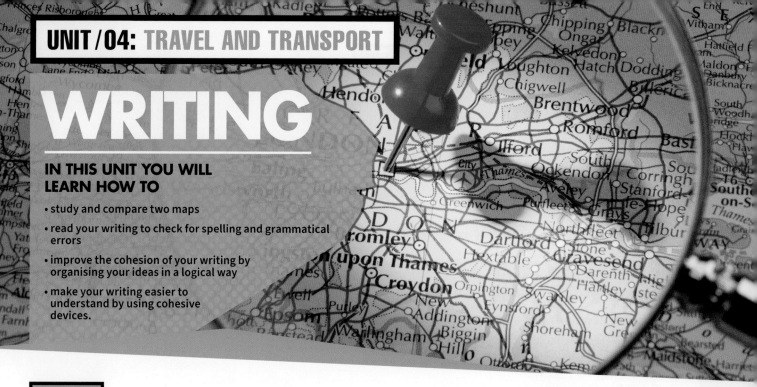

WRITING

IN THIS UNIT YOU WILL LEARN HOW TO

- study and compare two maps
- read your writing to check for spelling and grammatical errors
- improve the cohesion of your writing by organising your ideas in a logical way
- make your writing easier to understand by using cohesive devices.

LEAD-IN

01▶ In Writing Part 1, you may be asked to write about one or more maps.

The box contains useful vocabulary for this type of task. Complete the labels on the maps 'Now' and 'Twenty years ago' with the correct word from the box.

TIP 01

Some of this vocabulary may already be labelled on the maps in the exam.

bridge	church	east	residential area	farm	fields	hills	motorway
north	pond	west	skyscraper	river	south	stadium	windmill

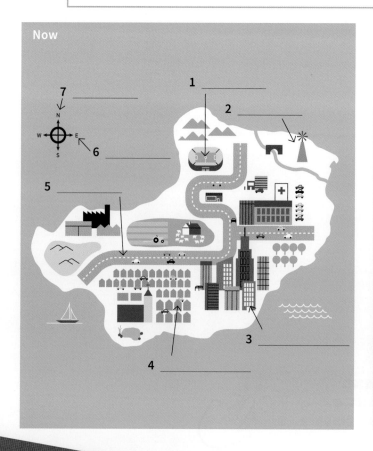

Now

1 _____
2 _____
7 _____
6 _____
5 _____
3 _____
4 _____

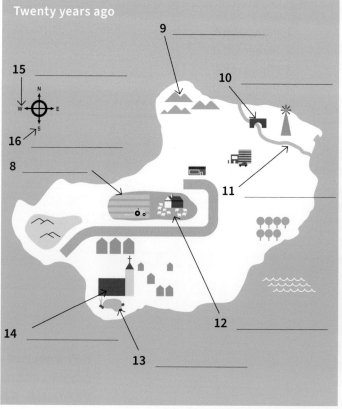

Twenty years ago

9 _____
15 _____
10 _____
16 _____
8 _____
11 _____
14 _____
12 _____
13 _____

02 ▷ Study both maps of the island ('Now' and 'Twenty years ago'), and discuss these two questions with a partner.

1 Which features have changed? *More houses have been built.*

2 Which features have remained the same?

TIP 02

For this task it is important to use prepositions of place appropriately.

03 ▷ Think about your own town. What changes have taken place over the last ten years? Write sentences using some of the verbs in the box.

modernised	replaced	expanded	increased
knocked down	built	renovated	developed

Over the last ten years, more shops and residential areas have been built in my area.

Discuss your notes with a partner. Are your sentences similar or different?

GRAMMATICAL ACCURACY

04 ▷ Read this sample answer and correct the errors that you find. There are five spelling mistakes and five wrongly used tenses.

You need to focus on grammatical accuracy in the Writing test.

SAMPLE ANSWER

Looking at the two maps, it is evident that this irland changed dramaticaly in the last twenty years. There has been a great deal of development in the south of the island. A motorway has been building threw the centre. This divides the existing farm from a newly built hotel, skyscraper and increased residential area. The church and pond, however, still remain the same as they always were.

There are new developments at the north end of the island. Behind the hills, there is a football stadium. Furthermore, in the east of the island a large hospital has built with space for car parking, to the east of the hills are the windmill and bridge, features of the original island.

Overall, the island has being developed significantally over the last twenty years. This development was occurred in both the south and north of the island, providing more facilites for the people living there.

05 ▷ Write the errors and your corrections in the table.

Spelling	Tenses
1 irland — island	1
2	2
3	3
4	4
5	5

Answer these questions.

1 Which tense is mainly used here?
2 Why is this tense used?

COHERENCE AND COHESION

07▷ **Study these two maps which show how Mumbai has changed.**

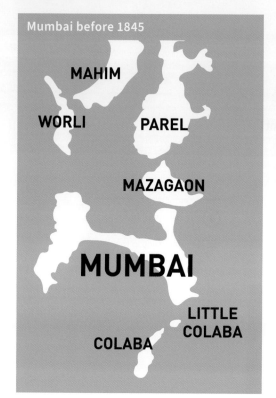

Mumbai before 1845

MAHIM

WORLI   PAREL

MAZAGAON

MUMBAI

LITTLE
COLABA
COLABA

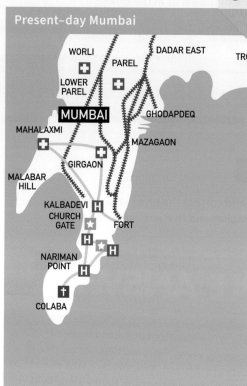

Present–day Mumbai

WORLI   DADAR EAST   TRO
        PAREL
LOWER
PAREL
MUMBAI   GHODAPDEQ
MAHALAXMI
                MAZAGAON
        GIRGAON
MALABAR
HILL
KALBADEVI
CHURCH
GATE   FORT

NARIMAN
POINT

COLABA

> ◎ Two other aspects you must take into consideration in the exam are coherence and cohesion:
>
> **Coherence** – Is it easy to understand? Are your ideas organised in a logical way?
>
> **Cohesion** – Are your ideas connected together well?

08▷ **Read these sentences which compare the two maps.**

1 These two maps show that, since 1845, Mumbai has changed considerably.
2 There are railway lines which run through the central area, as do many major roads.
3 One feature which has remained the same, however, is the names given to the areas of Mumbai.
4 In particular, it has many facilities such as hotels, cinemas, churches and hospitals.
5 There is also a harbour, located to the east of Mazagaon.
6 Looking at the map of Mumbai today, we can see it is now a highly developed area with lots of facilities.
7 Overall, therefore, these two maps clearly illustrate that this area has changed significantly since the 1800s.
8 Furthermore, there are also several transport links which now connect this area together.
9 Before 1845, Mumbai was made up of seven different islands, as opposed to the one mainland which exists today.
10 For example, the south part of the city is called Colaba after the original island, while the north part is called Worli and Parel, and the east part Mazagaon.

09 ▷ At the moment, the order of the sentences in exercise 8 is not coherent or logical, making the meaning difficult for the reader to understand. Put the sentences in a logical order by answering these questions.

1 Which sentences would you put in the introduction?
2 Which sentences would you put in the first paragraph, describing what has changed?
3 Which sentences would you put in the second paragraph, describing what has remained the same?
4 Which sentences would you put in the summary at the end?

10 ▷ Look at how the devices in this table are used in the sentences in exercise 8.

1 Adding an idea	2 Similarity	3 Highlighting	4 Contrast	5 Summary
furthermore	as do	in particular	as opposed to	overall
also				

In order to make a text read well, you need to use 'cohesive devices'.

These are words or short phrases which help guide the reader through your writing by linking sentences and paragraphs. Good use of these devices will make what you have written easy to follow. Without them, your writing may be difficult to read, with too many short sentences.

11 ▷ This box contains more words and short phrases which help to link your ideas together. Write the words in the correct column in the table.

in addition	in comparison	in conclusion	in contrast	particularly
moreover	similarly	to conclude	to summarise	what is more

12 ▷ Complete the sentences with words from the box. More than one answer may be possible.

1 Fifty years ago there weren't any main roads in this town, _____ to the developed area, which can be seen today.
2 The maps illustrate how the school has developed over the last five years. There is now a computer lab and, _____ , extra classrooms have been built.
3 _____ , both maps show how the facilities in the park have improved over the last year.
4 The south end of the island has changed the most, _____ the residential area, which has increased dramatically in size.
5 The first map shows that the area has many shops and restaurants; _____ , the second map features a large area used for leisure.

13▶ Use the information and language from this lesson to answer this Writing Part 1 task.
You should spend about 20 minutes on this task.

The following maps show some of the changes that have taken place in Dubai in recent decades.

Summarise the information by selecting and reporting the main features, and make comparisons where relevant.

Write at least 150 words.

Clock Tower Roundabout, Dubai

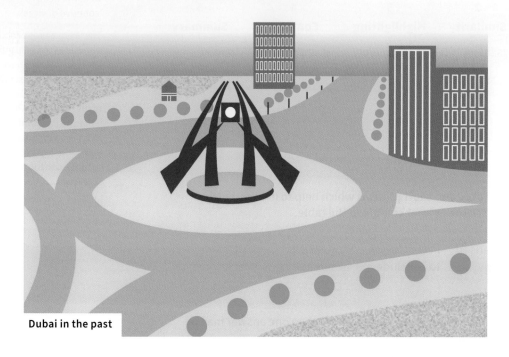

Dubai in the past

Present-day Dubai

GO ONLINE AND
COMPLETE UNIT 4
WRITING
EXERCISES 1–3

UNIT /04: TRAVEL AND TRANSPORT

LISTENING

IN THIS UNIT YOU WILL LEARN HOW TO

- identify the main subject of conversations
- identify the functions that speakers use
- match questions and options (e.g. solutions to advantages/ disadvantages).

01 ▷ Some people are talking about transport problems. What is the problem in each case? Listen to five conversations and choose from the list, A–E.

30

A A method of travel	Conversation 1 _____
B A travel plan	Conversation 2 _____
C Using the bicycle or car	Conversation 3 _____
D The bus service	Conversation 4 _____
E The next train	Conversation 5 _____

02 ▷ Listen again and identify the type of function that the speakers use in each conversation. Choose from the list, F–J.

30

F Expressing doubt	Conversation 1 _____
G Persuading	Conversation 2 _____
H Complaining	Conversation 3 _____
I Proposing	Conversation 4 _____
J Enquiring	Conversation 5 _____

03 ▷ Match the functions F–J with each of these sentences from the conversations.

1 Well, shall we take the train? _____

2 I really think you should do some more exercise. _____

3 Excuse me, could you tell me …? _____

4 Are you sure? I really don't think that's a good idea. _____

5 I don't believe it! _____

 We use language like this to perform these everyday functions and others, such as requesting, agreeing, disagreeing and advising. You will hear speakers in this lesson using some of these functions.

[MATCHING QUESTIONS]

04▷
31

You will hear two students working on a university project. They are talking about a transport problem. What is the problem? Choose from the list, A–D.

A The number of road accidents in the town has risen.
B There are not enough buses and they are too crowded.
C There is too much traffic in the town centre.
D The train service into the town has been losing money and may close.

TIP 04

In the exam, the questions follow the order of information in the recording. The answer to each question is the letter that appears next to the correct option in the box.

05▷
32

The students are discussing the details of the problem. Listen to the conversation and match each place, A, B or C, with the correct location, 1–4. There is ONE more location than you need.

A Town Hall
B Starview Cinema
C Arts Centre

Location 1: at the junction of East Road and Station Road
Location 2: by the main roundabout
Location 3: at the shopping centre
Location 4: by Central Park

06▷
33

Now the students are discussing possible solutions to the traffic problem and possible disadvantages to each. Listen to the conversation and match the disadvantages, A–D, with the solutions, 1–4.

A It will cause problems with deliveries for businesses.
B It will move traffic into residential areas.
C It will cost too much.
D People won't use it much.

1 Bus and cycle-only lanes
2 Park and ride
3 Pedestrian area and one-way system
4 Tram transport system

07▷
34

Listen to the students' discussion about costs and match the costs, A–F, with the solutions, 1–4. There are TWO more costs than you need.

A £10m
B £15m
C £20m
D £23m
E £25m
F £30m

1 Tram transport system
2 Bus and cycle-only lanes
3 Park and ride
4 Pedestrian area and one-way system

08▷
35

Listen to the discussion of the likely benefits of each proposal and match the proposals, A–D, with the benefits, 1–5. There are fewer proposals (A–D) than benefits (1–5), so letters may be used more than once.

A Park and ride
B Bus and cycle-only routes
C Pedestrian area and one-way system
D Tram transport system

1 Better public transport
2 More visitors
3 Better health
4 Less pollution and congestion
5 Greater safety

TIP 08

In the Listening test, there are not always the same number of questions (numbers) and options (letters). Sometimes, there are fewer options than questions, so you will need to choose the same option more than once. Sometimes there are fewer questions than options, so you will not need to use all the options.

36

Sophie and Robert used functions A–G. Listen to extracts from their conversations and write the function used in each. There is one more function than you need.

A Proposing / suggesting

B Approving / accepting

C Expressing doubt / reservations

D Complaining

E Disagreeing

F Persuading

G Correcting

Extract 1 _____

Extract 2 _____

Extract 3 _____

Extract 4 _____

Extract 5 _____

Extract 6 _____

[EXAM SKILLS]

37

10▷ Listen to Jane and Bill, who are discussing the results of a survey about changes to their town, Ashtown, over the last 25 years, and choose the correct answer, A, B or C.

1 In Bill's opinion, why are there fewer buses in Ashtown?

   A The buses are old and uncomfortable.

   B Fares have gone up too much.

   C There are not so many routes.

2 What change does Bill think has benefited the town centre the most?

   A the construction of a bypass

   B the development of cycle paths

   C the banning of cars from certain areas

3 Which area does Bill think most people are employed in?

   A manufacturing

   B services

   C education

What changes have been made to the facilities? Choose FIVE answers from the box and write the correct letter, A–G, next to facilities 4–8.

Action

A it has moved to a new location

B it is now used for a different purpose

C it uses more technology than in the past

D it has been closed down

E it is less popular than it used to be

F it has been sold to a different organisation

G it has been expanded

Facilities

4 railway station car park

5 cinema

6 indoor market

7 library

8 art college

GO ONLINE AND COMPLETE UNIT 4 LISTENING EXERCISES 1–3

SPEAKING

IN THIS UNIT YOU WILL LEARN HOW TO

- plan your long-turn answer for Speaking Part 2
- use the correct sequencing words to give your answer a clear structure
- understand sentence stress when using sequencing words
- deal with follow-up questions after your long turn.

LEAD-IN

01▷ Ask and answer these questions with a partner.

1 What different places have you been to on holiday?
2 Have you ever been to the desert? What about a city break?
3 What kind of transport have you used during holidays in the past?
4 Have you ever travelled anywhere alone?

[PREPARING FOR SPEAKING PART 2]

02▷ Listen to the instructions the examiner gives at the start of Speaking Part 2 and choose the correct answer.

38

1 You can choose the topic for Speaking Part 2. / The examiner will give you a topic.
2 You have one minute to make notes. / You have lots of time to make notes.
3 You should make notes on the paper provided. / You can make notes on the task card.
4 The maximum time to talk is two minutes. / You can talk as long as you like.
5 You can stop talking if you have nothing to say. / You should keep talking until the examiner stops you.

03 ▶ Look at the task the examiner gave the student in exercise 2.

TIP 03

The sections on the task card should usually be taken in order, so it reads like a real story where you set the scene in the beginning, then give your opinions at the end.

Describe an exciting journey you once took.

You should say:

- when and where you went on the journey
- what kind of transport you used
- what happened on the journey

and explain what you remember most about the journey.

04 ▶ Complete this table with your own ideas, then practise asking and answering the questions with a partner.

TIP 04

It sometimes helps if you add some questions of your own to the task, to give you more to say.

When and where you went on the journey	Where did I go?
	When did I go?
	Who did I go with?
What kind of transport you used	What kind of transport did I use?
	Why did I use that kind of transport?
	What do I remember about the transport?
What happened on the journey	Interesting point 1
	Interesting point 2
	Interesting point 3
And explain what you remember most about the journey	What do I remember? (Item 1)
	Why do I remember it?
	What do I remember? (Item 2)
	Why do I remember it?

0 5 ▶ Close your books and listen to the student attempting the task in exercise 3. Look at the pictures and listen again. As you listen, put the pictures in the order they happened.

 You need to use the correct sequencing words during the long turn so that the examiner can understand what happened from beginning to end.

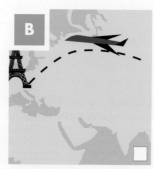

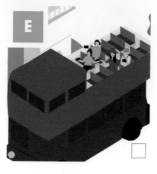

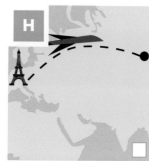

06 ▷ Use the words from the box and your ideas from exercise 4 to plan your own answer to the task. Then practise your answer with a partner.

after	until	as	and	because	before	in order to
now	once	or	since	although	when	whether
while	yet	so	but	where		

PRONOUNCING SEQUENCING WORDS

07 ▷ Listen to sentences 1–5. Decide whether the words in bold are stressed or unstressed. Underline the stressed words.

40

1 I boarded a plane to **Paris**, which was rather **exciting** as I had never done that before.
2 Since I come from China, **it** took a long time to arrive, **but when** I got there, the first thing I did was go to the Louvre Museum.
3 I **had** trouble ordering **food** because I **don't** speak any **French**.
4 **Once** I had **eaten**, I then **took** a tour bus to the Champs Elysées **in order to** do a bit of shopping.
5 When I **got** back on the tour bus and **started** taking **pictures**, I dropped my **camera** over the side.

CHOOSING THE CORRECT SEQUENCING WORDS

08 ▷ Connect the sentence beginnings, 1–10, with the sentence endings, a–j, and the correct sequencing words. More than one answer may be possible.

1 This was rather exciting	but	**a** took a tour bus.
2 It took a long time to arrive	as	**b** I come from China.
3 It was a great experience	and	**c** started taking pictures.
4 I went to a restaurant	although	**d** I had eaten.
5 I went to the Champs Elysées to do a bit of shopping	then	**e** I went on to buy as much as I could.
6 I then took a tour bus	since	**f** I had never done that before.
7 I took the flight back to China	once	**g** I was pretty hungry around that time.
8 I got back on the tour bus	where	**h** next time I think I should study French.
9 I started taking pictures	after	**i** everything was over.
10 Once I had eaten, I	because	**j** I dropped my camera over the side.

DEALING WITH FOLLOW-UP QUESTIONS

09 ▶ Listen to THREE recordings, A, B and C, and answer these questions.

41

1 How many questions did the examiner ask?
2 What kind of questions did the examiner ask?
3 How long was the student's answer?

Share your ideas with a partner.

TIP 09

When ending the long turn, try to summarise what you have said.

[EXAM SKILLS]

10 ▶ Ask and answer these Speaking Part 1 questions with a partner.

1 Do you usually go on holiday every year?
2 Do you prefer to go to cities or the countryside?
3 Do you like to travel alone or with other people?
4 Why do people like to travel?

11 ▶ Answer the prompts in this Speaking Part 2 task. Try to talk for TWO full minutes.

Describe an exciting journey you once took.

You should say:

- when and where you went on the journey
- what kind of transport you used
- what happened on the journey

and explain what you remember most about the journey.

12 ▶ As you listen to your partner, try to think of TWO follow-up questions.
When your partner has finished, ask follow-up questions. For example:

Would you …?
Do you …?
Is there …?

GO ONLINE AND COMPLETE UNIT 4 SPEAKING EXERCISES 1–3

UNIT /05: BUSINESS AND WORK

READING

IN THIS UNIT YOU WILL LEARN HOW TO

- skim a text to identify facts, opinions and theories
- match a fact, opinion or theory with a person
- recognise the use of *will* and *going to* future forms
- match sentence beginnings and endings about a passage.

01 In the Reading test, you will be tested on your ability to identify facts, opinions and theories. Read statements 1–3 and decide which category they belong to: fact, opinion or theory.

1 I don't believe space tourism will ever be possible – it is far too dangerous.
2 According to experts, robots will soon reach human levels of intelligence.
3 The first working robot was introduced in 1961. It worked on a production line making cars for Ford.

02 With a partner, discuss statements 1 and 2 in exercise 1.

'Matching features' is a common task in the Reading test and is used with texts which contain opinions, theories or facts about different people. This type of question requires the student to match an opinion, theory or fact with a person or people.

0 3 ▶ Skim read the text to identify the main ideas.

TIP 0 3

Although matching features tasks are often about a person, they can also be about a place, year or thing.

Great entrepreneurs

A

Andrew Carnegie was one of the wealthiest businessmen of the 19th century.

Mostly self-taught, he started his career as a messenger boy and telegraph operator. By 1889, however, he had become the proud owner of Carnegie Steel Corporation, the largest company of its kind. Famous not only for his success and wealth, he was equally well known for his generous contribution to society. During the last 18 years of his life, it is estimated that he donated roughly $350 million to charities, foundations and universities.

B

Another success story of the 19th and 20th centuries was the founder of the Ford Motor Company, Henry Ford. Responsible for manufacturing an automobile which could be afforded by the masses, he made a significant impact on society and became incredibly wealthy. Primarily, his success was achieved by using the 'assembly line'* to manufacture his cars. Before this, employees of other manufacturers would work in groups to build one car at a time. The moving assembly line meant that each individual was responsible for a specific job.

This division of work allowed cars to be produced more quickly and efficiently. With the addition of the world's first automatic conveyor belt*, it is estimated that Henry Ford's factory was soon producing a car every 93 minutes.

C

Estée Lauder started her own beauty company in 1946. Her business, which includes product lines such as Estée Lauder, MAC Cosmetics and Clinique, has had incredible success. Born in Queens, New York, in 1908, she started her first beauty company with a skin cream developed by her uncle – a chemist by profession. Recognised as an innovative businesswoman, Lauder became one of the richest self-made women in the world. She believed her success came from producing high-quality products and focusing on excellent customer service.

D

Steve Jobs made his fortune by creating some of the most popular products of all time. Born in 1955 in San Francisco, California, Jobs co-founded Apple Computer with Steve Wozniak in 1976, when Jobs was just 21. The project started in the family garage and together they revolutionised the computer industry with products such as the iPod, iPhone, iPad and Mac.

*assembly line – a line of machines and workers in a factory that a product moves along while it is being built or produced

*conveyor belt – a continuously moving piece of rubber or metal used to transport objects from one place to another

0 4 Make notes about the main ideas in each paragraph and discuss them with a partner. Did you focus on the same points?

0 5 Is the text mainly factual, theoretical or opinion-based?

TIP 0 5

Identifying whether the text is mainly **factual**, **theoretical** or **opinion-based** will help you understand the question better and decide what type of information you are looking for.

0 6 Read these statements connected to the text and underline the key words in each.

1 established a fast and economical way to produce a popular product
2 started their first company with a family member
3 began by inventing products at home
4 focused on creating first-rate items and looking after clients
5 a charitable entrepreneur, who gave a great deal of wealth away

0 7 Look back at the text and write down synonyms for key words in the statements. (Not every key word has a synonym in the text.)

TIP 0 7

When approaching this type of task, always try to look in the text for words or phrases which are **similar** to those in the question. The **same** words are rarely found in both the question and the text.

0 8 Look at the list of entrepreneurs. Match each statement from exercise 6 with the correct entrepreneur, A–D. (You may use any letter more than once.)

Entrepreneurs
A Andrew Carnegie
B Henry Ford
C Estée Lauder
D Steve Jobs

TIP 0 8

Make sure your answer is based on the **information in the text** and not on your personal knowledge of the subject.

TIP 0 8

Be careful! Some of the people in the list could be distractors, you may not need to use all the letters, and the people mentioned may be used in several sections.

0 9 Read through these steps and put them in the correct order.

Approaching matching features tasks

a Decide if the text is mainly factual, opinion-based or theoretical.
b Read the sentence before and after each option (e.g. list of names) in the passage and match the information to a statement.
c Read all the instructions carefully.
d Match a statement to a name / option.
e Skim read the whole passage to gain a general understanding.
f Scan both the passage and question and identify:
 • the options in the passage (e.g. the list of people)
 • key words in the statements
 • synonyms in the passage for words in the statements.

◎ IELTS passages are usually longer than the example given in exercise 3, so it is important to arrive at the correct answers as quickly as possible.

● ● ●   ◁ ▷

HOME	TECHNOLOGY	SCIENCE	BUSINESS	SEARCH	

BUSINESS IDEAS OF THE FUTURE

A The most successful entrepreneurs are those who predict the needs of the future earlier than the competition. No new business start-up is without risk, but the benefits can be immeasurable. Inventions such as the automobile, the internet and the iPad were all initially met with a high degree of criticism, so it is important to maintain the belief that anything is possible! Below are just a few of the business ideas expected to be successful in the future.

B Travelling to space used to be possible only for governments or large aerospace companies. This is no longer the case, however, and several private companies have planned tourist missions into space which are going to take place in the next few years. Consulting firm Futron Corporation predict that the space tourism industry will be worth $1.3 billion and have more than 25,000 customers in the next five to ten years. Space tourism pioneer Peter Diamandis also predicts that space hotels are going to be big business, with companies from around the world already working on such projects. Not everyone, however, is as convinced about the prospect of space tourism. Jeffrey Jones, a member of the Center for Space Medicine at Baylor College, warns that even a short journey into space could cause serious health problems for tourists of average or poor health.

C Another idea comes from a company in New Zealand called Martin Aircraft. They have produced the first commercially available jetpack, which they plan to start selling next year. Initially, they will be sold to shops and cost approximately $150,000. The craft will work for short trips only, approximately 30 minutes, and manage speeds of up to 74 kph and an altitude of 914 m. The CEO of the company, Peter Coker, notes that, as well as being used by the rich for pleasure, they could also be useful in search-and-rescue operations.

D Growing meat in a laboratory is an idea which, understandably, appeals greatly to animal rights activists. Jason Matheny, founder of the not-for-profit company New Harvest, also feels that producing meat in this way would satisfy a growing global demand for meat. It would also be healthier, more energy-efficient and sustainable. The Dutch scientist Professor Post, who served up the world's first laboratory-grown beef burger, predicts that 'cultured meat' will mean the end of traditional cattle farming within decades. Tracey Hayes, the CEO of the Northern Territory Cattlemen's Association in Australia, admits that although this technology could be damaging to the worldwide beef industry, it would not affect Australia, as cattle farming is a great Australian tradition.

E According to a recent prediction made by the United Nations, in the future, 86% of people living in developed countries will live in cities. With this in mind, an idea called 'vertical farming' has emerged. Essentially, vertical farming comes from the belief that cities should not rely on rural areas for food but should grow their own  crops by creating multi-storey, high-tech greenhouses. The idea for vertical farms came from the ecologist Dickson Despommier, who turned his knowledge of parasites* into a way of looking at cities.

F Daniel Kluko of Green Spirit Farms predicts that software will be used to look after these multiple farms remotely. For example, an app on a smartphone or tablet will be able to handle the day-to-day care of crops. Kluko also believes that this use of technology will help to keep costs to a minimum, allowing vertical farms to compete with traditional farms.

*parasite – a plant or animal that lives on or inside another plant or animal in order to get food

1 1 ▸ Decide whether the text is mainly factual, theoretical or opinion-based.

1 2 ▸ Look at statements 1–5 and the list of people.

This person believes this new idea

1 could be used to save lives.
2 could be harmful.
3 is best controlled using technology.
4 would fulfil a worldwide need.
5 could have a significant impact on
  an existing business.

List of people

A Jeffrey Jones
B Daniel Kluko
C Peter Coker
D Peter Diamandis
E Jason Matheny
F Professor Post

1 3 ▸ Scan the text and statements and identify:

1 the list of people in the text
2 the key words in the statements
3 synonyms in the text for words in the statements

1 4 ▸ Match each statement with the correct person.

TIP 1 4

Be careful of distractors. Do not simply choose the name which is nearest to the key information – you need to read the whole section to locate the correct answer.

GRAMMAR FOCUS: FUTURE: *WILL* AND *GOING TO*

---

1 5 ▸ Look at the extract taken from the previous text and answer these questions using *will*, *going to*, or *both*.

1 Which future form is used to express a planned action?
2 Which future form is used to express a prediction?

This is no longer the case, however, and several private companies have planned tourist missions into space, which **are going to take** place in the next few years. Consulting firm Futron Corporation predict that the space tourism industry **will be worth** $1.3 billion and have more than 25,000 customers in the next five to ten years. Space tourism pioneer Peter Diamandis also predicts that space hotels **are going to be** big business, with companies from around the world already working on such projects.

1 6 ▸ Complete the sentences using the correct future form. More than one answer may be possible.

1 In the future, robots _____ do many of our manual tasks.
2 The new invention _____ to be revealed to the public tomorrow, according to the schedule given to the media.
3 A Are you going to the exhibition on space travel this afternoon?
   B I'm not sure, maybe I _____ .

MATCHING SENTENCES

17 Another type of question in the Reading test is matching sentence beginnings and endings. Complete each sentence beginning, 1–5, with the correct ending, A–E.

1 Aside from the job itself,

2 A positive work environment makes

3 If you're looking for a new job,

4 Having a sense of balance between work and personal life

5 Employees should work in an environment

A assessing the work environment is very important.

B improves job satisfaction among employees.

C the work environment is very important to an employee.

D where they are not afraid to suggest ideas for improvement.

E employees feel good about coming to work.

18 Read these tips about the matching sentence beginnings and endings task, and highlight key information.

1 The questions follow the order of the text.

2 The questions may test only part of the whole text.

3 The sentence endings may look grammatically similar.

4 Focus on the sentence beginnings as you will not use all of the sentence endings.

5 Look for similar words, not matching words.

19 Read the text on page 90 again, then look at these sentence beginnings.

1 Starting a new business can be difficult

2 The first jetpack available to the public

3 Animal rights activists would definitely

> **TIP 19**
>
> Remember that the sentence beginnings follow the order of the text.

20 Scan the text for the relevant section and then match each sentence beginning with the corresponding paragraph (A–F).

21 Now read the sentence endings and match them with the beginnings in exercise 19. There are more endings than you need.

a will not be able to travel far.

b but if you have money you should try.

c ban eating meat.

d support the idea of producing meat in a laboratory.

e but the rewards can be great.

22 Read each completed sentence and check both meaning and grammar are correct.

EXAM SKILLS

GO ONLINE AND COMPLETE UNIT 5 READING EXERCISES 1–4

23 Refer again to the text on page 90 and complete sentences 1–5 with the correct endings A–G. There are two more endings than you need.

1 New ideas that are not always believed in

2 It has been predicted that accommodation in space

3 The invention which has been created to enable people to fly

4 It has been predicted that in years to come

5 The price of producing food in the city

A is currently available only to the rich.

B the majority of the population will be living in urban areas.

C at first are still worth following.

D will be kept to a minimum using technology.

E will be possible in the future, based on the evidence of current projects.

F is not as high as on traditional farms.

G will not be possible in the future.

UNIT / 05: BUSINESS AND WORK

WRITING

IN THIS UNIT YOU WILL LEARN HOW TO

- analyse an 'advantages and disadvantages' essay task
- plan your ideas and organise them into paragraphs
- use linkers to make your essay easy to read.

## LEAD-IN

01 ▷ Look at the photos and discuss the questions which follow with a partner.

 In Writing Part 2 you may be asked to write an essay on the advantages and disadvantages of a particular topic.

Working in the country

TIP 01

Remember to present both sides of the argument and also to give your opinion in Writing Part 2.

Working in the city

1 What are the advantages and disadvantages of working in the city and working in the country?

2 Where would you prefer to work and why?

PLANNING YOUR ANSWER

 Planning your answer for Writing Part 2 is vital to writing a successful essay. Effective planning will ensure your essay is:

- **relevant** – i.e. answers the question.
- **structured** – i.e. clearly organised in paragraphs.
- **coherent** – i.e. is easy for the examiner to read.

02▷ Read these statements. Have you experienced any of these problems?

If you don't plan:
- you can write a lot of information but not always answer the question.
- you can write too much, too little, or run out of ideas half-way through.
- you may not provide a clear structure for examiners to follow easily.

03▷ Discuss these questions with a partner.

1 How long do you currently spend planning your essays?

2 How long do you think you should spend planning?

3 What methods do you use to plan (visual plans, lists, etc.)?

ANALYSING THE TASK

 The first step in the planning process is to analyse the task. Spending enough time reading and analysing the task will ensure that your answer is relevant. In order to analyse the task, you must first highlight the **topic** and **task** words:

- **topic** words indicate what needs to be **discussed**.
- **task** words indicate what needs to be **done**.

For example:
Many students these days choose to work abroad after graduating. Discuss the advantages and disadvantages of this.

Topic words: *student, work abroad, after graduating*

Task words: *discuss, advantages, disadvantages*

04▷ Look at these sample tasks and underline the topic and task words in each.

1 Some people believe that entering the workplace after school is far more beneficial than studying at university. To what extent do you agree or disagree with this statement?	2 In order to get a job these days, many people do unpaid internships (work experience). What are the advantages and disadvantages of these internships?	3 Stress caused by work is becoming a major problem worldwide. What are the reasons for this? How could this problem be tackled?

05▷ Compare your answers with a partner. Did you choose the same words?

BRAINSTORMING YOUR IDEAS

After analysing the task, it is important to start brainstorming your ideas.

Brainstorming is a technique which allows you to think about all your ideas in relation to a subject without having to worry about factors such as spelling, grammar, structure, etc.

There are several ways of brainstorming. The mindmap and linear plan below are just two examples.

Experts believe that, over the next decade, robots will be doing many of the jobs currently done by humans. Discuss the advantages and disadvantages of this.

Visual plans/Mindmaps

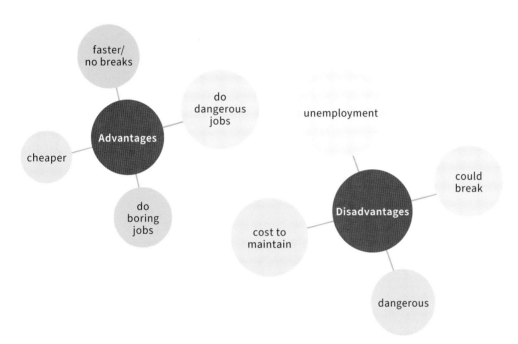

Linear plans/Bullet points

Advantages	Disadvantages
faster, no breaks	unemployment
do dangerous jobs	cost to maintain

 Look at these tasks and brainstorm ideas for each with a partner.
Try using both methods to plan your essay and decide which suits you best.

1 The advantages and disadvantages of wearing a uniform to work.
2 The advantages and disadvantages of working for a big company instead of a small, family-run business.

Although your ideas do need to be relevant, it is more important to concentrate on the **quality** of your English.

STRUCTURING YOUR IDEAS

 Once you have analysed the task and brainstormed your ideas, you can begin to structure your essay.

Here is a possible structure for an advantages/ disadvantages essay.

Introduction	Paragraph(s) 1/2	Conclusion
Rephrase the question	Discuss advantages	Summary of the main points
	Paragraph(s) 3/4	Minimum word limit: 250 words
	Discuss disadvantages	You must use your own words
		Make sure you group your ideas together
		It is a good idea to state your own opinion here

07 ▷ Use this paragraph planner to structure one of the essays you brainstormed in exercise 6.

Paragraph planner

Introduction

Main body 1

Main body 2

Conclusion

TIP 07
It is never a good idea to memorise a model answer, as you are very unlikely to come across exactly the same question in the exam.

USING LINKING WORDS

 Once you have planned an essay which is organised well, you need to make sure your ideas are linked together. This will make it easier for the examiner to read and will also improve your exam score.

08 ▷ Read the task and sample essay, and complete it with linking words from the box. Words can be used more than once.

also	consequently	for example	furthermore	however
whilst	in conclusion	in contrast	therefore	

TIP 08
You will gain extra marks for using linking words appropriately.

Experts believe that over the next decade, robots will be doing many of the jobs currently done by humans. Discuss the advantages and disadvantages of this.

SAMPLE ESSAY

In the future, experts predict that robots will be doing many of the tasks currently done by humans. **1** _____, there will be many advantages and disadvantages for society. In this essay, I will discuss both the positive and negative aspects of this new development.

The biggest advantage robots will bring to the workplace is their ability to work quickly and accurately. **2** _____, they don't need to take breaks or have holidays. This would **3** _____ mean that having a robot worker would be much more economical than employing a human.

Another great advantage of using robots in the workplace is that they can perform tasks that are thought to be dangerous, **4** _____, working on busy roads or underground. They can **5** _____ do the jobs humans don't want to do, such as cleaning the house or dealing with rubbish.

6 _____, there are also many disadvantages to robots entering the workplace. The most significant disadvantage is that many humans would be left unemployed. **7** _____, if a robot was to stop working, this could cause major problems for a company which relied heavily on the technology. A robot which wasn't working properly could also be very dangerous in some cases. The cost of maintaining these robots could also be very expensive.

8 _____, as can be seen from the points made in this essay, there are both advantages and disadvantages to having robots enter the workplace. **9** _____ there are many advantages to this, a significant negative impact would be the loss of jobs for humans. If managed in the right way, **10** _____, I feel that overall the advantages would outweigh the disadvantages.

---

0 9 ▷ Answer these questions with a partner.

1 How long should you spend planning your answer?
2 What methods can you use to plan your answer?
3 Are you marked on the quality of your ideas or your English?
4 Does it matter if not all your essay is relevant to the topic?
5 Is it a good idea to memorise a model answer?
6 How many words do you need to write?
7 Is it a good idea to include your own opinion in this type of essay?

GO ONLINE AND COMPLETE UNIT 5 WRITING EXERCISES 1–3

EXAM SKILLS

1 0 ▷ Use the information and language from this lesson to answer this Writing Part 2 task. You should spend about 40 minutes on this task.

Write about the following topic:

In the past, most people used to travel to their place of work. With increased use of computers, the internet and smartphones, more and more people are starting to work from home.

What are the advantages and disadvantages of this development?

You should use your own ideas, knowledge and experience, and support your arguments with examples and relevant evidence.

Write at least 250 words.

TIP 1 0

Before answering the question, remember:
• Analyse
• Brainstorm
• Structure

LISTENING

IN THIS UNIT YOU WILL LEARN HOW TO

- use notes to follow a talk or lecture
- identify information needed to complete notes or sentences
- recognise the language of comparison and contrast to predict ideas in a talk.

LEAD-IN

01 ▶
42
In this lesson you will hear two lecturers talking about different types of business in the UK. Listen to the introduction and match the type of business with the correct description, A, B or C.

TIP 01

In the Listening test the recorded instructions will tell you about the speaker and the topic.

Type of business

| sole trader   partnership   limited liability company |

A _____
- personal and business finances are separate
- easier to borrow money
- corporation tax

B _____
- personal and business finances are not separate
- no shares
- income tax

C _____
- personal and business finances may be/may not be separate
- members own business together
- income tax

IDENTIFYING CORRECT NOTES

02▶

43

When you listen for information to complete notes in the Listening test, you need to listen carefully to identify and select the correct information. Look at notes A–E and listen to another lecturer talking about the structure, advantages and disadvantages of being a sole trader. Decide which notes are correct and which are not. Correct any notes which are wrong.

> A A sole trader can start a business without registering with Companies House.
>
> B Employing other people is not possible for a sole trader.
>
> C Sole traders must pay tax on their earnings every month.
>
> D A sole trader might pay more tax than a company pays.
>
> E Lately, more people like teachers and computer programmers are becoming sole traders.

[COMPLETION TASKS]

03▶

44

In the Listening test, you may need to complete notes with ONE OR TWO WORDS AND/OR A NUMBER from the recording. In this exercise, the lecturer is talking about the structure, and the advantages and disadvantages of partnerships. Listen and complete the notes with the correct words or phrases from the box.

accounts   borrow money   contracts   pay debts   tax

1 Partnership: easier to _____ than sole trader

2 If simple partnership fails, all partners may lose personal possessions to

_____

3 LLP members must send _____ to Companies House

4 LLP better chance of getting _____ from larger organisations

5 Members of partnership may pay more _____ than owners of limited liability companies

04▶

45

In the Listening test you might need to complete sentences which summarise the information from the listening with ONE OR TWO WORDS AND/OR A NUMBER. The lecturer is now talking about the structure, advantages and disadvantages of limited liability companies. Listen and complete the sentences.

1 Shareholders in a limited liability company do not lose their _____ _____ or property to pay debts because liability is limited to the business.

2 A limited company must have a registered address where the company keeps its _____ and _____ .

3 The shareholders must pay _____ _____ on any money they take out of the company as a salary.

4 For many people who think about setting up a business, it is a good idea to start as a _____ _____ and form a limited company later.

TIP 04

In the Listening test you will not hear the same words that you read, but you will hear the same information in the same order.

05▶ The lecturer is discussing the advantages and disadvantages of the different business structures, using various expressions to compare and contrast them. Listen and use the words and phrases in the box to complete the notes.

It is important to understand when a speaker is making comparisons and contrasts as it can help you predict and choose the correct information to answer questions. In the Listening test, you may need to complete notes which summarise the information in the recording and show how the different points are connected.

| however | similarly | the negative side | the other hand | the same is true |

Business structure	Advantages	Disadvantages
Sole trader	Cheap and straightforward to start Control of decision-making	On 1 _____ , danger of losing personal goods and property to pay debts May pay more tax More difficult to get contracts
Partnership	Useful that one partner can run the business if the other partner is absent Easier to borrow money than for a sole trader In a limited liability partnership, personal possessions and property are protected	On 2 _____ , it might be difficult to run the business effectively if there are serious disagreements Regarding taxes, 3 _____ of partnerships as sole traders In a simple partnership, 4 _____ , members are personally responsible for business debts
Limited liability company	Personal possessions and property are protected Corporation tax is usually lower than income tax	Annual return and company accounts must be sent to Companies House 5 _____ , company records must be kept at the registered address

[EXAM SKILLS]

06▶ Listen to the lecturer presenting three different case studies to illustrate each business type. Complete the notes with information from the listening. Write TWO WORDS OR ONE WORD AND/OR A NUMBER in each gap.

TIP 06

It is essential that you use the correct spelling.

Sanjay and Tanya	1 Plan to set up business to provide _____ to _____ 2 Better to set up a _____ company if employ their own staff
Melissa and Jane	3 Intend to spend _____ on _____ to use in the business 4 Limited company best as have enough _____ and _____ to be successful
Barry	5 Could use one of his _____ 6 Could set up as sole trader, or start a limited company with relative as _____ _____

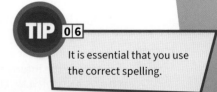

GO ONLINE AND COMPLETE UNIT 5 LISTENING EXERCISES 1–4

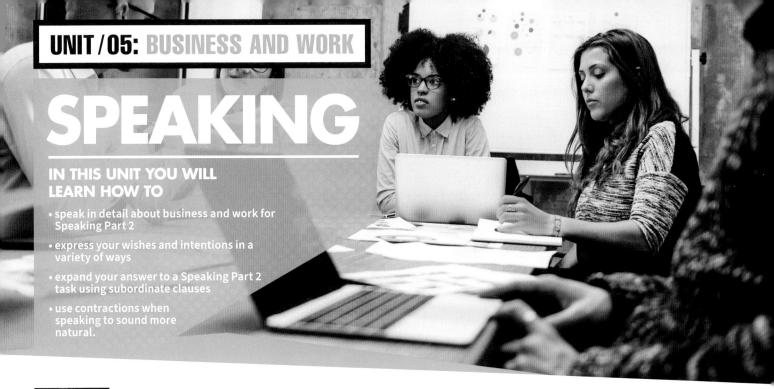

UNIT / 05: BUSINESS AND WORK

SPEAKING

IN THIS UNIT YOU WILL LEARN HOW TO

- speak in detail about business and work for Speaking Part 2
- express your wishes and intentions in a variety of ways
- expand your answer to a Speaking Part 2 task using subordinate clauses
- use contractions when speaking to sound more natural.

01 ▷ Match quotes 1–4 with the correct photo A–D.

1 I'd really love to be able to help children who are struggling with their studies.

2 I hope that one day I can help make new homes for people in our community.

3 I wish I could have the chance to look after people when they are ill.

4 I would like to be able to protect my community and make it safe for everyone.

02▷ Look at the expressions in the box, then discuss the careers in the photos with your partner.

I'd like to …	I'd probably hate …	I'd really love to …
I hope that one day I can …	I'm not convinced that I'd …	I'm not sure whether I'd …
I've always wanted to …	I wish that I could …	There is no way I'd …

DIFFERENT KINDS OF WORK

03▷ Look at these job postings. Match the postings 1–4 with the jobs a–d.

a architect   **b** babysitter   **c** DJ   **d** firefighter

---

JOB SEARCH

1 QUALIFICATIONS: Must hold childcare certificate

RESPONSIBILITIES: Responsible for making sure children complete their homework, ensuring child safety, and getting children into bed on time

PAY: Approx. $5 per hour

BENEFITS: Plenty of time to watch TV, or work on your studies

2 QUALIFICATIONS: Must be able to lift 60 kg and run with it for 5 minutes. Must have training in fire safety

RESPONSIBILITIES: Putting out fires, rescuing animals from trees, and putting yourself in danger every day

PAY: Approx. $50,000 a year

BENEFITS: Opportunities for promotion every 5 years, generous pension on retirement

3 QUALIFICATIONS: Must hold degree in Computer-Assisted Design

RESPONSIBILITIES: Ensuring new buildings are cost-effective and environmentally friendly

PAY: Approx. $100,000 per year

BENEFITS: Free accommodation upon project completion, small budget for stationery

4 QUALIFICATIONS: Must know the latest sounds making the charts

RESPONSIBILITIES: Working unsociable hours, keeping people entertained

PAY: Approx. $200 per session

BENEFITS: Travel budget included, although opportunities for a long career are limited

04 ▷ Complete this table with a partner, then discuss whether you would like to do each job.

Job	Qualifications / Characteristics needed	Responsibilities	Pay / Salary / Wage	Benefits (e.g. promotion, retirement)
Model				
Politician				
Reporter				
Sailor				

EXTENDING THE TASK CARD

05 ▷ Read this Speaking Part 2 task, then match the question words, 1–6, with the correct stem, a–f.

Describe a job that you would like to do for a day.

You should say:

- what kind of job it is
- what the daily responsibilities of the job are
- what characteristics you need for the job

and explain why you would like to do this job.

1 What …		a	usually does this kind of job?
2 Who …		b	is this job a good job to do?
3 When …		c	do you have to arrive at work?
4 Where …		d	do you have to go to do this job?
5 How …		e	special ability might you need to do this job?
6 Why …		f	can I apply for the job?

06 ▷ With a partner, add SIX extra questions to this task. Practise answering the task for TWO minutes each.

Describe a successful businessperson that you would like to meet.

You should say:

- who they are
- what kind of business they are in
- what characteristics make them successful

and explain why you would like to meet them.

1 What _____
2 Who _____
3 When _____
4 Where _____
5 How _____
6 Why _____

TIP **05**

If you have finished answering all the questions in the task, one useful technique is to think how you can expand your answers to each prompt by giving examples and making comparisons.

07 ▶ With a partner, use these sentences to start your long turn. If you run out of ideas, ask your partner to take over. Talk for at least TWO minutes on each topic.

1 I think I would be very interested in becoming a nurse for a day.
Being a nurse is very …

2 I've often thought about being in the army. As a soldier, you would get to …

3 I wonder whether it would be fun to be a police officer, at least for a day.
It would be very interesting to …

4 I'm not sure if I could ever do this, but it would be fascinating to be a pop star for a day. As a famous pop star, the first thing I would do is …

5 It would be fantastic if I could be a professional chef for a day.
The first thing I would make would be …

08 ▶ Look at these examples, which contain subordinate clauses, then complete sentences 1–5.

TIP 08

The successful use of subordinate clauses will increase your grammatical range as well as your overall fluency and coherence.

'I've often thought about going into business by myself, **which** *might be risky*, but …'

'I once worked as a receptionist in a hotel, **which** *was an interesting experience*.'

'I've always been an admirer of Bill Gates, **who** *is the one of the world's most successful businesspeople*.'

'I remember how the economy used to be in the past, **when** *people weren't as rich as they are now*.'

'I would like to work in South Korea one day, **where** *they are quick to adopt new technology*.'

1 I once worked as a _____ , **which** was _____ .
2 I've often thought about _____ , **which** might be _____ .
3 I've always been an admirer of _____ , **who** is _____ .
4 I remember how _____ used to be in the past, **when** _____ .
5 I would like to work in _____ one day, **where** _____ .

0 9

Listen to the speaker saying these pairs of sentences. The first example in each pair is not contracted, while the second example is.

1a I *would* love to work as a computer programmer.
1b I*'d* love to work as a computer programmer.
2a I *would not* like to be a pilot as I *do not* like heights.
2b I *wouldn't* like to be a pilot as I *don't* like heights.
3a I *will* apply for a position as a receptionist.
3b I*'ll* apply for a position as a receptionist.
4a I *will not* look for a job straight away after graduation.
4b I *won't* look for a job straight away after graduation.
5a I *should have* taken a part-time job at university.
5b I *should've* taken a part-time job at university.
6a If I *had* studied harder, I *could have* got the job.
6b If I*'d* studied harder, I *could've* got the job.

1 0

Use these prompts to say complete sentences to your partner. Make sure you contract the modal verbs.

1 I would love to …
2 I would not like to … as I do not …
3 I will apply for …
4 I will not …
5 I should have …
6 If I had …, I could have …

EXAM SKILLS

1 1

Ask and answer these Speaking Part 1 questions with a partner.

1 Have you ever had a part-time job?
2 What kind of job would you like in the future?
3 What kind of job is popular with young people in your country?
4 Is there a job that you would not like to do?

1 2

Answer the prompts in this Speaking Part 2 task. Try to talk for TWO full minutes.

Describe a successful business in your country.

You should say:

- what kind of business it is
- what kind of people work there
- why the business is successful

and explain whether you would like to work for that business or not.

GO ONLINE AND
COMPLETE UNIT 5
SPEAKING EXERCISES 1–4

READING

IN THIS UNIT YOU WILL LEARN HOW TO

- approach *Yes / No / Not Given* questions
- identify whether statements in questions match the writer's views
- use *so, too, either* and *neither* to agree or disagree with someone
- complete a summary with words from a box or words from a passage.

LEAD-IN

01 The environment is a common topic in IELTS. Match the words in the box with the definitions 1–8.

captivity	conservation	endangered	extinction
habitat	poach	species	threaten

1 the natural environment of an animal or plant
2 a situation in which a type of animal no longer exists
3 the protection of nature
4 situation where animals or plants may soon not exist because there are very few now alive
5 a group of plants or animals that share similar characteristics
6 be likely to cause harm or damage to something or someone
7 illegally catch or kill animals, especially by going onto land without the permission of the person who owns it
8 a situation in which an animal is kept in a zoo or a person is kept as a prisoner, rather than being free

YES / NO / NOT GIVEN TASKS

◎ *Yes / No / Not Given* tasks are common in the exam. The purpose of this task is to identify if the statements in the questions match the views or claims of the writer.

0 2 **Read this short text and answer the question.**

TIP 0 2

A 'view' is a personal opinion and a 'claim' is a statement made by the writer and presented as a fact.

> It is commonly believed that taking steps to protect the environment is morally the right thing to do. What is sadly evident, however, is that we all have friends and family who do not concern themselves at all with tackling this problem.
>
> The number one reason for this is that, for some, it is just inconvenient. Other people just do not feel that their contribution makes a difference. Fortunately, however, the majority of us do give it the attention it deserves and many people go to great lengths to ensure the planet is protected for future generations.

Look at the statements and write

YES   *if the statement agrees with the views in the text*

NO   *if the statement contradicts the view of the writer*

NOT GIVEN   *if it is impossible to say what the writer thinks*

1 Some people do not pay attention to environmental issues because they do not believe their involvement would make an impact.
2 Some people tackle environmental problems in the wrong way.
3 Most people do not care about environmental issues.
4 Some people do a great deal to protect the environment.

Which synonyms or words/phrases with a similar meaning to those in the text helped you to locate the answer?

0 3 **To help you approach this type of question with a longer text, put the steps in order.**

Approaching *Yes / No / Not Given* tasks

a Scan the text for these key words or words of a similar meaning.
b Choose *Yes*, *No* or *Not Given*.
c Underline these words in the text.
d Read the question statements carefully and underline key words.
e Read the instructions carefully.
f Read the sentence before and after the key words or synonyms in the text.
g Skim read the text to gain a general understanding of the topic.

TIP 0 4

In this type of task, the questions appear in the same order as the text.

Home   About   News   Top Stories   Community

THE ROLE OF THE MODERN ZOO

Initially seen purely as centres of entertainment, zoos were often heavily criticised in society for keeping animals captive. Nowadays, however, zoos have a lot more to offer than perhaps some people realise. Good zoos have changed their focus and are now responding to environmental problems, such as the decline in wildlife and loss of habitat. Indeed, scientists believe that a third of all animal and plant species on Earth risk extinction within this century.

The modern zoo, therefore, has developed dramatically as a major force in conserving biodiversity* worldwide. Zoos linked with the Association of Zoos and Aquariums participate in Species Survival Plan Programmes, which involve captive breeding, reintroduction programmes and public education to ensure the survival of many of the planet's threatened and endangered species.

Captive breeding is the process of breeding animals outside their natural environment in restricted conditions such as farms, zoos or other closed areas.

It is a method used to increase the populations of endangered species, in order to prevent extinction. One of the main challenges facing captive breeding programmes, however, is maintaining genetic diversity.* Zoo staff are fully trained in this area, and manage the programmes carefully to ensure genetic variation.

Another way in which zoos protect endangered species is through reintroduction programmes. These programmes release animals that have been in the zoo back into their natural habitats.

Finally, and perhaps most significantly, many zoos now concentrate on educating the public, particularly the younger generation. These zoos educate millions of visitors each year about endangered species and related conservation issues. Visiting the zoo not only raises money for conservation projects, but also reminds individuals about environmental issues.

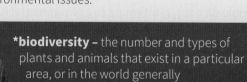

*biodiversity – the number and types of plants and animals that exist in a particular area, or in the world generally

*genetic diversity – the variety of genes within a species

Look at the statements and write

YES   if the statement agrees with the views or claims of the writer

NO   if the statement contradicts the view of the writer

NOT GIVEN if it is impossible to say what the writer thinks

1 Zoos have been very successful in protecting endangered species.
2 Putting endangered animals back into the wild to reproduce is a good way to increase their populations.
3 All zoos now focus on teaching people about animals facing extinction.
4 Zoo visits increase awareness of environmental problems.

0 5 ▸ *So, too, either* and *neither* can be used to agree or disagree with someone.

Study the sentences.

Agreeing with the speaker

'I love visiting zoos and seeing all the animals.' 'Me too.' / 'So do I.' / 'I do, too.'

'Really? I don't like seeing animals in cages.' 'Me neither.' / 'Neither do I.'

'I'm more interested in animals in the wild.' 'Me too.' / 'So am I.' / 'I am, too.'

Disagreeing with the speaker

A: I love visiting zoos and seeing all the animals.

B: I don't.

C: Neither do I. / Me neither.

A: Really? I'm fascinated by all the different animals.

B: I'm not.

C: I'm not either. / Neither am I.

0 6 ▸ Using the information in the box, answer these questions using *so, too, either* and *neither*. More than one answer is possible.

1 'I like exploring nature.' _____ **(agree)**

2 'I would love to go on a safari holiday.' _____ **(disagree)**

3 'I'm really interested in animal conservation.' _____ **(agree)**

4 'I don't know anything about endangered species.' _____ **(agree)**

SUMMARY COMPLETION TASKS

◎ There are two kinds of summary completion task in the Reading test. One provides a box with possible answers and the other requires you to choose the answers from the text.

For this type of task there are usually more words or phrases than gaps and some of the words or phrases might be distractors (words/phrases which look suitable but are not the correct answer).

0 7 ▸ Complete the summary of the previous text with a word from the list.

In the past, zoos focused mainly on **1** _____ the public. This is certainly not the case any more. Today, the role of good zoos is to take an active part in **2** _____ projects. Several methods are used to achieve this. One way to avoid the extinction of certain species is to ensure that animals within zoos breed. This is handled **3** _____ , however, to ensure genetic diversity. Another method is to release the animals back into their natural habitat. Perhaps the most significant role of the zoo, however, is its capacity to educate the general public about conservation and, more specifically, to inform the **4** _____ generation.

A carefully	E conservation
B quickly	F reproduce
C entertaining	G younger
D animal	

TIP 0 7

In the exam, the summary covers only a part of the whole text.

TIP 0 7

When you have chosen a word for each gap, make sure that your sentences are **grammatically correct**. This is a way of double-checking that you have the correct answer.

08 Answer these questions with a partner.

1 Which words from the list above are distractors?
2 In which spaces would they have been grammatically correct?

09 Skim read this text to understand the main ideas.

The mountain
GORILLA

As their name suggests, mountain gorillas live in forests in the mountains, at heights of around 2,400 to 4,000 m. The mountain gorilla's habitat is limited to protected national parks in two regions of Africa. They have thicker fur compared to other great apes and this helps them to survive in a habitat where temperatures often drop below freezing. Mountain gorillas also have shorter arms and tend to be a bit larger than other gorillas.

Currently there are fewer than 900 surviving and they are classed as critically endangered. They are endangered for several reasons, but most significantly because humans are moving further into their territory and consequently destroying their habitats. Human invasion also brings with it the risk of disease and the threat of being poached. Another problem the species faces is the area where they live, which is continuously troubled by war. Consequently, gorillas have been killed by bombs and war refugees have removed trees from the forests to create new homes and farms.

Many conservation projects have been set up to aid mountain gorillas and it is believed that their numbers may slowly be increasing. Nevertheless, they continue to face major threats from both loss of habitat and poaching.

10 Complete the summary using one word from the text.

Mountain gorillas are one of the most **1** _____ species in the world. With fewer than 900 surviving, there are several factors which have caused their decline. The biggest factor is humans moving into their areas and destroying their **2** _____ . The risk of being **3** _____ is another major reason.
In response to this decline in mountain gorillas, efforts have been made by **4** _____ groups to try and increase numbers.

TIP **10**

Decide what type of word you are looking for before scanning the text, e.g. noun, adjective, etc. ...

11 Using all the skills you have learnt in this lesson, read the text and answer the questions which follow.

HOW EFFECTIVE ARE CONSERVATION EFFORTS?

While many organisations put a considerable amount of effort into conservation projects, it is just not enough. Many of these efforts are effective short-term, but in the long term they simply do not work, due to a number of factors.

Whilst there remains a demand for exotic animals in society, endangered species will always be at risk of being hunted and poached. Poachers often target larger animals – animals which take a long time to repopulate, such as rhinos and elephants. The poachers are clever and use methods which are sometimes completely undetectable. A recent case involved 300 elephants being killed in Zimbabwe's largest nature reserve. Poachers put poison in the water holes, killing hundreds of elephants and destroying an entire ecosystem*.

Captive breeding is perhaps the most effective method of protecting animals from extinction, but this also has its problems. First, releasing animals from captive environments could introduce disease into wild populations. Secondly, after several generations in captivity, species could become less able to survive in the wild. Would they know how to hunt for food? Or how not to be killed by other animals?

Perhaps the biggest problem facing endangered species, however, is the increasing population of the human race. Although conservation measures have helped to prevent humans from completely destroying all natural habitats, human invasion will always be one of the greatest risks to threatened species.

* ecosystem – all the living things in an area and the way they affect each other and the environment

Look at the statements and write

YES   *if the statement agrees with the views in the text*

NO   *if the statement contradicts the view of the writer*

NOT GIVEN   *if it is impossible to say what the writer thinks about this*

1 Captive breeding programmes ensure that animals can cope in their natural habitat.
2 Poachers are good at hiding the way in which they kill animals.
3 Releasing animals into the wild after captive breeding has led to infections spreading.
4 Conservation projects have not made any impact on saving natural habitats.

Complete the summary using the list of words, A–L.

The problems faced by conservationists

A great deal of effort is put into conservation work in order to protect endangered species from becoming **1** _____ . Whilst some of these conservation efforts are successful to an extent, they are still not enough to safeguard certain species in the long term.

Culturally, these sought-after endangered **2** _____ are still valuable property and therefore they will always be at risk from **3** _____ . **4** _____ is perhaps the best method to ensure their survival, but is also problematic. After generations of being held in a **5** _____ environment, these species may lose their ability to cope in their natural habitat.

One of the most significant factors is the increase in the population of the human race, leading to many natural habitats being taken over and **6** _____ .

A lost	B poachers	C strange
D diseases	E extinct	F species
G protected	H human	I destroy
J captive breeding	K destroyed	L changed

GO ONLINE AND COMPLETE UNIT 6 READING EXERCISES 1–5

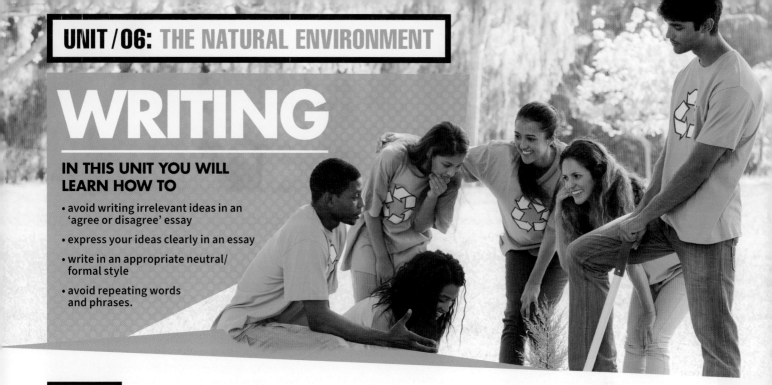

UNIT / 06: THE NATURAL ENVIRONMENT

WRITING

IN THIS UNIT YOU WILL LEARN HOW TO

- avoid writing irrelevant ideas in an 'agree or disagree' essay
- express your ideas clearly in an essay
- write in an appropriate neutral/formal style
- avoid repeating words and phrases.

LEAD-IN

01 ▷ Discuss these questions with a partner.

1 How often do you recycle? What kinds of thing do you recycle?
2 Do you try to save energy at home? What kinds of thing do you do to save energy at home?

02 ▷ Work in pairs. Read these statements and discuss whether you agree, disagree or agree to a certain extent with them. You must give reasons to support your opinion.

1 People should be fined if they do not recycle their household waste.
2 Environmental studies should be made compulsory in school.
3 These days people buy too much and this is one of the major factors affecting the environment.
4 Trying to save resources is a waste of time – it doesn't make a difference globally.

INCLUDING ONLY RELEVANT IDEAS

03 ▷ **Read this task and the sample answer, then answer the questions which follow.**

Some people believe that you should be fined if you do not recycle.
To what extent do you agree or disagree with this statement?

1 Underline the key words in the task.
2 Generally the sample essay answers the task, although the writer has also included some irrelevant information. Underline the irrelevant information in the sample answer.
3 Why do you think the writer has included this information?
4 What is the best way to ensure you do not include irrelevant information in your answer?

◎ Make sure that you answer the task by only including **relevant** ideas.

In order to ensure all your answer is relevant, you must read the task very carefully and underline key words. You must then spend time planning your answer.

USING AN APPROPRIATE STYLE

◎ You are being asked to write an academic essay in this task, so your language needs to be neutral/formal. You should avoid using abbreviations, bullet points and informal language.

04 ▷ **Rewrite these sentences so they sound more formal.**

1 Our environment is getting worse day by day.
2 We might not be able to see all of the bad things in our environment, but they are there for sure!
3 If this keeps going on, our families will struggle in the future.
4 There are many things our teens and families can do to help get rid of pollution, e.g. hand-wash our clothes, ride a bike to school/work etc.
5 There could be a solution to helping our environment if we
 • reach out to people who don't care about the environment
 • change their point of view
 • tell them how bad things are.

TIP 04

Using the passive can sound more formal than using the active. However, use the passive only if it sounds natural and you are confident about its correct use.

SAMPLE ANSWER

In some countries people are fined if they do not recycle. I agree strongly with this idea and think all countries should adopt this policy. Even though it would be difficult to manage, it would encourage people to take recycling more seriously.

Choosing not to recycle simply because you do not have the time is just not a good enough excuse when you consider the impact waste has on the environment. Recycling means used materials are converted into new products, reducing the need to consume precious natural resources.

It is not only recycling which helps protect the environment – there are also many other things that can be done, for example, saving energy or water when you are at home. This can be done by switching off lights or turning off the taps when not in use. People need to educate themselves about environmental issues and then take action.

Before a fine can be issued, however, the government has to provide clear guidelines about what can be recycled and where it can be recycled. Governments could do more to help environmental issues in general. For example, the government could fine companies that do nothing to help with environmental issues and reward those that do.

In conclusion, due to over-buying and not recycling enough, we are destroying our planet and experiencing problems such as global warming and natural disasters. Consequently, fining people for not recycling is the least we can do. The fine should be at least as much as a parking or speeding fine.

In order to get a good score in the exam you need to demonstrate a wide range of vocabulary, and it is important that you avoid repeating the same words as the task. For example:

In some countries people are fined if they do not recycle. I agree strongly with this idea and think all countries should adopt this policy. ✔

Not

Some people believe you should be fined if you do not recycle. I agree strongly with this idea and think people should be fined if they do not recycle. ✗

There are several ways you can avoid repeating the same words as the task. You can use

- pronouns, e.g. *he, she, it, this, that, these, those, one, both*
- synonyms or words and phrases with a similar meaning, e.g. *problem/issue*
- relative clauses, e.g. beginning with *which, that, who.*

0 5 ▷ Read the task and the sample answer, then complete it using the words and phrases from the box. The words can be used more than once.

increase in population	it
issue	planet's
they	these ideas

Overpopulation is the world's most serious environmental problem.
To what extent do you agree or disagree with this statement?

SAMPLE ANSWER

Overpopulation is indeed a growing concern in the developing world, causing many of the **1** _____ environmental problems. Although an increasing population does have a negative impact on the environment to an extent, the greatest problem is in fact caused by the way in which humans choose to live their lives. In the following essay, both **2** _____ will be discussed.

Overpopulation does have a serious impact on the world's environment for several reasons. An **3** _____ means more pollution, caused by more cars on the road, more factories, more farming and more household chemicals. Pollution is a significant environmental issue and **4** _____ can have a serious effect on human and animal health.

Overpopulation also means that natural resources are decreasing more rapidly. The modern world is consuming more than **5** _____ can produce. People are continuously buying more products and building more houses. Fresh water, oil and natural gas are just some of the resources which are in demand.

Perhaps overpopulation would not be an issue, however, if society changed the way in which **6** _____ lived. For example, in order to help these environmental problems, people could try to save natural resources by using less water or by consuming fewer products. **7** _____ could also try to reuse or recycle more. Pollution could also be kept to a minimum if people only bought organic food or tried to use their cars less.

In summary, although overpopulation is a significant problem when considering the environment, **8** _____ would be less of an **9** _____ if people made certain changes to their daily lifestyle.

[EXAM SKILLS]

0 6 ▷ Use the information and language from this lesson to answer this Writing Part 2 task.
You should spend about 40 minutes on this task.

Write about the following topic:

Most people do not care enough about environmental issues. To what extent do you agree or disagree with this statement?

Give reasons for your answer and include any relevant examples from your own knowledge or experience.

Write at least 250 words.

GO ONLINE AND COMPLETE UNIT 6 WRITING EXERCISES 1–4

LISTENING

IN THIS UNIT YOU WILL LEARN HOW TO

• complete a diagram showing a process

• answer multiple-choice questions

• understand the use of signposting words

• revise quantifiers with countable and uncountable nouns.

LEAD-IN

01▷

49

You will hear a lecture about the environment and energy sources. Listen to the first part of the lecture and complete the table with the energy sources from the box.

> fracking   petroleum   solar power   wave power

Renewable sources	Non-renewable sources
Hydroelectric power	Coal
Wind power	Natural gas

COMPLETING DIAGRAMS

02▶

You are going to hear a lecture about fracking (a method of obtaining gas from the ground). First, listen to descriptions of some words from the lecture and match them with the correct picture, A–D.

In the Listening test, you may have to listen and complete a diagram showing a process and what happens in a sequence of events. Some of the labels in the chart will be missing. You will need to listen and complete the missing labels.

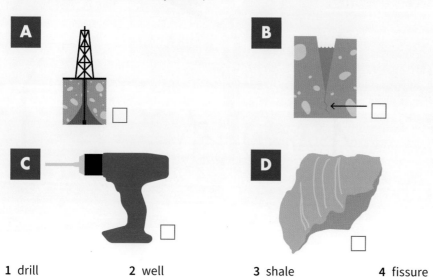

1 drill   **2** well   **3** shale   **4** fissure

03▶

Now look at the diagram below and discuss these questions with a partner.

1 Do you need to look at the whole diagram carefully to complete this type of task?
2 Do you need to understand all the words? What can you do if you don't understand some of the words?
3 Why is there a large circle in the diagram? What does it tell you?
4 The diagram shows you the sequence of events in the process. Can you find where it starts, where it goes and where it finishes?
5 What type of word do you think is missing in each case?

04▶

The lecturer is talking about the fracking process. Listen and complete the diagram with NO MORE THAN ONE WORD AND/OR A NUMBER for each answer.

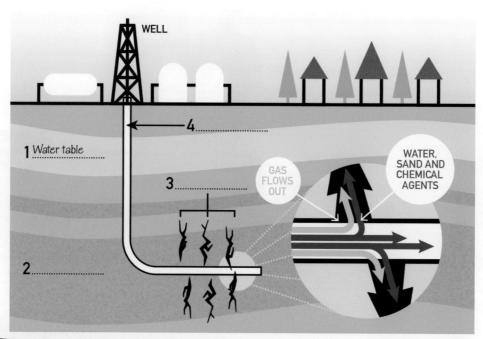

QUANTIFIERS WITH COUNTABLE AND UNCOUNTABLE NOUNS

Nouns in English can be either countable or uncountable. Some nouns can be both countable and uncountable, usually with differences in meaning.

'Quantifiers', like *some*, *many*, *few* and *all*, are used to refer to quantity. There are three types of quantifier – those which are used:

- only with countable nouns
- only with uncountable nouns
- with both types of noun.

05▶ **Choose the correct quantifier in these sentences.**

1 **Little / Few** of the renewable energy sources, such as wind and wave power, have been developed and used around the world.
2 Although coal is still widely used, **much / many** more gas is used instead these days.
3 **All / Every** non-renewable resources have negative effects on the environment.
4 **Several / Some** energy production in the UK comes from wind turbines.
5 There are not **a lot of / much** suitable sites for solar power in the UK.

06▶ **The lecturer is talking about fracking in different countries. Listen and complete the sentences with the quantifier from the box which correctly reflects what the lecturer says. There are more quantifiers than you need.**

TIP 06

Remember that you will hear the recording **only once** in the exam.

a little	more	all	every	few	fewer
a lot of	many	less	much	some	several

1 In Canada, _____ shale gas has been found in various areas.
2 Only a _____ Canadian regions have allowed fracking to take place.
3 In the USA, _____ of the requirement for gas is met by shale gas.
4 A great deal _____ shale gas is being produced in Australia now than a decade ago.
5 If fracking takes place in the UK, people might save _____ money on their gas bills.
6 There are far _____ people per kilometre in the USA than in the UK.

07▶ **Write the quantifiers from the box in exercise 6 in the correct place in the table.**

Used only with countable nouns	Used only with uncountable nouns	Used with both countable and uncountable nouns

[MULTIPLE-CHOICE TASKS]

 In the exam you will need to answer multiple-choice questions about a recording. You have three choices and must choose one correct answer. The two wrong answers are distractors: they seem as if they could be correct but are not.

08 The lecturer is talking about the benefits of fracking. Listen to the first part of the lecture, look at question 1 and choose the correct answer, A, B or C. Why is this answer correct?

53

1 Those who are in favour of fracking say that the main benefit is

A better energy supply.

B lower energy bills.

C increased electricity generation.

TIP 08

In multiple-choice tasks in the Listening test you will hear the answers in the same order as the questions.

09 Listen to the first part of the lecture again and make a note of the words and phrases in the listening which mean the same as the main part of the question and the correct answer.

53

10 With a partner, discuss why you think the other options are wrong.

TIP 10

It is important not to listen for words which are in the question. You must listen and understand the **idea** that the speaker is expressing and choose the answer **which means the same**.

11 Underline the important words and phrases in question 2, then listen and choose the correct answer, A, B or C.

54

2 When fracking starts in a new location

A local businesses lose many of their employees.

B companies bring in most of the workers needed.

C it creates more opportunities for businesses in the area.

TIP 11

Focus on the important parts of the question by looking at it carefully and underlining the words and phrases you think are key. Then listen and choose an answer. Make sure you listen to the end before making your final choice.

12 Did any of your underlined words and phrases help you choose the correct answer rather than the distractors? Why? / Why not?

13▶ Look at questions 3 and 4 and underline the words and phrases you think are significant. Then listen to the next part of the lecture and choose the correct answer, A, B or C.

TIP 13

Focus on the ideas that the questions and options express, not the words themselves.

3 Although burning gas produces carbon dioxide,
   A it does not produce chemicals which are harmful to the body.
   B the amount produced is slightly less than from coal and oil.
   C it produces much less water than coal and oil burning produces.

4 Some people think that using more gas from fracking to produce energy means that
   A 50% less electricity will be produced than now.
   B more water can be used in the production of coal and oil.
   C there will be more time to work on environmentally friendly sources of energy.

14▶ The lecturer is talking about people's concerns about fracking. Before you listen, underline the words and phrases in the statements that you think are important, so that you can recognise words and phrases which express the same ideas in the recording. Then listen and choose the correct answer, A, B or C.

1 One of the environmental concerns is that
   A increased use of shale gas will significantly raise carbon dioxide levels.
   B using shale gas in some areas will not benefit the environment overall.
   C countries that use shale gas will still use high levels of oil and natural gas.

2 Fracking may not be economically beneficial because
   A it can reduce the value of homes in the areas where it takes place.
   B after five years of fracking, production can fall significantly.
   C the levels of gas in the ground are unlikely to be sustainable.

3 One medical concern related to fracking is that
   A the quality of the water supply in some areas can be badly affected.
   B poor air quality causes breathing problems in healthy people.
   C workers are passing on illnesses to local people.

4 Fracking has not been able to take place in some places because
   A local people have managed to prevent it.
   B the authorities are waiting for better information about its effects.
   C some countries want to follow the example of France.

15▶ Check your answers, then think about why the other options are wrong and discuss your reasons with a partner.

UNDERSTANDING SIGNPOSTING TO FOLLOW A TALK

 To help listeners follow a lecture or talk, speakers often use 'signposting'. This involves words and expressions that tell the listener what the speaker is going to say, for example: saying how many main points there are, giving examples, emphasising a point, summarising what has been said, etc.

16 ▶ **Listen again to the lecturer talking about people's concerns and write signposting words and expressions from the box in the table. Write the correct function for each expression: sequencing (SE), contrast (C), addition (AD), summarising (SU), topic change (T) or attitude (AT).**

56

TIP 16

Signposting can help you know where you are up to with the exam questions because these occur in the same order as the script. If you get lost, signposting words and expressions may help you find your way back to the right question.

| clearly | earlier | to begin with | secondly | now | while |
| that | first | to summarise | what's more | last | |

	Signposting word/expression	Function
	___To begin with___ , let's look at the environmental concerns.	SE
1	The _____ and possibly most significant environmental concern is …	
2	_____ , it is likely that, although countries which produce shale gas …	
3	_____ , there are serious pollution problems …	
4	The _____ environmental concern connected with drilling is that of earthquakes.	
5	_____ I'd like to turn to the economic concerns.	
6	_____ there's clearly an increase in economic activity …	
7	As I mentioned _____ , there are a lot of concerns …	
8	_____ , a lot more research needs to be done …	
9	So _____ , there are significant environmental …	
10	We can see that the future is very uncertain, and _____ is what I'd now like to discuss.	

[EXAM SKILLS]

1 7 ▶ The lecturer is talking about the future of fracking and other forms of energy. Listen and choose the correct answer, A, B or C.

1 The problem with fracking is that it
   A has caused carbon dioxide levels to rise by more than a third.
   B will not help countries meet their energy requirements.
   C will make the world climate warmer by 1 degree Celsius.

2 One result of climate change is
   A lower levels of rain in some parts of Europe.
   B serious problems for food production in some African regions.
   C increased risk of ice in populated areas by the sea.

3 A reason renewable energy sources are not being developed quickly is that
   A fracking is the best way to reduce global warming at the moment.
   B governments want to find other long-term solutions.
   C energy companies are afraid the cost will affect their businesses.

4 To develop renewable sources further
   A commercial organisations need external help.
   B governments need to produce less gas and oil.
   C countries should work together to change their economies.

5 Environmental groups believe that
   A fracking can help reduce global warming in the short term.
   B non-renewable sources can continue alongside renewable sources.
   C only renewable sources will be able to provide energy in the future.

> **GO ONLINE AND COMPLETE UNIT 6 LISTENING EXERCISES 1–3**

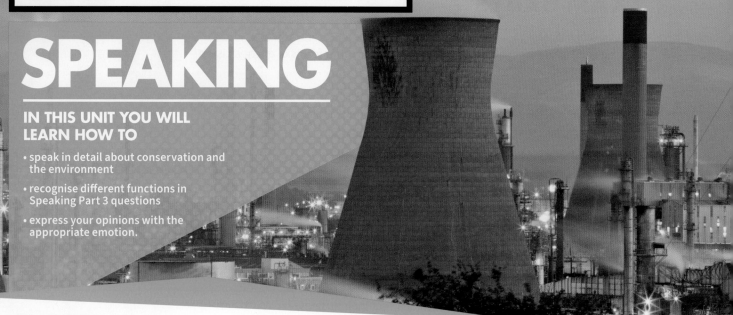

UNIT / 06: THE NATURAL ENVIRONMENT

SPEAKING

IN THIS UNIT YOU WILL LEARN HOW TO

- speak in detail about conservation and the environment
- recognise different functions in Speaking Part 3 questions
- express your opinions with the appropriate emotion.

 Discuss these questions with a partner.

1 What is the most beautiful place you have ever visited?
2 Do you think that global pollution is a serious problem?
3 Does the place where you live have a lot of pollution?

0 2 ▶ With a partner, complete the table with words from the box. Some words can go in both columns.

acid rain	carbon monoxide	drought	~~earthquakes~~	tornados
landslides	volcanic eruptions	~~oil spills~~	radiation leaks	tsunamis
sinkholes	thunderstorms	floods	forest fires	

Natural disasters	Man-made problems
earthquakes	oil spills

0 3 ▶ Complete the sentences using words from the table. More than one answer may be possible.

1 Humanity is to blame for the increase in _____ emissions around the world.

2 _____ result in many homes and public buildings being burnt down.

3 Proper care of important facilities will result in fewer _____ .

4 We cannot really prevent _____ but we can take steps to make buildings safer in case they happen.

5 _____ causes significant damage to homes and businesses.

6 Protection against _____ will involve the cooperation of local people and local government.

0 4 ▶ Which of these environmental factors are a threat where you live? Discuss with a partner.

acid rain	carbon monoxide	volcanoes	landslides	chemical spills
floods	freezing temperatures	tornados	earthquakes	

PRONUNCIATION: SILENT LETTERS IN ENGLISH

0 5 ▷
58
Some letters in English are 'silent' when spoken, or sound different from the spelling. Listen to these examples.

Scenic – the first 'c' is silent – this word is spoken as /ˈsiː.nɪk/

Business – the 'i' is silent – this word is spoken as /ˈbɪz.nɪs/

0 6 ▷
59
Listen to these words. Underline the letter(s) in each word which are silent or which sound different from the spelling.

1 calendar
2 foreigner
3 should
4 guest

5 autumn
6 honest
7 light
8 doubt

9 castle
10 yoghurt

MAKING TIMED NOTES

0 7 ▷ Look at these Speaking Part 2 tasks.

A Describe a place in your country that is famous for its natural beauty.

You should say:

- where that place is
- what kind of place it is
- what makes it beautiful

and explain why this place is famous in your country.

B Describe a place of natural beauty that you have visited.

You should say:

- when you visited this place
- what kind of scenic features the place had
- what you remember most about the place

and explain whether you would like to visit the place again.

0 8 ▷ Discuss these questions with a partner.

1 Which points in the tasks require *more* information?
2 What *kind* of information will you need for each point?
3 *How many* examples will you need for each point?
4 What *tense* will you need for each point?

0 9 ▷ Thinking about your answer to question 1 in exercise 8, make notes for tasks A and B in just 60 seconds. Use your notes to talk for TWO minutes on each topic.

TIP 0 9

You have only one minute to make notes so it is a good idea to practise making them with a stopwatch or timer.

1 0 ▷ Compare your notes with a partner. Try to talk about task A for TWO minutes using your partner's notes. Were you able to complete the task? If not, advise your partner how the notes can be improved, based on your answers to question 1 in exercise 8.

1 1 ▶ Here are two sets of notes for task B in exercise 7. Which set of notes do you think would be easier to write in just 60 seconds?

1

1 The Victoria Falls, on the border of Zimbabwe and Zambia. I went two years ago.
2 It's a waterfall. Lots of water, loud noise. It's the largest across at 1,738 metres.
3 It's huge, very tall. You often seen rainbows in the water.
4 It's a UNESCO world heritage site. Visitors come from around the world to see it.
5 Would like to visit again with my family this year.

2

Victoria Falls	International visitors
Waterfall	1,738 metres wide
Zimbabwe/Zambia	Rainbows
Two years ago	Noisy
UNESCO world heritage site	Visit with family

RECOGNISING AND USING DIFFERENT FUNCTIONS

1 2 ▶ Match questions 1–5 with a function from the box.

> assess   compare   explain   predict   suggest

1 So, what do you think will happen to the environment in the future?
2 What can governments do to help the environment?
3 Is there any difference between environmental issues now and those in the past?
4 Have schools done enough to inform children about environmental problems?
5 Why have private businesses not done more to help the environment?

 Part 2 of the Speaking test asks you to **describe** something, for example a place in your country. Remember that questions in Part 3 could ask you to do some (or all) of the functions in the box in exercise 12.

1 3 ▶ Read this transcript of a student answering a Speaking Part 3 question. Write the correct function from the box in the gaps before each phrase. Some functions can be used more than once.

How can we do more to protect the environment?

Well, that's a tough question. **1** _____ In the past, we didn't know much about the effect we were having on the environment **2** _____ as we didn't have access to much scientific knowledge back then, **3** _____ whereas now we know much more about the world and how it works and
4 _____ this knowledge has been so useful in helping us to protect the environment. **5** _____ The science has improved, **6** _____ so I think that we might start to discover new ways to reduce pollution in the future
7 _____ that are much better than those we have at the moment.
8 _____ Perhaps the government could spend more money on promoting environmental responsibility to companies, although **9** _____ it is by no means certain this will have the desired effect.

TIP **1 3**

Questions in Speaking Part 3 ask you about society as a whole, rather than you and your personal experience.

EXPRESSING OPINIONS: CERTAINTY AND DOUBT

1 4 ▶ **Complete the table using words from the box.**

almost	~~certainly~~	clearly	definitely	indeed	~~likely~~
maybe	might	no doubt	occasionally	of course	perhaps
seemingly	surely	unlikely	will		

Certain	Careful
certainly	likely

 When we give opinions we often want to express **how sure** we are about our feelings or claims:

- *If things do not improve quickly, there is **no doubt** that the environment **will** suffer.* **certain**
- *If things do not improve quickly, it is **possible** that the environment **might** suffer.* **careful**

1 5 ▶ **In Speaking Part 3, you should be prepared to have an opinion about any statement or topic. For statements 1–9, put a tick ✔ to show whether the speaker is agreeing or disagreeing.**

Statement	Agree	Disagree
That's true.	✔	
1 That's right.		
2 I'm not sure about that.		
3 That's also how I feel about it.		
4 I have to side with you on that one.		
5 Me neither.		
6 That's incorrect.		
7 I beg to differ.		
8 You might have a point there.		
9 I'm afraid I don't share that point of view.		

 Certain words can be used to make these statements stronger. For example:

*I **just** don't share that point of view.*
*That's **totally** incorrect.*
*I **definitely** have to side with you on that one.*
*That's **100%** true.*

16 ▷ For statements 1–5, write how much you agree or disagree with the statement. Then, using the example phrases in exercise 15, tell your partner whether you agree or disagree with each statement, remembering to express yourself strongly where necessary.

Statement	Strongly agree	Agree	Disagree	Strongly disagree
1 Governments should do more to prevent environmental damage.				
2 We are not responsible for damage to the environment.				
3 Global warming is not caused by humans.				
4 Factories do enough to prevent environmental accidents.				
5 Children should be educated about protecting the environment.				

[EXAM SKILLS]

17 ▷ Ask and answer these Speaking Part 1 questions with a partner.

1 Is there a place of natural beauty in your country?
2 Are there fewer places of natural beauty now than in the past?
3 Do you do anything to help the environment?
4 What is the most serious problem facing the environment today?

18 ▷ Answer the prompts in this Speaking Part 2 task. Try to talk for TWO full minutes.

Describe an environmental issue facing your country.

You should say:

- what kind of problem it is
- how long the problem has existed
- what effect the problem has had on people

and explain what we can do to solve the problem.

19 ▷ With a partner, discuss these Speaking Part 3 questions.

1 What is the cause of most environmental problems in the world?
2 Is there much more environmental damage now than in the past?
3 What more can governments do to solve environmental issues?
4 How can we educate children to protect the environment?

GO ONLINE AND COMPLETE UNIT 6 SPEAKING EXERCISES 1–3

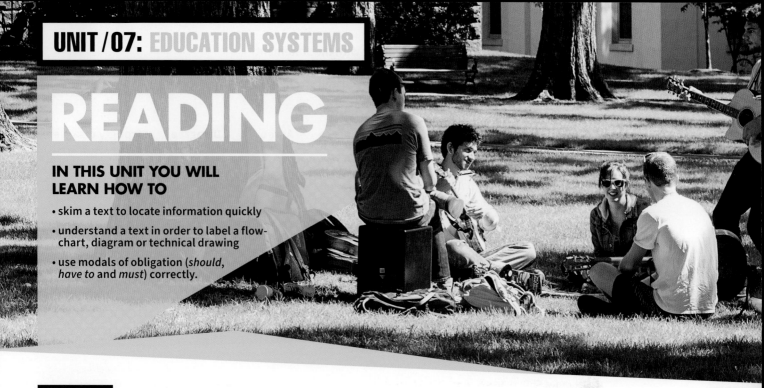

UNIT / 07: EDUCATION SYSTEMS

READING

IN THIS UNIT YOU WILL LEARN HOW TO

- skim a text to locate information quickly
- understand a text in order to label a flow-chart, diagram or technical drawing
- use modals of obligation (*should*, *have to* and *must*) correctly.

LEAD-IN

0 1 ▷ Read these signs displayed in a local university.

> No smoking on **campus**.

> All **assignments** should be submitted to the student information centre by the deadline given by your tutor.

> All undergraduates must attend the **lecture** on study skills on Thursday.

> Information on teacher training courses is available from the **Faculty** of Education.

> To **enrol** on extra courses, please visit the university website.

> To find out how to **fund** your university course, visit our careers centre on the first floor.

> The university offers a selection of courses for both **undergraduates** and **postgraduates**. For more information on our **Bachelor's degrees** for undergraduates or our **Master's degrees** for postgraduates (students who already have a first degree), please take a prospectus or visit the student information centre.

0 2 ▷ Match the words in bold in the notices with definitions 1–10.

1. a formal talk given to a group of people in order to teach them about a subject
2. to become or make someone become an official member of a course, college or group
3. to provide money for an event, activity or organisation
4. a piece of work or job that you are given to do
5. the land and buildings belonging to a college or university
6. a particular department at a college or university, or the teachers in that department
7. a higher university qualification that usually takes one or two more years of study after your first degree or qualification
8. a student who is studying for their first university degree
9. a university degree that is given after a course of study that usually takes three or four years
10. a student who has one degree and is now studying at a university for a more advanced degree

COMPLETING FLOW-CHARTS

0 3 In the Reading test you may be given a flow-chart to complete. Look at this chart, ignoring the gaps for the moment.

Applying to study at university in Australia (for international students)

Step 1 – Choose a university and enrol

Once you have chosen, you can apply
1 _____ to the university for a place.

Step 2 – Apply for a student visa

Once you have confirmation of **2** _____
and adequate **3** _____ for the first year,
you can apply for your visa.

Step 3 – Book your flight and accommodation

You can book your flight online and each university
has an accommodation team that can help you find a
place, especially for **4** _____ students.

0 4 Study the chart again and answer these questions.

1 What does the title suggest the chart is about?
2 What information is given by the main headings?
3 What type of word is missing from the text in 1–4 (e.g. noun, adverb, etc.)?
4 Can you guess what any of the missing words are?

0 5 Read this short text and then complete the flow-chart using ONE WORD ONLY from the text.

Studying abroad as an international student can be an enriching experience. If you have a good level of English, you will face the difficult decision of deciding which university you would like to apply to. Once you have chosen, you can contact the university directly in order to apply.

In order to successfully obtain a place at university, you will need to get a visa to study at the university of your choice. In order to obtain a visa, you will need proof of admission to the college. You will also need to show that you have enough funds for the first year of study. After you have done this, you can apply for a visa. Once you have received a visa, you can start to look for flights and also try to find somewhere to live. This is something that you don't need to worry about, as each university has an accommodation team to help you. Furthermore, preferential treatment is given for new students from abroad.

0 6 Read through the flow-chart again, with the gaps completed, and ask yourself these questions.

1 Are your answers grammatically correct?
2 Does the flow-chart make sense?

TIP 0 3
Often it is not necessary to understand every single word in the diagram or chart, so try to focus on key words and phrases.

TIP 0 4
The answers do not always come in the same order as the text.

TIP 0 5
Numbers and hyphenated words count as one word in IELTS.

07 In the Reading test, you may also be asked to complete a chart or diagram. Study this chart, ignoring the gaps for the moment, then answer the question.

	Monday	Tuesday	Wednesday	Thursday	Friday
9.00–12.00	1 _____		3 _____		Lecture
12.00–15.00					
15.00–18.00	Private study	2 _____	Tutorial	Private study	5 _____
18.00–21.00		Cinema club		4 _____	

What does the chart illustrate?

08 Read this text and complete the gaps in the chart using NO MORE THAN TWO WORDS AND/OR A NUMBER.

UNIVERSITYLIFE

University life is quite different to life at school or college. One of the most significant differences is the amount of time you spend at university, either attending lectures or tutorials. At school you spend about 30 hours a week studying in the classroom. At university, there is much less contact time and therefore you must have a great deal of self-discipline. At the moment I have to attend three lectures a week, all in the morning. In the afternoons, I use my time for private study, either working on assignments or revising for exams. That is unless I have a scheduled tutorial. Tutorials are an opportunity to work through assignments or topics in small groups. In some countries they are also referred to as 'seminars'. I attend tutorials weekly, one in the middle and one at the end of the week.

Another important part of university life is making sure you become involved in other activities, such as clubs or sport. You should choose something you will enjoy or something new. This will help you make friends and enjoy your time away from home. Towards the end of the week, I have football training in the evening and on Tuesday evening I attend the cinema club.

GRAMMAR FOCUS: MODAL VERBS OF OBLIGATION: *SHOULD, HAVE TO* AND *MUST*

09 Look at phrases a–c taken from the text and answer the questions which follow.

a I <u>have to</u> attend three lectures a week
b you <u>must</u> have a great deal of self-discipline
c you <u>should</u> choose something you will enjoy

1 Which of these statements expresses advice?
2 Which two of these statements express an obligation?
3 Which of these statements expresses a strong obligation?
4 What is the negative form for each of these statements?
5 What is the past tense for each of these statements?

1 0 Complete the sentences to show strength of obligation.
More than one answer is possible.

1 I _____ study harder. (**strong obligation**)

2 I _____ go to school today. (**no obligation**)

3 You _____ revise for your exams this weekend. (**advice**)

4 You _____ be late for lessons. (**strong negative obligation**)

◎ Note the difference between *mustn't* and *don't have to*.

You **mustn't** cheat in exams. / You **don't have to** study tonight.

Mustn't means it is not allowed or is a bad idea; *don't have to* means something is optional.

1 1 Study these university signs. Which sentence in each pair is most likely to be correct and why?

1a
YOU MUST NOT EAT
IN CLASSROOMS.

1b
YOU DON'T HAVE TO
EAT IN CLASSROOMS.

2a
YOU DON'T HAVE TO
CHEAT IN THE EXAM.

2b
YOU MUST NOT CHEAT
IN THE EXAM.

3a
You don't have to return your library book to the reception desk – you can also use the boxes provided.

3b
You must not return your library book to the reception desk – you can also use the boxes provided.

LOCATING THE ANSWER QUICKLY

1 2 Study the diagram and then skim read the text below.

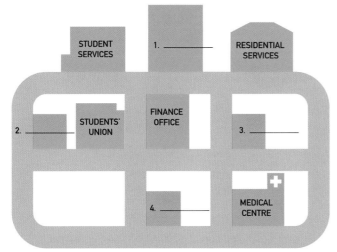

STUDENT SERVICES

1. _____

RESIDENTIAL SERVICES

2. _____   STUDENTS' UNION

FINANCE OFFICE

3. _____

4. _____   MEDICAL CENTRE

TIP 12

Locating the answer quickly is important as it allows you more time for other reading tasks which take longer.

Another significant difference between university and high school is the size of the campus. A university campus is much bigger and is often spread around a city, meaning that sometimes you have to walk to different areas of the city to attend lectures. Usually, however, each faculty is located in a building with classrooms and lecture halls close by.

The main student facilities tend to be in just one area. Universities have a variety of services to offer students, from areas for sport and relaxation, to places for quiet study.

I do most of my assignments in the university library, situated next to residential services and just behind the finance office. When I have finished, I like to relax, by going either to the gym or the students' union. Conveniently, both are close by, near student services. The students' union is a great place to have something to eat or drink and socialise with friends.

The university also offers help in finding a job. Advice is given by the careers centre, which is just behind the medical centre. Generally, though, if you need any advice on where to find things, just go to the main reception, in front of the finance office.

13▶ Complete the gaps in the diagram using NO MORE THAN TWO WORDS AND/OR A NUMBER. Try to locate the answers as quickly as possible.

14▶ Answer these questions with a partner.

1 Do the answers come from the whole text?
2 Which words helped you locate the relevant information quickly?

◎ Sometimes in the exam, you may get a diagram which is a technical drawing of a machine or invention, or something from the natural world.

TIP 13

These types of diagram may be difficult to understand at first, but it is important not to panic and to focus on what you do understand. This type of question is testing your understanding of the text, not your technical knowledge.

TIP 15

Make sure you copy the spellings correctly, especially for technical words.

15▶ Study this diagram, then read the text below. Write NO MORE THAN TWO WORDS from the text for each answer.

6 Carriage return lever

5 _____

2 _____

4 _____

3 _____

1 Key

Can you imagine being a student at university before computers? Before the technological revolution in the 1980s, if you didn't want to write by hand you had to use one of these machines – a typewriter.

It's called a typewriter because you are able to write on the page with pieces of type. The metal bars have letters on them, which allow you to write on paper neatly.

So how does it work? First, you need to press down on one of the keys and the lever* makes another lever called the type hammer move up towards the paper. The type hammer has the metal bar with the letters attached to it at the end. Just before the letter hits the paper a piece of cloth with ink on it called the ribbon moves upwards between the type and the paper. The letter then appears in ink on the piece of paper.

When you take your finger off the key, a spring makes the hammer move back to where it was before. At the same time, the carriage, which is the cylinder-shaped part at the top where the paper is held, moves to the left. You can therefore continue to write the word that you want. When the carriage gets to the end of a line you hear a bell. When you hear the bell, you press the carriage return lever on the left-hand side of the typewriter, which moves the paper up, so that you can continue writing on a new line.

* lever – a long bar that you use to lift or move something by pressing one end

UNDERSTANDING EXPLANATIONS

16 How were the words explained in the text?

> lever   ribbon   carriage return lever

 Technical terms or explanations can be given using these methods:

- footnote
- an explanation in the text
- an explanation given by the surrounding context.

17 Read this short text explaining how the modern computer works and answer the question which follows.

INPUT

The mouse and keyboard are input units: ways of getting information into your computer. Most computers store all this information on a hard drive (a huge magnetic memory). However, smaller computer-based devices like digital cameras and mobile phones use other kinds of storage, such as flash memory cards.

Many computers now have LCD screens, capable of displaying high-resolution graphics, such as very clear and detailed photographs. Many computers also have loudspeakers and can be connected to a printer.

PROCESSING

The computer's processor, also known as the central processing unit, is a microchip* buried deep inside. As it is used it becomes incredibly hot and a fan prevents the computer from overheating.

*microchip – a very small part of a computer or machine that does calculations or stores information

How were words explained in the text: by footnote, explanation in the text or explanation given by surrounding context?

a hard drive
c high-resolution
b flash memory cards
d microchip

18 Using your understanding of the text, complete this diagram. Write NO MORE THAN TWO WORDS from the text for each answer.

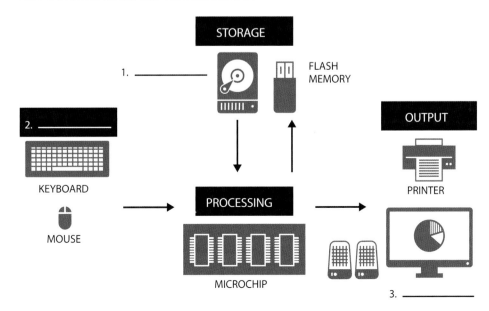

EXAM SKILLS

19 ▶ Read this text and complete this diagram using NO MORE THAN TWO WORDS AND/OR A NUMBER.

Common Australian University Qualifications

Undergraduate Study

| Bachelor Degree (General) 3 Years | Bachelor Degree **1** _____ 4 Years | Bachelor Degree with **2** _____ Bachelor Degree + 1 Year |

Postgraduate Study

| Master Degree **3** _____ 1 Year | Master Degree (Part-time) 2 Years | **4** _____ 3–4 Years |

The most common degree from an Australian university is a three-year bachelor degree in a field such as arts, business or science. Professional degrees such as engineering or law are completed over four years. Veterinary and dentistry degrees take five years and medical degrees take up to six.

A bachelor degree with 'honours' is usually achieved by doing an extra year of study at a more advanced level. Honours programme placements are offered to students with high bachelor-degree grades, particularly in the final year.

Admission to postgraduate programmes is based on achievement in previous university studies and, for some courses, on professional experience as well.

Masters courses are typically one year in duration for full-time study (or two years when completed part-time). MBAs may require one or two years of full-time study but are most commonly one and a half years.

To be accepted onto a doctoral programme, you need high achievement in a masters degree or to have a bachelor degree with at least upper-level second-class honours. A doctoral degree is assessed based on a dissertation, although coursework may feature in the first year. Generally this degree will last three to four years.

GO ONLINE AND COMPLETE UNIT 7 READING EXERCISES 1–6

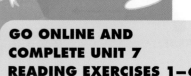

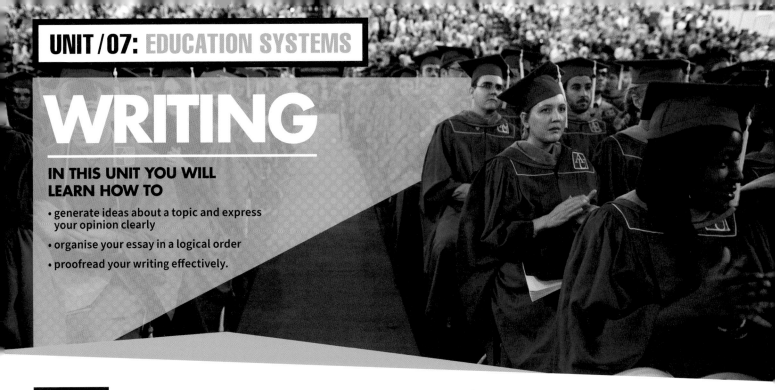

UNIT /07: EDUCATION SYSTEMS

WRITING

IN THIS UNIT YOU WILL LEARN HOW TO

- generate ideas about a topic and express your opinion clearly
- organise your essay in a logical order
- proofread your writing effectively.

0 1 ▷ Using some of the expressions in the box, discuss questions 1–7 with a partner.

For me, …	I think / believe …	In my experience, …	In my opinion, …
In my view, …	Personally, I think …	To my mind, …	

◎ Many of the Writing Part 2 tasks require you to give your opinion. In order to prepare for this type of task, it is a good idea to practise generating ideas about different topics by having debates with classmates or friends.

1 Are maths and science more important than the arts?

2 Should students be punished for arriving late at school?

3 Should all schoolchildren be required to wear a uniform?

4 Is homework necessary?

5 Should mobile phones be allowed in the classroom?

6 Is going to university the best way to get a good job?

7 Many students choose to take a 'gap year' to travel or work before going to university. Is this a waste of time?

0 2 ▷ Discuss this question with your partner.

Which of the expressions in the box are suitable only for spoken, not written English?

ORGANISING YOUR WRITING

03 ▶ In order to express your opinion clearly, you need to have a structure which is easy for the reader to follow. Put statements 1–9 into one of these categories.

Introduction _____

Main body _____

Conclusion _____

1 Restate your opinion
2 Examples of your experience – if relevant
3 Supporting ideas
4 Each paragraph should express one main idea
5 The function of the essay, e.g. *This essay will discuss …*
6 Rewrite the question using your own words
7 Introduce the topic
8 A summary of your main ideas
9 Give your opinion

TIP 03

Although you are very unlikely to come across a question in the exam that you have discussed before, you may already have thought about a similar topic.

04 ▶ Using the information from exercise 3, read this task and put the paragraphs in the sample answer in the correct order.

Nowadays, some parents feel that schoolchildren are given too much homework.

In your opinion, should homework time be reduced or banned altogether?

Give reasons for your answer and include any relevant examples from your own knowledge or experience.

TIP 04

Your opinion needs to be made clear throughout, as the writer has done in this sample answer, in order to achieve a good score in this part of the Writing test.

SAMPLE ANSWER

A ☐

Homework also teaches children the discipline needed to complete work to a deadline – a very important life skill. It also helps parents to become involved in their child's learning. By helping with homework, parents can understand what is being learnt at school and encourage their child to become interested in the topic.

B ☐

To conclude therefore, homework does have a value at school and should not be banned altogether. It is also very important, however, that homework does not dominate a child's time at home. There must also be adequate time for family, friends and sport.

C ☐

It is also important to note, however, that homework time should be limited and too much homework could have a negative impact on a child's ability to learn. Too much homework could be very stressful for a child and ruin their enjoyment of being at school. Homework should be limited to one hour every evening, so children have the time to become involved in other important activities, such as sport or music lessons.

D ☐

Homework is a common feature of school life. Giving students some homework is a useful exercise. Too much homework, however, can cause a great deal of unnecessary stress for pupils. In the following essay, I will discuss the reasons for this view.

E ☐

Homework is a beneficial tool in the school week for several reasons. Most importantly, it teaches pupils to work independently and to practise the skills or knowledge acquired during lesson time. They are able to work on projects or extended pieces of work, which they have to research either in the library or using the internet.

When you are writing within a time limit and under exam conditions, it is easy to make silly errors. It is important, therefore, to spend the last few minutes checking through what you have written so you do not lose marks unnecessarily. In order to check your work properly, you need to consider:

- punctuation – have you used full stops, capital letters and commas appropriately?
- grammar – have you used the correct tenses and the correct prepositions?
- spelling – are all the words spelt correctly?
- word count – have you written at least 250 words? (It is quicker to count lines instead of words.)
- handwriting – is your handwriting clear? Are there any words which are not clear and need rewriting?

All of these aspects need equal attention and you will lose marks if they are not considered carefully in your answer.

05 ▶ Look at this exam task and the sample answer, which contains 20 common errors. Correct the sample answer, considering all the points in exercise 4.

Home-schooling is becoming increasingly popular. What do you think the reasons are for this? Do you think home-schooling is more beneficial than attending a private or state school?

SAMPLE ANSWER

Nowdays, many parents are choosing to home-schooling there children rather than sending them to a private or state school. There is perhaps many reasons for this, but I believe the main reason is that many schools are not seen as safe any more. In some areas, schools can be very violent and fighting is a common problem, I do not believe that homes-schooling is always more beneficial to the student than state school, but in some cases it can be. In the following essay, I would discuss this idea further.

If you are lucky enough to be able to attend a good school, with only minor disipline problem, then I think attending a state school is better for you than being educated in home. school is more than just learning about different subjects, it is also a place were you can make new friends and learn to socialise. School also gives you the opportunity to join teams and clubs. subjects are also taught by people who have been trained in that particular area.

If, however, this is not the case, and you have to attend a school with poor disipline or somewhere you feel very unhappy, home-schooling could be more beneficial. It is better to learn in a comfortable enviroment, where you feel safe than in disruptive one. in order for home-schooling to be sucessful, however, your teacher needs to be knowledgeble and follow a set curriculim.

To summarise, therefore, home-schooling is more beneficial if the child is in a situation which is making them very unhappy.

EXAM SKILLS

06 ▶ Use the information and language from this lesson to answer this Writing Part 2 task. You should spend about 40 minutes on this task.

Many students choose to take a gap year before starting university, to travel or gain work experience. Do you think this is a good idea or a waste of time?

Give reasons for your answer and include any relevant examples from your own knowledge or experience.

Write at least 250 words.

GO ONLINE AND COMPLETE UNIT 7 WRITING EXERCISES 1–5

TIP 06

The clearer your handwriting, the easier it will be for the examiner to understand your answer.

TIP 06

When you have checked your answer, make any corrections neatly. Do not waste time rewriting the whole answer – it is better to use this time for planning and checking.

UNIT /07: EDUCATION SYSTEMS

LISTENING

IN THIS UNIT YOU WILL LEARN HOW TO

- listen to and understand a description
- complete a chart, diagram or sentences based on a talk or dialogue
- use notes to follow what a speaker is saying.

01▶

60

In this lesson you will hear a discussion and a lecture about education in the UK. Listen to seven short conversations and write 1–7 in the table to show which type of education the people are mainly talking about.

Type of education	Conversation	Information
Nursery		
Primary school		
Secondary school		
Sixth form college		
Further education college	1	
University		A
Adult education		

Sixth form college

Nursery school

60

02 ▶ Read the information A–G about different educational institutions in the UK. Listen again and write A–G in the table to show the correct information for each type of education.

A This is usually the first time students become completely independent. It's normal in the UK for these students to study in places a long way from their homes.

B You can take courses in all kinds of subjects, usually after work or at the weekend. The courses are usually quite cheap.

C The purpose of a vocational course is to prepare students for work in a certain profession, like hairdressing or car mechanics.

D Students no longer study in one classroom, but have to go to different classrooms depending on the subjects that they are studying.

E Parents can choose to send their children here. Many places are free, but parents often have to pay.

F When children are required to start full-time education, the majority of them go to this institution.

G Although students can prepare to pass exams for university entry at their schools, they can also choose to go to this special institution for two years.

Further education

Adult education

[CHARTS AND DIAGRAMS]

 This exercise helps you to focus on the words you will need to complete a chart by giving you two choices. The prompts that help you choose the correct answer are the **ages of the children**, so you should pay careful attention to those.

TIP 03

Before you listen for information to complete a chart or diagram, you should look at the chart or diagram carefully and think about the **type** of information that is required.

03▶

61

The lecturer is talking about the education system in England and Wales up until the age of 16. Listen and choose the correct answers in the table.

Key stage	Ages	School and school years	Assessments	Compulsory subjects include
0	4/5	**1 Nursery /** Reception	None	
1	5–7	Primary: **2 Infant /** Junior	Key stage 1 Teacher Assessments	
2	7–11	Primary: **3 Infant /** Junior	Key stage 2 **4 Standard Assessment Tests /** Teacher Assessments	**7 Modern Foreign Languages /** Citizenship
3	11–14	Secondary	Key stage 3 **5 Standard Assessment Tests /** Teacher Assessments	
4	14–16	Secondary	Key Stage 4 **6 Standard Assessment Tests /** General Certificates of Secondary Education	

04 ▶ The lecturer is talking about post-16 educational opportunities – the choices which pupils can make between the ages of 16 and 18. Listen and complete the diagram. Write ONE OR TWO WORDS in each gap.

TIP 04

If there are arrows in the diagram, you can use these to help you listen for the answers.

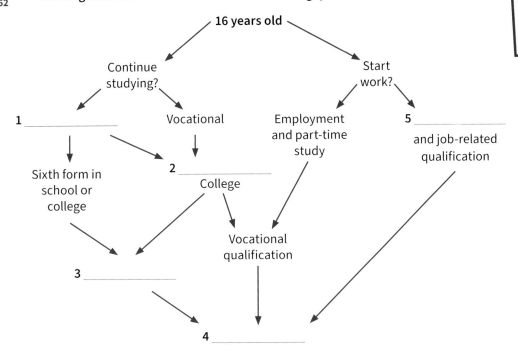

16 years old

Continue studying?

Start work?

1 _____

Vocational

Employment and part-time study

5 _____ and job-related qualification

Sixth form in school or college

2 _____

College

Vocational qualification

3 _____

4 _____

[COMPLETING SENTENCES]

05 ▶ A school student is discussing how to apply for university with a teacher. Listen and choose the correct word in each sentence.

1 Register on the UCAS (University and Colleges Admissions Service) website, enter your personal details and choose **five** / **seven** universities which offer a course you want to study.

2 Write your personal **statement** / **assessment**, telling the universities about you and why they should offer you a place.

3 The **reference** / **advice** will be supplied by your UCAS adviser at school.

4 Each university on your list examines your application and decides whether to make an offer. Offers may be **conditional** / **provisional**, which means you have to get certain grades.

5 If your exam results meet the requirements, the university will **confirm** / **renew** the offer and you can accept or reject it.

6 Many universities use a **clearing** / **reapplying** system to offer unfilled places on their courses to students who did not get high enough grades for their first-choice university.

06 ▶ Practise following the direction of a conversation by choosing the correct notes. A student who has just started university is discussing his course with a tutor. Listen and choose the correct notes (a or b) for 1–5.

64

1a Students usually attend a seminar after they have been to a lecture.

1b Students usually attend a lecture after they have been to a seminar.

2a Students usually attend tutorials every three weeks to discuss their progress with the tutor.

2b Students usually attend tutorials every two weeks to discuss their progress with the tutor.

3a The assessment over the whole course is 60% course assignments and 40% exams.

3b The assessment over the whole course is 40% course assignments and 60% exams.

4a Course assignments should be no fewer than 2,000 words.

4b Course assignments should not be more than 3,000 words.

5a Every assignment should have at least three academic references and five non-academic ones.

5b Every assignment should have at least five academic references and three non-academic ones.

[EXAM SKILLS]

07 ▶ A student who is about to finish university is discussing opportunities for further study with a tutor. Listen and complete each sentence with NO MORE THAN TWO WORDS.

65

1 If you want to teach in a school, the best option is to complete a _____ _____ in Education.

2 You can also apply to study on a _____ of _____ course.

3 If you want to do a _____ _____ like a PhD, it may take at least three years to complete.

4 A _____ _____ provides a good opportunity to gain commercial experience in your chosen profession.

5 If you want to find work, a good idea would be to attend a _____ _____ , which gives you the opportunity to talk to many potential employers in one place.

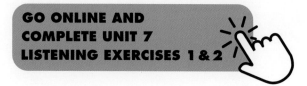

GO ONLINE AND
COMPLETE UNIT 7
LISTENING EXERCISES 1 & 2

UNIT /07: EDUCATION SYSTEMS

SPEAKING

IN THIS UNIT YOU WILL LEARN HOW TO

- speak in detail about education
- consider reasons, causes and effects for different Speaking Part 3 situations
- make suggestions or recommendations.

0 1 ▷ **Discuss these questions with a partner.**

1 What kind of school do you currently attend?

2 Is there anything about your school you would like to improve?

3 Have you ever thought about attending school in a different country?

4 What do you think schools will be like in the future?

TALKING ABOUT EDUCATION

02▷ Complete the sentences with words from the box.

academic	curriculum	discipline	essays	grades
graduation	private tutors	teachers	technical	tests

1 Our _____ are quite strict and give us lots of homework. They are also responsible for _____ and if you don't do your homework, your parents might get a letter!

2 I'm really worried about our high school _____ – my parents want me to get good _____ .

3 At university, we need to learn how to write in a more _____ style. It's different from the way we used to write at school, so many students need help from _____ at first.

4 The _____ at my school includes lessons on speaking, reading and listening to English, and I also have to write a lot of _____ .

5 Our school teaches a number of _____ subjects like electronics and electrical engineering, so I hope to get a good job in those areas after _____ .

03▷ Using the words from the box and your own ideas, describe the education system in your country to your partner. Use themes 1–4 to help you (both UK and US names are given).

1 nursery school/kindergarten
2 primary school/elementary school
3 secondary school/high school
4 university/school

TIP 03

Education is a common topic in IELTS, so you may be asked about your educational history or context in Speaking Parts 1, 2 or 3.

GIVING REASONS FOR YOUR ANSWER

04▷ In Speaking Part 3 you need to speak at length about a topic. To do this, you may need to provide reasons to expand your opinions. With a partner, brainstorm some reasons to support these opinions.

1 The school system in our country is one of the best in the world.
2 The school system in our country is in need of improvement.
3 Too many people in our country go to university.
4 Many people in our country are not ready to get a job when they leave school.
5 Technology has brought many great developments in education.
6 Technology is making education more stressful.

TIP 04

In Speaking Part 3, you need a wide vocabulary to speak about various topics at length and make your meaning clear.

05▷ Use these prompts to link your reasons together, then say them to your partner.

1 There are several reasons why …
2 The first reason is that …
3 The second reason is that …
4 Another point to consider is that …
5 The biggest / main reason is that …

TALKING ABOUT CAUSE AND EFFECT

0 6 ▶ In Speaking Part 3, you might also have to talk about the causes and effects related to a topic. With a partner, brainstorm some possible causes for the problems in the table.

Problem	Causes
a Parents have to spend a lot of money on private education.	**1** *Because students are under a lot of pressure to get good grades.* **2** _____ **3** _____
b Students do not have enough free time to socialise.	**1** *Due to the fact that they have to study from morning until night.* **2** _____ **3** _____
c Many students have reported that they are unhappy with studying English.	**1** *As they have to spend a lot of time memorising lists of vocabulary.* **2** _____ **3** _____

0 7 ▶ With a different partner, brainstorm some possible effects of the causes in the table.

Cause	Effect
a Because students are under a lot of pressure to get good grades	**1** *Parents have to spend a lot of money on private education.* **2** _____ **3** _____
b Due to the fact that they have to study from morning until night	**1** *Students do not have enough free time to socialise.* **2** _____ **3** _____
c As they have to spend a lot of time memorising vocabulary	**1** *Many students have reported that they are unhappy with studying English.* **2** _____ **3** _____

MAKING SUGGESTIONS USING MODAL VERBS

0 8 ▶ Speaking Part 3 questions often ask you to make suggestions or recommendations. Make some suggestions about your country's education system by completing these sentences.

1 In order to improve our education system, the government **should** _____ .

2 Teachers **should** _____ to improve their students' grades.

3 Students **must** _____ to improve their chances of getting a job after graduation.

4 Parents **have to** _____ with teachers to help their children do better at school.

5 Our country **must** _____ in order to compete internationally.

> **TIP 0 8**
>
> You should study the way that *should*, *must* and *have to* are used and try to include them in your responses.

0 9 ▶ For each sentence in exercise 8, give a reason for your answer. This may include some causes and effects.

In order to improve our education system, the government should change the testing system. The main reason is that because we only study to pass our tests, we find it difficult to use our knowledge in real-life situations.

effect   cause   suggestion

1 0 ▶ Your class is going to make a 'time capsule' that will be opened in the year 3000. You can include only TEN items in the capsule. In small groups, decide which items you will include, and justify your selection. To do this, try to give reasons, causes, effects and suggestions. Use the table to help you.

Item	Why?
a picture of the students in the class	The main reason is that the people who open the capsule should know who buried it. Otherwise, they might not be able to understand the objects inside.
1	
2	
3	
4	
5	
6	
7	
8	
9	
10	

1 1 ▶ Once your group has decided on TEN items, present your list to the class, giving reasons, causes, effects and suggestions. Your class now has to decide on the final TEN items to be selected.

12 Write the contraction of the pronoun and verb in these sentences and then practise saying them.

1 She would _____ often give us extra homework before our exams.

2 The problem with studying late at night is that it is _____ hard to remember the next day what you learnt.

3 I know that if I work harder, I will _____ get good grades.

In speech, we often shorten words like *would, will* and *is* to make contractions, for example:

- *I would → I'd*
- *I will → I'll*
- *That is → That's*

13 Listen to the contractions in these sentences, then practise saying the sentences to your partner.

66

1 **I'd** suggest going to bed earlier or you **won't** be able to remember what **you've** learnt.

2 We **mustn't** push young people into studying too hard, or **they'll** drop out of school.

3 **That's** not the right solution. Instead, we **should've** banned homework for pupils some time ago.

EXAM SKILLS

14 Respond to the prompts in this Speaking Part 2 task. Try to talk for TWO full minutes.

Describe a problem with the education system in your country.

You should say:

- what kind of problem it is
- how long the problem has existed
- what effect the problem has had on education

And explain what we can do to solve the problem.

15 Listen to a student answering these Speaking Part 3 questions. Note down any reasons, causes, effects or suggestions they give. Then answer the questions with your own ideas.

67

1 What is the effect of private tutoring on education?

2 Is private tutoring more important today than it was in the past?

3 What more can governments do to reduce the need for private tutoring?

4 How can we encourage more parents to teach their children at home?

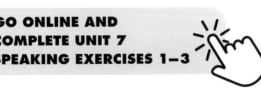

GO ONLINE AND COMPLETE UNIT 7 SPEAKING EXERCISES 1–3

READING

IN THIS UNIT YOU WILL LEARN HOW TO

- find factual information in a text to decide if a statement is *True*, *False* or *Not Given*
- practise identifying *Not Given* questions
- recognise and use the first and second conditional correctly.

LEAD-IN

0 1 ▷ Read these three short texts, describing some of the most interesting festivals in the world.

0 2 ▷ Discuss these questions with a partner.

    1 Which one of these festivals would you most like to attend and why?

    2 Which one of these festivals would you least like to attend and why?

LA TOMATINA SPAIN

La Tomatina is the world's biggest food fight! It is always held on the last Wednesday of August every year in Bunol, a town near Valencia in Spain. Because it is such fun, it has become very popular and officials have had to limit the event to 20,000 people by issuing tickets. More than 100 metric tons of over-ripe tomatoes are thrown in the street during the event.

TRUE / FALSE / NOT GIVEN QUESTIONS

 True / False / Not Given questions are a common feature of the exam. They are similar to *Yes / No / Not Given* questions, but instead of being opinion-based, these questions relate to **factual information only**.

03 Read statements 1–3 relating to the short texts in the lead-in, and decide if they are *True*, *False* or *Not Given*.

TIP 03
The questions are in the same order as the text.

1 Any number of people can attend La Tomatina.
2 The mud festival is used to sell a beauty product.
3 On Dia de los muertos people do the same activities their loved ones enjoyed in life.

BORYEONG MUD FESTIVAL
SOUTH KOREA

A cosmetics company in South Korea created a line of beauty products which featured mud from the Boryeong mud flats as a main ingredient. The company did not want to spend money on advertising, so the Boryeong Mud Festival was born. This allowed potential customers to feel the benefits of the special mud. The festival is home to mud slides, a mud prison, mud pools and mud skiing. You can also enjoy live music, acupuncture and a fireworks display.

DIA DE LOS MUERTOS (DAY OF THE DEAD)
MEXICO

This Mexican holiday is celebrated throughout Mexico and around the world. The holiday focuses on remembering friends and family members who have died. It is particularly celebrated in Mexico, where the day is a bank holiday. Activities involved in the holiday include building private altars, cleaning the graves of loved ones and telling funny stories about dead relatives. Street parties, parades and festivals are also a common feature of the celebration.

0 4 ▷ In exercise 3, which word makes statement 1 false?

0 5 ▷ In exercise 3, which word/phrase in the text makes statement 2 true?

0 6 ▷ Read this short text and answer the questions which follow.

Birthdays take place once a year and celebrate the day you were born. Many people have a party on their birthday and socialise with family and friends. A birthday cake, with candles on the top, is often presented at this celebration, together with gifts and cards.

Answer *True*, *False* or *Not Given*.

1 The candles on the cake often represent your age.
2 Everyone has a party on their birthday.
3 Presents are often given on birthdays.
4 Everyone likes birthdays.
5 Birthdays are celebrated differently around the world.

0 7 ▷ Here is a summary of the advice given in the previous section. Complete the tips using ONE word from the box in each gap. There is one word you do not need.

carefully	change	order	rely	same	synonyms

Tips

· Do not **1** _____ on matching words in the text and question to decide on your answer.
· Answers are in the same **2** _____ as they appear in the text.
· *True* means that the information is the **3** _____ as in the text, not similar.
· Read the relevant part of the text very **4** _____ .
· It is useful to look for **5** _____ , as the words in the question are rarely the same as those in the text.

0 8 ▷ Using the tips in exercise 7, read the texts and then decide if these statements agree with the information given in them.

Look at the statements and write

TRUE   *if the statement agrees with the information*
FALSE   *if the statement contradicts the information*
NOT GIVEN   *if there is no information on this*

1 The Dragon Boat Festival celebrates when Qu Yuan was saved by the people who stopped the fish eating him.
2 When the Harbin Ice and Snow Festival first began, only the Chinese entered the competition.
3 If conditions allow, the exhibits at the Harbin Ice and Snow Festival are displayed when the official festival is over.
4 There are a variety of things to do and see at the Lantern Festival.
5 Chinese New Year is also known as the Spring Festival.

Perhaps the hardest part of this type of question is understanding when the information is *Not Given*.

It is important to remember here that your answers must be based on the information in the **text only** and not from your own knowledge of the subject (or an educated guess).

HARBIN ICE AND SNOW FESTIVAL

Another spectacular festival hosted by the Chinese is the Harbin Ice and Snow Festival. This is an annual winter festival which takes place in Harbin, Heilongjiang, China, and is now the largest ice and snow festival in the world. Initially, the majority of participants were Chinese, but it has since become an international festival and competition. The festival includes the world's biggest ice sculptures. Officially, the festival starts on 5th January and lasts for one month. However, exhibits often open earlier and finish later, weather permitting. The ice sculptures are displayed throughout the city.

CHINESE FESTIVALS

If I could visit any country to be a part of their celebrations and festivals, it would be China. China is home to some of the most beautiful celebrations on the planet – celebrations filled with colour and meaning.

DRAGON BOAT RACING

The Dragon Boat festival, also known as the Duanwu Festival, has been celebrated in China for more than 2,000 years. The festival occurs on the fifth day of the fifth month of the Chinese lunar calendar. The celebration emerged after the Chinese scholar, Qu Yuan, threw himself into the Mi Lo river in protest against the government of the time. Qu Yuan was drowned and the people were unable to find the body, so to prevent the fish from eating him, the locals threw rice patties into the river. Ever since then, rice dumplings or *zongzi* are prepared and eaten during this festival season. Other activities include drinking a special drink called *realgar* and dragon-boat racing to the sound of beating drums.

CHINESE NEW YEAR

By far the biggest celebration in the Chinese calendar, however, is Chinese New Year. In fact, the lantern festival signifies the end of this long celebration, which begins on Chinese New Year's Eve. It is a holiday filled with dragons, fireworks, symbolic clothing and flowers. Chinese New Year is a time for families to get together. The New Year's Eve dinner is called Reunion Dinner, and is believed to be the most important meal of the year. Families of several generations sit together, enjoying food and socialising.

LANTERN RIDDLES

Also in January there is the Lantern Festival, or the Shangyuan Festival, which is celebrated on 15th January of the Chinese lunar calendar. This festival marks the return of spring and is regarded as a day for appreciating family and the bright full moon. There are several different activities involved in this celebration, appealing to all age groups. These include: watching fireworks or solving the riddles* featured on the lanterns.

*riddle – a strange and difficult question that has a clever and often funny answer

GRAMMAR FOCUS: FIRST AND SECOND CONDITIONALS

09 ▸ **Read statements a and b and answer the questions which follow.**

a If I have the time this weekend, I will come to the Dragon Boat Festival with you.

b If I could attend any festival in the world, it would be the carnival in Rio de Janeiro.

1 In which statement does the speaker believe that attending the festival is unlikely to happen?

2 In which statement does the speaker believe that attending the festival may happen?

3 Label each statement as either the first or second conditional.

4 Using the examples, complete these rules with these words: *past simple*, *present simple*, *infinitive*, *would*.

> **Rules**
> First conditional
> *If* + **5** _____ , ... *will* + **6** _____
> Second conditional
> *If* + **7** _____ , ... **8** _____ + infinitive

10 ▸ **Complete the sentences with suitable verbs, using either the first or second conditional form.**

1 If you _____ to the festival in town tomorrow, there _____ crowds of people. You did say you were going.

2 If I _____ the time, I _____ to more festivals. I am just too busy with other things.

3 If I _____ the time, I _____ bake a cake for the party. I should be able to do it this evening.

4 If I _____ enough money, I _____ celebrate New Year in Australia. I just don't have the money at the moment.

5 If he _____ this fancy dress costume this afternoon, he _____ be very hot in this summer heat.

EXAM SKILLS

11 ▷ Read the text and answer the questions which follow.

In January or February, Venice plays host to the most magical of carnivals. During the carnival, the city is filled with a mass of masked party-goers, posing and dancing, in an attempt to reinvent one of the great traditions of the city. Naturally, it is very crowded and hotels and restaurants are expensive, but it is a unique occasion and a great time to experience this beautiful city.

The carnival was first held in Venice in the 11th century and lasted for over two months. Activities involved a series of formal parties in St Mark's Square and playing games for money. Regardless of social status, participants wore costumes and masks. Images of the time and occasion are still displayed throughout the city today. During the 18th century, however, this period of festivities came to an end, and the carnival did not return until 1979. Today, the carnival is extremely popular with people eager to dress up and parade around the city in their masks and costumes.

The weekends are the busiest times at the carnival – the final weekend in particular. During the festivities, you can enjoy live music and take part in a large open-air festival. Costumes are also a major feature of the occasion and there is even a competition to judge the best one. The best ones are usually displayed at the centre of carnival festivities, in the breathtaking St Mark's Square. Numerous shops in Venice sell these costumes and masks in preparation for this great event.

Perhaps the most attractive aspect of the Venice carnival, though, is the variety of masked balls and parties there are to attend. You do have to pay for these, however, and they can be quite costly. One of the most expensive parties is the Valentine's Grand Masquerade Ball, held on February 14th at the Palazzo Flangini.

Do these statements agree with the information given in the text?

Look at the statements and write

TRUE   *if the statement agrees with the information*

FALSE   *if the statement contradicts the information*

NOT GIVEN   *if there is no information on this*

1 Before the 20th century, only the rich participated in the carnival.

2 The Venice carnival was banned in the 18th century.

3 The most popular days at the carnival are during the week.

4 None of the festivities take place outside.

5 In order to take part in the costume competition you need to be Italian.

6 There are few places in Venice where you can purchase your costume and mask.

7 The tickets for the Valentine's Grand Masquerade Ball are worth a lot of money.

GO ONLINE AND COMPLETE UNIT 8 READING EXERCISES 1–4

WRITING

IN THIS UNIT YOU WILL LEARN HOW TO

- identify and approach a 'problems and solutions' essay question
- plan and write an essay answering both parts of the question
- write a suitable introduction and conclusion
- revise past, present and future tenses.

LEAD-IN

01 Discuss these statements with a partner. Can you suggest solutions to any of these problems?

1 Formal celebrations can make some people nervous.

2 Nowadays many children do not fully appreciate the presents they are given.

3 Celebrations such as birthdays or New Year can make some people feel lonelier than usual.

4 Some people believe it is too expensive to get married these days.

5 Some celebrations have become too much about money and the reasons behind them have been forgotten.

> ⊚ In the Writing test, you may be asked to write a 'problems and solutions' essay using statements similar to those in the lead-in.

02 Look at the pairs of sentences. Each pair includes a sentence with good advice and a sentence with bad advice, based on mistakes often made by students. Next to each statement, put a ✔ for good advice and a ✗ for bad advice.

1a Planning is not necessary for this type of question. ✗

1b Planning is particularly important for this task. ✔

2a Discuss only two or three problems/solutions in detail.

2b Include as many problems/solutions as you can.

3a Read and analyse the question very carefully.

3b Skim read the question and base your answer on the key words.

4a A solution does not need to be given for every problem you mention.

4b Each problem mentioned should have a solution.

5a Your answer must have a clear structure.

5b Structure is not necessary for this task.

03▷ Skim read this sample answer to understand the main idea.

Some celebrations have lost their original meaning and these occasions have become too much about spending money. What problems can this cause? What could be done to change the situation?

SAMPLE ANSWER

Introduction

There are several national or international celebrations throughout the year which are dominated by shops and companies taking the opportunity to make large profits. Heavy advertising campaigns, which begin well in advance of the celebration itself, mean that some people pay very little attention to the actual reason behind the event. In the following essay, I will discuss some of the problems this causes and also offer some solutions. ←

Main Body

One of the main problems with some celebrations being too focused on spending money is that it means for some people the occasion might cause stress and unhappiness. This could be created by worrying about what gifts to buy or by not having any money to buy presents. ←

Main Body

Perhaps the most significant problem, however, is that the true meaning of the celebration is forgotten. Most celebrations are about appreciating life and spending time with friends and family. As a result of focusing on presents and money, this is often forgotten, and the buying of gifts can actually cause arguments between loved ones. ←

Main Body

I believe the solutions to these problems, however, are simple. First, it is the duty of schools and parents to educate the younger generation, teaching them the true meaning of each celebration. Secondly, and perhaps more importantly, people should limit the number of presents they give and receive, consequently putting less emphasis on that part of the occasion. ←

Conclusion

In conclusion, therefore, there are several negative effects associated with celebrations becoming too focused on spending money – effects which, for some, can cause unhappiness and stress. In order to prevent this from happening in the future, the younger generation need to be educated fully on the true meaning of celebrations and generally people should put less importance on buying and receiving presents. ←

04▷ Complete the boxes next to the sample answer with descriptions a–e.

    a Summary of the discussion

    b What is the solution? How will it solve the problem?

    c Second problem and reasons for this/examples

    d First problem and reasons for this/examples

    e Rephrase the question and say what the essay is about

WRITING INTRODUCTIONS AND CONCLUSIONS

 Look at the sample answer again and answer these questions.

Introduction

1 Which words rephrase the question?

2 Which words indicate what the writer is going to discuss?

Conclusion

3 The conclusion summarises information taken from which paragraphs?

4 Is there any new information included in the conclusion?

5 Does the conclusion copy the exact wording used in the main body of the essay?

6 Is the last sentence a prediction or recommendation?

TIP 05
If you have time, you can finish your conclusion with a prediction or recommendation.

UNDERSTANDING THE QUESTION

06 ‘Problem and solution’ essay questions may not always be phrased in the same way. Study these examples and answer the questions which follow.

A

In the modern world, spending money is a major focus of many of our celebrations and the meaning behind these events has become less important.

Suggest measures which could be taken to solve this problem.

B

Spending too much money on gifts has led to numerous problems and the true meaning of many celebrations has less importance these days.

Identify these problems and suggest ways in which these issues might be tackled.

C

Nowadays most people pay little attention to the real meaning of many celebrations, due to a growing focus on spending money on gifts.

What are the negative aspects of this and what can be done to minimise the bad effects?

D

Focusing on spending money during times of celebration is a significant problem and many people pay little attention to the true meaning of these events.

What are the reasons for this and how could these problems be solved?

1 What other ways are there of saying *what solutions can you suggest*?

2 What other ways are there of saying *problems*?

3 Which of these essay questions requires a different kind of answer?

07▶ Read this sample answer and complete it using the correct form of the verbs in the box.

close	do	discuss	give	ignore	pass	want

Celebrations such as New Year can make some people feel lonelier than usual.
What are the reasons for this and how might this issue be tackled?

SAMPLE ANSWER

For those with family and friends close by, New Year can be a happy occasion. For many, however, for a whole variety of reasons, it can be a very lonely time and can make people feel more alone than usual. In the following essay, I **1** _____ the reasons for this and how the problem could be solved.

One of the reasons some people feel lonelier at New Year is because the event **2** _____ a great deal of attention by the media and many people feel pressure to be doing something spectacular. There is, therefore, a large expectation to be around crowds of people.

Another reason is because at New Year many businesses **3** _____ for the holiday. Consequently, people often do not have the option of keeping busy at work or socialising with colleagues. A third reason is that New Year tends to be a time when people think about the year which **4** _____ and their life in general. Therefore, if someone does not have company at this time, it can make them feel lonelier.

In order to tackle this problem, people should not pay too much attention to the media at this time. If they do not have anything planned, they should treat it as an ordinary day. If they **5** _____ to think about the year which has passed, they should **6** _____ it on a different day, when there is no pressure to feel happy.

In summary, loneliness can be a problem for some people at New Year. In order to tackle this, the media should **7** _____ and lonely people should treat the date as an ordinary day.

[EXAM SKILLS]

08▶ Use the information and language from this lesson to answer this Writing Part 2 task. You should spend about 40 minutes on this task.

Write about the following topic:

Organising a large family celebration such as a wedding can often create problems.

What can be the problems associated with organising a large family event and what solutions can you suggest?

Give reasons for your answer and include any relevant examples from your own knowledge and experience.

Write at least 250 words.

GO ONLINE AND COMPLETE UNIT 8 WRITING EXERCISES 1–7

LISTENING

IN THIS UNIT YOU WILL LEARN HOW TO

- identify key information in summaries and tables to guide your listening
- classify information as you listen
- listen carefully to complete summaries and tables.

LEAD-IN

01▶

68

Listen to these short extracts from talks and complete the table to show the type of event each speaker is talking about.

Speaker	Event
	Music festival
	Arts and crafts festival
	Poetry and literature festival
	Food festival
1	Sports festival
	Technology fair

[SUMMARY COMPLETION]

In the Listening test you may have to complete a summary with words from the recording. You may need to write up to *three words and/or a number* in each gap. Before you listen, you need to look at the summary and gaps and think about:

- what the topic is
- what the missing information could be
- what kind of words you can put there (nouns, verbs, adjectives, adverbs, etc.).

You also need to pay attention to key words and phrases in the summary which will help you to listen carefully for the correct words.

02 ▷ The speaker, Dr Saunders, is talking about the preparations for a recent arts festival at a university. Before you listen, look at sentences 1–4 and underline the key words and phrases. Listen and choose the correct alternative in each sentence to create a summary of his talk. (You may hear both alternatives, but the context should help you make the correct choice.)

TIP 02

Remember that the information on the recording is in the same order as in the summary.

1 The festival has grown in four years from having mostly music and performing arts in the first year to including other art forms, most recently **painting and crafts / photography and films**, especially from the university students.

2 Dr Saunders is particularly encouraged by the number of **students / professional artists** who took part in the latest festival.

3 The festival visitors stayed at the university and at the city college, with the students helping with the **accommodation / catering** arrangements.

4 The aims of the festival include extending the university's reputation and giving students the chance to get experience of organising events, mainly as **paid workers / volunteers**.

03 ▷ Listen to Dr Saunders' review of the festival and complete the sentences in the summary. Write up to TWO WORDS AND/OR A NUMBER in each gap.

 TIP 03

Before you listen, look at each sentence and underline the key words and phrases to help you focus on listening for the correct words.

- At 12,500, visitors were up by 10% on the previous year.
- The **1** _____ event was the most popular with many different entries and high levels of attendance.
- One of the main musical attractions had to call off through illness and a replacement could not be found in time, so money had to be returned to the customers.
- The crafts exhibition was **2** _____ despite the variety and quality of crafts on display, so it needs to be reviewed.
- Although there was good security present, **3** _____ , which were worth about £3,000, were stolen so there is a need for better security in future.
- There were some complaints about accommodation because many visitors booked it very late. Unfortunately, the extra accommodation which was supplied was of a **4** _____ .
- More volunteers are needed as some visitors did not get enough information.
- A lot of money was spent on **5** _____ to work with the volunteers but they were possibly not worth the money, so suggestions for reducing costs in that area are welcome.
- The programme needs to be updated and there needs to be more **6** _____ , such as advertising and sponsorship, from local companies for the next festival.

[COMPLETING TABLES]

 In the Listening test you may have to complete a table with words from the recording. The table will have information in clear categories, so before you listen, you need to look at the categories with gaps and think about what **kind** of information is required in each gap. This will help you to listen carefully for the correct missing words.

04▶

71

A lecturer, Dr Reynolds, and two students, Sangita and Lawrence, are discussing the festival programme. Listen and choose the correct alternative in these notes.

Discussion on events		
Event	**Sangita**	**Lawrence**
Music	Artist in reserve 1 **Student band /** **Well-known local band**	Unlikely for the main act to be unable to play in future 2 **Book local band for the last night / Book local band every night**
Crafts	Have clothes separate from other crafts	Make more of the fashion section 3 **Show clothes, glass and pottery / Show only clothes**
Theatre and poetry	Performances in students' own languages	4 **Have students' plays and poems / Have only famous plays and poems**
Photography	5 **Have only digital photographs displayed / Have digital and non-digital photographs displayed**	Only have photographs displayed digitally

05 ▶ Dr Reynolds, Sangita and Lawrence are discussing the practical aspects of the festival. Listen and complete the notes with ONE WORD AND/OR A NUMBER.

72

TIP 05

Remember to look at the different categories in the notes and think about what information would come under that category. This will help you to focus on the correct words when listening.

TIP 05

You may need to write up to **three words and/or a number** in each gap in the exam.

Discussion on organisation		
Aspect of organisation	**Sangita**	**Lawrence**
Accommodation	Use holiday accommodation for **1** _____ .	Having young people at the festival helps the university in future.
Catering	Encourage students to give their ideas and offer to use their own **2** _____ skills.	Agrees
Professional help/ volunteers	Former students would organise it better.	The **3** _____ did not work well as they saw the festival as just a student event.
Security	Windows were open. Everyone should be more careful and take personal **4** _____ for security.	Nothing to add, as there were security guards around all the time.
Finance	It's a good idea for businesses to sponsor or advertise as long as they respect the spirit of the festival.	Students might not be happy with commercial organisations taking a role. Businesses can sponsor specific events and present **5** _____ .

[EXAM SKILLS]

0 6 ▶ Dr Reynolds is telling Dr Saunders about the students' suggestions. Listen and complete the table with NO MORE THAN TWO WORDS AND/OR A NUMBER.

73

Suggestions from the discussion on the festival		
	Suggestion and reason accepted	**Suggestion and reason rejected**
Music	Local bands and student bands: encouraging people to take part	Using replacement bands: too complicated
Crafts	Fashion show: good idea as it can involve many international students	Stop pottery and glass exhibition: need to encourage all **1** _____ of art, not just the popular ones
Theatre and poetry	Plays and poems by students: it would help to raise **2** _____ Works in different languages: help international students feel more at home and valued	–
Photography	–	Digital and non-digital exhibition: not next year because of the **3** _____
Accommodation	–	Using the holiday park: unlikely to be ready in time, but a good possibility for future festivals
Catering	Encourage students to take part in cooking: helps their **4** _____	–
Professional help/ volunteers	Find better organisers: have a better selection system	Using former students instead of professional organisers: not really possible – too much trouble to find and employ them
Security	Encourage students to be more careful: it will increase **5** _____ among students	–
Finance	Encourage businesses to sponsor events and advertise: would encourage more interest in the university and improve relationships with business	Encourage students to have more events to raise money: would take their attention away from their **6** _____

GO ONLINE AND COMPLETE UNIT 8 LISTENING EXERCISES 1–3

SPEAKING

IN THIS UNIT YOU WILL LEARN HOW TO

- speak in detail about celebrations and special events
- make comparisons between the past and the present, or between similarities and differences
- use words and phrases that show 'concession' to look at both sides of an argument
- stress key words to make comparisons.

LEAD-IN

01 ▶ With a partner, describe what you can see in the photos below and then discuss these questions.

1 What kind of things do people celebrate in your country?
2 What do you do to celebrate birthdays in your country?
3 Are any of the celebrations in your country known throughout the world?
4 Do you enjoy public holidays and celebrations?

Often Speaking Part 3 questions will ask you to compare the importance of a topic in the past and present. Look at this sample Part 3 question:

Do you think that national celebrations are less important now than they were in the past?

When answering this type of question, it is useful to consider all sides of the debate.

0 2 ▶ **With a partner, complete this chart. Complete each sentence in at least two different ways.**

We can use *more* or *less* to compare the ideas in the chart:

Celebrations were *more* important in the past *than* now because ...
Celebrations were *less* important in the past *than* now because ...

0 3 ▶ **With a partner, decide whether celebrations are more important now than in the past. Use *more* and *less* in your answer, and give reasons using your ideas from the chart.**

TIP **0 3**

Develop your responses by using a range of tenses and by adding more information in your answer.

MAKING PAST/PRESENT COMPARISONS WITH *WOULD*

To offer more information in questions which ask for a comparison between the present and the past, it helps to consider the differences between what people **would** or **used to** do in the past and what they do now.

04 ▸ With a partner, brainstorm some popular events that you know about and write them in the first column of the table. Then complete the table with your shared ideas.

	Event	Things people would do in the past	Things people do now
1	Chinese New Year	In the past, people would get together with their families and celebrate at home.	Now, people like to watch the fireworks at the harbour.
2			
3			
4			
5			
6			

LOOKING AT BOTH SIDES OF THE ARGUMENT

In Speaking Part 3, you should try to consider both sides of an argument. You can do this by using words such as *although*, *even though* and *while* to add information about one side of the argument, then adding information about the other side. For example:

Although many people still celebrate Valentine's Day each year, it is possible that they focus too much on presents.

Even though preparing for the carnival takes a lot of time, it is an important part of our culture.

While the Battle of the Oranges is supposed to be fun, it leaves a lot of mess for people to clean up!

When we present both sides of the argument using these words, it is called 'concession'.

05 ▶ With a partner, consider one positive and one negative statement about a festival you have attended. Then make a positive and negative statement about a festival you would like to attend. Make a balanced argument using a concession for each one. Use the pictures on page 163 and those here to help you.

Although the Battle of the Oranges gets very messy, it's such a colourful experience.

TIP 05

You can also make concessions with sentence openers such as:
The problem is, …
The trouble is, …
The thing is, …
The disadvantage of that is, …
On the other hand, …

Glastonbury Music Festival

Albuquerque International Balloon Fiesta

DISCUSSING SIMILARITIES AND DIFFERENCES

06 ▶ We can make categories for ideas about similarities and differences. Using the festivals you chose in exercise 4, complete this table.

Event	Season	Location	Procedure	Meaning
Rio Carnavale	Spring	Brazil	Street dancing and performance	Celebration of different cultures

07 ▶ Using the information in the table, talk about how these festivals are similar and different with a partner. Can you think of any other categories to describe the festivals?

TIP 07

Another useful way of comparing things is to focus directly on the differences. For example:
The main difference between Chinese New Year and new year celebrations in my country is …

08 ▷ Using the adjectives in the box (as well as your own ideas), compare and contrast the four festivals with a partner.

astonishing	colourful	dramatic	emotional	entertaining	exhausting
impressive	incredible	memorable	mysterious	peaceful	serious

TIP **08**

When we compare, we focus on the **similarities**. When we contrast, we focus on the **differences**.

PRONUNCIATION: CONTRASTIVE STRESS

09 ▷ Often we can emphasise differences by stressing key words. Listen to the sentences and underline the words which the speakers stress.

74

1 I prefer spending time with my family on my birthday rather than spending time with them at New Year.

2 This holiday is much more exciting than that holiday.

3 These ideas might be better for a celebration than those ideas.

4 Some people don't enjoy public holidays as much as other people I know.

10 ▷ Write THREE sentences comparing different things with your own ideas. Say them to a partner, stressing the key words to show contrast.

[EXAM SKILLS]

11 ▷ Ask and answer these Speaking Part 1 questions with a partner.

1 Do you have any special festivals in your country?

2 What kind of festival is most popular in your country?

3 Are there any international festivals that you would like to attend?

4 Are there any festivals or celebrations you don't enjoy?

12 ▷ Answer the prompts in this Speaking Part 2 task. Try to talk for TWO full minutes.

Describe a public holiday in your country.

You should say:

- what the holiday is celebrating
- when the holiday occurs
- what people do on that holiday

and explain why you like / dislike that holiday.

13 ▷ Listen to a student answering these questions. Then practise asking and answering them with a partner.

75

1 What is the difference between how people celebrate special events today compared with the past?

2 Should we learn about the special events of other countries in school?

3 What will special events be like in the future?

4 Do we spend too money on special events like Valentine's Day or birthdays?

GO ONLINE AND COMPLETE UNIT 8 SPEAKING EXERCISES 1—3

ANSWER KEY

Unit 1   THE MAN-MADE ENVIRONMENT

READING

1 **Location:** beach, city centre, mountains, countryside, remote island
Building type: skyscraper, bungalow, mansion, castle, garage
Style: glamorous, simple, traditional, modern, spacious
Rooms: cellar, gym, dining room
Parts of a room: staircase, floor, ceiling, window
Materials: wood, marble, leather, stone

3 2 skimming   3 skimming   4 scanning   5 scanning   6 skimming

6 1 names, verbs, adjectives, numbers
3 Antilia (Mumbai, India)
4 1 f   2 d   3 c   4 e   5 g   6 a   7 b

7 1 Mukesh Ambani   2 27   3 marble
4 the lotus flower and the sun   5 168   6 600

8 1 C   2 E   3 F   4 A   5 B   6 D

9 1 e   2 f   3 g   4 c   5 b   6 a   7 h   8 d

10 1 9 / nine   2 man-made snow   3 clean their room(s)

11 1 mythical island   2 guests   3 architecture

12 **Present continuous:** an action which is not complete, happening at the time of speaking
Present simple: repeated actions, general facts, opinions

13 1 lives   2 believes   3 correct   4 clean
5 is entertaining

14 1 is working   2 am / 'm renting   3 think
4 are / 're building   5 cleans

15 1 (newspaper) publisher   2 Julia Morgan   3 $3.5 million
4 3 / three   5 attend formal dinner(s)   6 California / California state
7 Europe   8 mother   9 15 / fifteen years
10 every continent   11 zebras
12 (the) expensive maintenance

WRITING

1 2 line   3 horizontal axis   4 vertical axis   5 bar chart   6 bar
7 key   8 title   9 pie chart   10 segment   11 table   12 column
13 row

2 1 The world's most expensive cities
2 The cost per square metre in US dollars
3 Cities
4 The cost per square metre in each city
5 shortest – Monaco; tallest – New York / Singapore
6 Monaco, Hong Kong and London very similar; New York and Singapore significantly more expensive
7 Home ownership in some European countries
8 Percentage of people owning their own homes
9 Some European countries
10 Romania has the largest percentage of homeowners and Switzerland the smallest.
11 Most of the countries have similar figures, except for Romania.
12 Romania has a much higher percentage of homeowners than the other countries.
13 Average house size in selected countries
14 Different countries
15 Australia / Hong Kong
16 Australia / USA
17 Average size of houses in selected European countries
18 Two: country / size
19 Denmark
20 Italy
21 France / Germany

3 1 The pie chart provides information about the average house size in selected countries and the table in selected European countries.
2 the USA   3 45 m²   4 selected   5 most houses in Europe are much smaller than in the selected non-European countries
6 Hong Kong

4 The writer did not make any errors with spelling or punctuation, but should not have included opinions ('This is perhaps because it is such a large country'; 'This is most probably due to the size of each country').

5 2 Increase   3 Climb   4 Go up   5 Rocket   6 Soar   8 Decrease
9 Decline   10 Go down   11 Plummet   12 Plunge   13 Drop
Possible other words: *Rise* – surge, shoot up, peak; *Fall* – reduce, collapse, tumble, diminish, sink, dip

6 1 rocket, soar   2 plummet, plunge

7 1 rose   2 remains / has remained / remained   3 has decreased
4 are going to go up   5 have rocketed

8 **Big change:** dramatic, substantial, significant
Small change: slight, modest
Gradual or no change: steady, stable, unchanged

9 1 significant / substantial / dramatic
2 steady
3 slight / modest
4 unchanged / stable / steady

10 1 C   2 A   3 B

11 **Big change:** dramatically, substantially
Small change: moderately
Gradual change: gradually, slowly, consistently
Quick change: sharply, rapidly

12 1 significantly / considerably / substantially / dramatically
2 slightly / moderately
3 gradually / steadily / slowly / consistently
4 sharply / quickly / rapidly

14 1 B Dubai   2 C Hong Kong   3 A London

15 1 went up, plummeted dramatically
2 remained, peak, rise
3 increased steadily, decreased substantially, went up

16 *Sample answer*
The bar chart shows how many people aged 25–34 either rent or have bought a house in the UK. Furthermore, it illustrates this change over an eleven-year period.

The number of home owners within this age range has decreased substantially since 2004. In 2004, nearly 60% owned their own home, whereas in 2014 this dropped to under 40%. There was a gradual decrease in home ownership over the eleven-year period which was more significant from 2009 to 2014. Only in 2011 and 2012 did the number remain stable at just over 40%.

The rental market, however, has increased dramatically over the same eleven-year period. From 2004 to 2014, the number of people renting has risen by nearly 30%. Again, this has been a gradual increase in most years, rising by just a few percent each year. In 2014, the rental market reached a peak at just under 50%.

In conclusion, therefore, it is easily apparent from this bar chart that for people between the ages of 25 and 34, the rental market is increasing each year, whereas the buyers' market is decreasing.

LISTENING

1 1 C   2 B   3 A

2 1 ground floor, two-bedroom   2 first floor, two double bedrooms, one bathroom   3 two levels, large double bedroom, smaller double, third bedroom, spacious living room, large kitchen / dining room

3 1 Churchill Road   2 Three / 3   3 Two / 2   4 garden
5/6 (a) cooker   6/5 (a) dishwasher   7 1 / one o'clock   8 Eliot
9 07863 905073

4 1 £53.72   2 472 km   3 01897 625730   4 110 m x 55 m   5 B1074

5 1 £350,000   2 4.3 x 3.28 m   3 30 x 10 m   4 4.91 x 3.95 m
5 4.2 x 3.55 m

6 1 name, address and home phone number
2 mortgage from bank and deposit in bank account
3 two months (three at the most)
4 C (she wants to move in before her children start school)

8 1 B   2 C   3 A   4 B   5 A

SPEAKING

2 1 Eight / 8 questions
2 *Wh-* questions – *Where, Who, When, Why; Would* questions; *Yes / No* questions with *Is* and *Do*
3 where (you) live; shopping
4 Approximately 15–20 seconds; 3–4 sentences per question

3 **Home:** pretty big house, two floors, garden, shared bathroom, city centre, about five minutes' walk, a 20-minute bus ride, I'm (pretty) happy with the location, Well, I don't like, shared house, the trains can be a little loud

Shopping: shopping centre, cinema, ice-rink, hang out, famous brands, gets very full, everything is in one place, clean and comfortable, entertainment, under one roof, local market, styles and brands, old-fashioned

7 1 b   2 d   3 a   4 f   5 c   6 e

10 **Other topics:** sport, healthcare

11 2 ac / comm / o / da / tion   3 ar / chi / tec / ture
4 con / struc / tion   5 es / ca / la / tors   6 in / ha / bi / tants
7 mon / u / ment   8 mu / se / um   9 res / i / den / tial
10 sta / di / um   11 coun / try / side   12 en / vi / ron / ment
13 ge / og / ra / phy   14 re / gion / al   15 temp / er / a / tures
16 sce / ne / ry

Unit 2   LEISURE AND RECREATION

READING

1 1 Muhammad Ali   2 Michael Jordan   3 Serena Williams
4 David Beckham   5 Jack Nicklaus

2 1 Boxing   2 Basketball   3 Tennis   4 Football   5 Golf

3 1 B   2 A   3 B   4 C   5 A

4 1 B   2 B

5 1 1: opinion   2: factual
2 yes, most appropriate answer chosen
3 yes, *appeal, successful athlete*; no, matching words are often misleading
4 *referred to himself as*

6 1 questions, instructions   3 key   4 Scan   5 wrong

7 1 B, D   2 B, C   3 A, B

8 1 Complete: 1, 3   Question: 2
2 1 Text: *powerful*, Question: *strong*; Text: *determination*, Question: *self-belief*
2 Text: *be important*, Question: *focused on*; Text: *training to be tennis stars*, Question: *tennis training*; Text: *education*, Question: *studies*
3 Text: *speed of thought*, Question: *thinks quickly*; Text: *powerful shots*, Question: *can hit the ball hard*
3 1 Answers: *fashion*, Text: *fashion*
2 Answers: *home*, Text: *home*; Answers: *training*, Text: *training*; Answers: *star*, Text: *star*
3 Answers: *hit*, Text: *hit*; Answers: *third fastest*, Text: *third fastest*; Answers: *opponents*, Text: *opponents*
4 In questions 1 and 2, no, the same words are not used in the text and the correct answers. In question 3, both the text and one of the correct answers use the word *hit*.

9 past simple, past continuous, present perfect

10 1 she was playing …, Serena hit …
2 playing a match / hitting a serve
3 Long, continued action: playing a match; short, finished action: hit a serve
4 yes

11 1 whilst they were training
2 past continuous, past simple

12 1 was playing, rang
2 fell, (he was) running
3 started
4 was raining

13 *Possible answers*
a he threw the ball to his opponent
b he was scoring a goal   c he heard a loud noise

14 B

15 1 B   2 C   3 B   4 B

WRITING

2 1 USA, USSR and Germany 2 Norway 3 France
4 1 Introduction 2 Main body 3 Main body 4 Summary
5 1 yes 2 separate 3 both
6 1 introduction 2 main body 3 summary
8 1 C 2 A 3 D 4 B
9 (significantly) more successful than
10 achieved far more gold medals, slightly more silver and bronze medals, a little more successful than Great Britain, the same number of medals
11 1 slower / more slowly 2 further / farther 3 colder; more successful
   4 more interesting 5 better 6 more often 7 older
   8 more gracefully
12 easily (apparent), far (more), slightly (more), a little (more), roughly (the same)
13 1, 2, 5
   3 and 4 just describe facts taken directly from the table (i.e. no interpretation has taken place)
14 *Possible answers*
   1 The most successful country is the USA, which has won over 2,500 medals.
   2 The line graph shows that Germany and Great Britain have won a similar number of medals.
   3 The second most successful country is the USSR, which has won fewer than half the medals of the USA.
15 *Sample answer*
   The two charts give information about the gender and number of athletes who have entered the Games since they started. The bar chart illustrates the number of men and women entering the Games, whereas the line graph shows the number of participants.

   It is evident from the bar chart that, until 2012, there were always significantly more men entering the Games than women. In 1924 and 1952, there were hardly any women entering the Games, yet in 1952 there were over 4,000 male participants. In 2012, however, the number of female athletes rose significantly to nearly 5,000, only approximately 1,000 fewer than male participants.

   The line graph shows a similar trend, with the number of participants increasing throughout the century. The most significant increase occurred between 1984 and 2012, when the number of athletes rose from just over 6,000 to over 10,000 in 2012.

   To summarise therefore, since 1924 the number of athletes entering the Olympic Games has increased dramatically. This is particularly the case for women, who are now represented in nearly the same numbers as male participants.

LISTENING

1 1 crossroads 2 junction 3 bend 4 flyover
   5 traffic lights 6 roundabout
2 1 flyover 2 traffic lights 3 roundabout 4 bend 5 crossroads
   6 junction
3

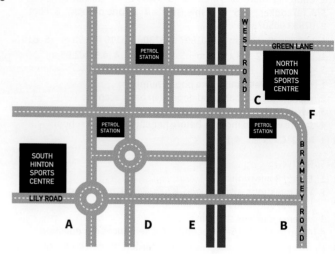

4 A 2 B 5 C 4 D 1 E 3
5 1 badminton 2 gymnastics 3 weightlifting 4 basketball
   5 table tennis 6 weightlifting
6 1 nets 2 balls 3 mats 4 bars 5 bats 6 bench
7 A: 2 B: 1, 6 C: 3, 4 D: 5

SPEAKING

1 A hiking B movies C karate / kickboxing D swimming
   E football F video games G surfing the internet H gym
   I reading
3

👍	🤷	👎
I like …	I don't know if I like …	I don't look forward to …
A lot of people like …	I'm not sure whether I like …	I hate …
I'm very keen on …	I don't know much about …	I'm not a big fan of …
I often enjoy …	I'm not really interested in …	Not many people like …

4 *Possible answers*
   1 I love listening to K-Pop BECAUSE it's really exciting.
   2 I sometimes enjoy mountain climbing BUT I prefer watersports.
   3 I don't like spending money SO I prefer staying at home.
   4 I'm not really interested in watching football on TV AND my friends don't really like it either.

7 Possible answers
  1 I like it because it's cool in summer, keeps me fit and is good for my back.
  2 I enjoy it because it's exciting, I can follow my favourite team and it's cheaper than going to the match.
  3 I love it because it's relaxing, good for my vocabulary and inspiring.
  4 This is because I love good stories, special effects and to escape my everyday life.

11 1 Ryan **Giggs** was a **famous** player for Manchester **United**; he played **hundreds** of games.
  2 At London **2012**, the United **States** was top of the **medals** table, followed by **China**, then Great **Britain** and Northern **Ireland**.
  3 Last **weekend**, I **was** going to go to the **gym** but I **decided** not to **bother**.
  4 Michael **Jordan** is the **number one all-time points scorer** in the NBA **playoffs**, although Lebron **James** is catching **up**.
  5 I **ran** in the **New York marathon** last **year**. I thought I was **never** going to make it to the **end**!

12 1 positive   2 negative   3 negative   4 positive

13 2 I like swimming, but I wish there were more places to swim where I live.
  3 I've always liked fishing but I don't have time to do it any more.
  4 I'm really excited about all the new video games that will come out soon. I can't wait!

15 1 I didn't think Mayweather would [beat / defeat / lose to / knock out] Pacquiao in that boxing match.
  2 It has always been a dream of mine to [play / compete / win / qualify / represent my country] at Wimbledon.
  3 I try to [exercise / train / compete / play] about three times a week, so that I can keep playing well.
  4 I [support / watch] Liverpool Football Club. I've been a fan for a very long time.
  5 Their international football team [shoot / tackle] plenty of times during a game but usually [score] very few goals.

Unit 3 THE NEWS AND MEDIA

READING
2 1 A   2 D   3 C   4 B
5 1 B   2 A   3 D   4 D
6 1 T   2 T   3 T   4 T   5 T
7 1 the most popular way   2 66%   3 several methods   4 25%
  5 survey   6 on a weekly basis
8 1 reaction   2 opinion   3 cause and effect
  4 summary   5 description   6 account
9 B reason / factual   C cause and effect
  D problems / factual   E opinion   F summary
10 2 it was also revealed – past simple passive
  3 social networks are being used selectively – present continuous passive
  4 there has been growing concern by researchers – present perfect passive
11 The passive is commonly used in formal writing. Also, in sentences 1–3, the agent is not important (e.g. in sentence 1 we are not interested in *who* uses social media to break news).
12 2 has been delayed (present perfect) / is delayed (present simple)
  3 were named (past simple)
  4 is being developed
13 1 … is blamed for all the wet weather.
  2 … was found unconscious in his Manhattan apartment.
  3 … has been recovered from a sunken Spanish ship.
  4 … is being celebrated today.
14 1 Questions and instructions   2 Synonyms   3 No   4 Yes   5 No
15 1 E   2 A   3 B   4 C   5 F   6 B

WRITING
1 1 e   2 g   3 c   4 d   5 a   6 f   7 b
2 First, Secondly, Thirdly, Next, Then, After that, Finally
3 Set 3
5 1 No   2 No   3 Yes – although it's better to use synonyms if possible
6 1 First   2 Secondly   3 Thirdly   4 Then / After That   5 Finally
10 Present simple passive (are assigned, are booked, are allocated, is reviewed … edited, are loaded … saved); passive used with a modal: can be cut
11 1 A local news story is chosen.
  2 The story is accompanied by a picture.
  3 A good first line is thought of.
  4 The main body of the article is written.
  5 The article is checked for errors.
  6 A good title is invented.
  7 The article is submitted to a local newspaper.
12 A 3   B 5   C 2   D 4
13 *Sample answer*
The diagram illustrates a method called 'lithography', a process used for printing newspapers. After the image is transferred onto a press plate, it goes through several rollers before being successfully printed onto paper.

First, the plate is passed through dampening rollers, which provide a mixture of water and chemicals. This is to dampen the non-image areas. Secondly, the plate passes through a set of ink rollers, in order for the ink to stick to the image area. Thirdly, the plate goes through the blanket cylinder. This is to squeeze out the water and the inked image area is picked up. Finally, the plate passes through the impression cylinder. The paper then runs between the impression cylinder and blanket cylinder, pressing the image onto the paper. After that, the paper is dried with hot and cold air and put on the delivery pile.

Overall, the diagram shows that there are four sets of rollers used, before the image is transferred onto paper.

LISTENING
1 1 B   2 C   3 A
2 *Topic 1: Modern art*
  Positive: Speaker 3
  Negative: Speaker 2
  Neutral: Speaker 1
  Topic 2: Combating climate change
  Positive: Speaker 1
  Negative: Speaker 2
  Neutral: Speaker 3
3 B
4

	Pluto expedition	Mars expedition	Moon expedition
Simon	Positive	Neutral	Neutral
Maria	Positive	Positive	Negative
Dr Thornton	Negative	Positive	Neutral

5 1 B   2 A   3 C   4 A   5 B   6 C

6

Conversation	Key words/expressions	Positive/Negative/Neutral
1	I don't see how	Negative
2	certainly, definitely	Positive
3	well, (to be honest,) I'm not really worried	Neutral
4	I'm all for that, a good thing	Positive
5	I can't seriously believe that, I really don't think	Negative
6	It's all the same to me, it shouldn't matter	Neutral

7 C is correct

8 1 She mentions that the Pluto project is successful, but doesn't say the same about the Mars project, so A cannot be right.
  2 There is information about using robots and machines to start a colony, but that is connected with a Chinese project on the moon, so B cannot be correct.
  3 The Mars project will last six months and Dr Thornton says that is just the right length of time for the group, so C must be correct.

9 1 **Correct answer:** B
  Distractor: A
  (The participant's mother is ill, not the participant, so it is a problem unconnected to the project.)
  2 **Correct answer:** B
  Distractor: A
  (Dr Thornton clearly states that no one else can come in once the project has started.)
  3 **Correct answer:** B
  Distractor: A
  (Simon agrees with Dr Thornton, who says the work should be shared.)

11 1 C She mentions that she is a psychology tutor, and that many types of people take part in studies like this, but she is particularly interested in how people get on when they are locked away together.
  2 A She is not surprised that these problems happen. She sees Maria's point that it's not a television series or soap opera, but she thinks it's positive that the first sign of anger came only after three months.
  3 B Simon refers to environmental problems, but not caused by Joe. He also talks about solving problems, but this refers to the problems with conflict, not the environment. He mentions that Joe managed to repair the ventilation system.

12 1 B 2 A 3 C 4 B 5 C 6 A

SPEAKING

2 *Possible answers*

Newspapers	
Advantages	**Disadvantages**
1 Professionally written	1 Only one opinion on a news story
2 Different types of newspaper appeal to different readers	2 Selective in what is published
3 A wide range of story types within one newspaper	3 Uses a lot of natural resources to produce

The internet	
Advantages	**Disadvantages**
1 Mostly free	1 Hard to decide which news sources to trust
2 All content available to view easily	2 Not always suitable for children
3 Can copy and paste text and pictures into school/college work	3 Facts not always checked

Radio	
Advantages	**Disadvantages**
1 Accessible to people of all ages	1 No visual information
2 Can listen in the car without distraction	2 Easy to miss information
3 Free	3 Lots of advertisements

Television	
Advantages	**Disadvantages**
1 24-hour coverage	1 Stories generally given a short amount of time
2 High-quality pictures and sound along with story	2 Often includes commercials
3 Often includes interviews with experts in real time	3 Not much opportunity for interaction

5 These sentences are spoken with the correct intonation:
  2 B 3 B 4 A 5 A 6 B

9 1 B 2 D 3 E 4 C 5 F 6 G 7 A

10 2 Large numbers of rocks and stones were removed (by volunteers) to rescue people.
  3 Survivors were pulled from the collapsed buildings (by rescuers).
  4 Many people were injured (by falling building).
  5 Survivors were taken to hospital (by helicopters).
  6 Many children were left homeless (by the earthquake).
  7 The city was struck (by the earthquake) at 10.00 am.

Unit 4 TRAVEL AND TRANSPORT

1 1 h 2 a 3 i 4 b 5 c 6 j 7 g 8 d 9 e 10 f

3 b

4 b

5 1 A **Words to underline:** best attractions, avoid, queues, Early morning, good time, take photographs, meet the locals
Summary: Good to get up early

   B **Words to underline:** good idea, useful phrases, the language, as much as possible, respond, people who make an effort
Summary: Speak the language, even if you make mistakes

   C **Words to underline:** delays, cancellations, do not allow, ruin, not to get frustrated, unable to communicate, native, more polite, more effective, body language, better trip, plans to change, funny side, wrong
Summary: Don't get upset if plans change or you can't communicate with the locals

   D **Words to underline:** Before, find out, people and customs, integrate more easily, not do anything to offend, more you know, gaining the most
Summary: Find out as much as possible about the people and culture before you go

   E **Words to underline:** Do not just socialise, travellers, start conversations, locals, key, best and cheapest, talking regularly, better chance of learning the language
Summary: Talk to the local people to get the most from your trip

   F **Words to underline:** real feel, a few hours, watching daily life, colours, smells and sounds, surround
Summary: Spend time sitting and observing everyday life

   3 **Paragraph B:** vii   **Paragraph C:** iii   **Paragraph D:** i
Paragraph E: viii   **Paragraph F:** v

7 1 **a** present perfect, past simple   **b** past simple
c present perfect continuous, present continuous passive
   2 **past simple:** past form of verb
present perfect: has / have + past participle
present perfect continuous: have / has + been + verb + -ing
present continuous passive: is being + present participle (-ing form)

8 1 b 2 a 3 c

9 1 have / 've been travelling
   2 got up
   3 has been cancelled / was cancelled
   4 have / 've been sunbathing
   5 have / 've visited
   6 went

10 1 f 2 g 3 c 4 b 5 d 6 e 7 a

11 1 Do not use the same heading twice.
   2 Keep track of time.
   3 Read the shortest paragraph first.
   4 Ignore words you do not understand.

12 **Paragraph A:** vi   **Paragraph B:** iii   **Paragraph C:** v   **Paragraph D:** i
Paragraph E: iv   **Paragraph F:** ix

1 1 1 stadium 2 windmill 3 skyscraper 4 residential area
      5 motorway 6 east 7 north 8 fields 9 hills 10 bridge
      11 river 12 farm 13 pond 14 church 15 west 16 south

2 1 A motorway has been built through the centre of the island.
      A hospital has been built in the east of the island.
      A skyscraper has been built in the south of the island.
      The residential area has increased in size.
   2 The farm and fields have remained the same.
      The church and pond near the residential area have remained the same.

5 *Spelling errors*
   2 dramaticaly – dramatically   3 threw – through
   4 significantally – significantly   5 facilites – facilities
   Tense errors
   1 changed – has changed   2 building – built
   3 has built – has been built
   4 has being developed – has been developed
   5 was occurred – has occurred

6 1 present perfect
   2 because there is a connection between the past and present

9 1 1, (9)
   2 (9) 6, 2, 4, 8, 5 (sentence 9 could go in the introduction or the first paragraph)
   3 3, 10
   4 7

11 1 moreover, in addition, what is more
   2 similarly
   3 particularly
   4 in contrast, in comparison
   5 to summarise, in conclusion, to conclude

12 1 in comparison / in contrast   2 what is more / in addition / moreover
   3 To summarise / In conclusion / To conclude   4 particularly
   5 in contrast

13 *Sample answer*
When comparing these two maps, it is evident that this area has changed significantly. It has definitely become more modern and busier.
In both maps the only feature which remains completely the same is the clock tower in the middle of the roundabout. In the past, there were a few buildings at the side of the road, but the area was mainly covered in sand.
Today, however, the map is quite different: the area by the road is covered with skyscrapers and the road itself is heavily used due to the increase in the number of people driving cars and the amount of traffic. In addition, trees have been planted around the edge of the roundabout.
Overall therefore, the area has become significantly more developed and populated. Numerous skyscrapers fill the roadside and it is no longer possible to see areas of sandy desert.

LISTENING

1 Conversation 1: D   Conversation 2: E   Conversation 3: B
  Conversation 4: C   Conversation 5: A

2 Conversation 1: H   Conversation 2: J   Conversation 3: I
  Conversation 4: G   Conversation 5: F

3 1 I   2 G   3 J   4 F   5 H

4 C (All the other issues are mentioned, but are not the main problem
  under discussion, and the number of accidents has actually fallen.)

5 Location 1: B   Location 2: C   Location 4: A

6 1 B   2 D   3 A   4 C

7 1 F   2 A   3 B   4 E

8 1 D   2 C   3 B   4 A   5 C

9 Extract 1: E   Extract 2: B   Extract 3: G   Extract 4: A   Extract 5: F
  Extract 6: C

10 1 C   2 B   3 C   4 G   5 A   6 F   7 C   8 B

SPEAKING

2 1 The examiner will give you a topic.
  2 You have one minute to make notes.
  3 You should make notes on the paper provided.
  4 The maximum time to talk is two minutes.
  5 You should keep talking until the examiner stops you.

5 1 D   2 A   3 B   4 I   5 L   6 C   7 F   8 E   9 G   10 J   11 K
  12 H

7 1 I boarded a plane to **Paris** [stressed], which was rather **exciting**
    [stressed] as I had never done that before.
  2 Since I come from China, **it** [unstressed] took a long time to arrive,
    but when [unstressed] I got there, the first thing I did was to go to
    the Louvre Museum.
  3 I **had** [unstressed] trouble ordering **food** [stressed] because I **don't**
    [unstressed] speak any **French** [stressed].
  4 **Once** [unstressed] I had **eaten** [stressed], I then **took** [unstressed]
    a tour bus to the Champs Elysées **in order to** [unstressed] do a bit
    of shopping.
  5 As I **got** [unstressed] back on the tour bus and **started** [unstressed]
    taking **pictures** [stressed], I dropped my **camera** [stressed] over
    the side.

8 *Possible answers*
  1 This was rather exciting AS / SINCE / BECAUSE I had never done
    that before.
  2 It took a long time to arrive AS / SINCE / BECAUSE I come from
    China.
  3 It was a great experience ALTHOUGH next time I think I should
    study French.
  4 I went to a restaurant AS / SINCE / BECAUSE I was pretty hungry
    around that time.
  5 I went to the Champs Elysées to do a bit of shopping WHERE / AND
    I went on to buy as much as I could.
  6 I then took a tour bus ONCE I had eaten.
  7 I took the flight back to China AFTER everything was over.
  8 I got back on the tour bus AND started taking pictures.
  9 I started taking pictures BUT I dropped my camera over the side.
  10 Once I had eaten, I THEN took a tour bus.

9 1 5
  2 *Yes/No* questions and *Would* questions
  3 The candidate took around 5–10 seconds to answer each question.

Unit 5   BUSINESS AND WORK

READING

1 1 opinion   2 theory   3 fact

4 A **Andrew Carnegie**
  One of the wealthiest businessmen of 19th century
  Self-taught
  1889 became owner of Carnegie Steel Corporation
  Donated approx. $350 million to charities, foundations and
  universities
  B **Henry Ford**
  Founder of the Ford Motor Company
  Made cars affordable to the masses
  Introduced assembly line and conveyor belt – could make a car every
  93 minutes
  C **Estée Lauder**
  Started her beauty company in 1946
  First product was skin cream developed by uncle
  Believes success due to high-quality products and excellent
  customer service
  D **Steve Jobs**
  Co-founder of Apple Computer with Steve Wozniak
  Started company in 1976 at age of 21
  Revolutionised the computer industry – iPod, iPhone, iPad, Mac

5 factual

6 & 7
  1 fast – quickly, every 93 minutes
    popular – the masses
  2 family member – uncle
  3 at home – family garage
  4 first-rate – high-quality
    looking after clients – customer service
  5 gave … wealth away – donated

8 1 B   2 C   3 D   4 C   5 A

9 1 c   2 e   3 a   4 f   5 b   6 d

11 2 The text is mainly opinion-based.

13 1 **Paragraph B:** Peter Diamandis, Jeffrey Jones
    Paragraph C: Peter Coker
    Paragraph D: Jason Matheny, Professor Post
    Paragraph F: Daniel Kluko
  2 1 save lives
    2 harmful
    3 controlled using technology
    4 fulfil a worldwide need
    5 significant impact … existing business
  3 1 save lives – search-and-rescue
    2 harmful – serious health problems
    3 controlled using technology – an app … will be able to handle
    4 fulfil a worldwide need – satisfy a growing global demand
    5 significant impact … existing business – mean the end of
      traditional

14 1 C   2 A   3 B   4 E   5 F

15 1 going to   2 both

16 1 will / are going to   2 is going   3 will

17 1 C   2 E   3 A   4 B   5 D

18 1 questions, order
  2 part of the … text
  3 grammatically similar
  4 Focus … sentence beginnings
  5 similar words

20 1 A   2 C   3 D

21 1 e   2 a   3 d

23 1 C   2 E   3 A   4 B   5 D

WRITING

1 *Possible answers*
   Country
   Advantages: more physical work, healthier, more enjoyable, less stressful
   Disadvantages: lower pay, less opportunity for promotion, difficult in bad weather
   City
   Advantages: higher pay, busy, exciting, lots of opportunities
   Disadvantages: tiring, busy, difficult to get to work

4 1 **Task:** extent / agree / disagree
      Topic: workplace after school / more beneficial / university
   2 **Task:** advantages / disadvantages
      Topic: get a job / unpaid internships
   3 **Task:** reasons, How … tackled
      Topic: stress / major problem

6 1 Wearing a uniform

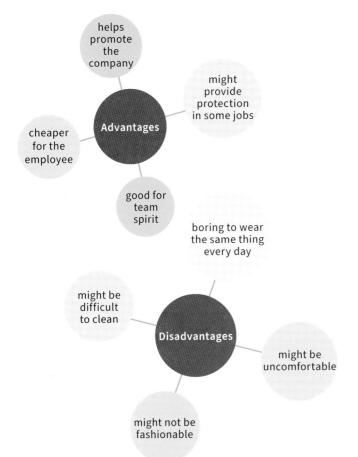

2 Working for a big company

Advantages	Disadvantages
Meet more people	Less personal
More opportunities for promotion	Perhaps limited to one type of task

8 1 Consequently   2 Furthermore / Also   3 therefore
   4 for example   5 also   6 In contrast / However
   7 Also / Furthermore   8 In conclusion   9 Whilst   10 however

9 1 approximately ten minutes
   2 mindmaps, linear plans, bulleted lists, etc.
   3 your English
   4 Yes, your answer must all be relevant.
   5 No, because it is unlikely you will have an essay in the exam with exactly the same title.
   6 a minimum of 250
   7 yes

10 *Sample answer*
The way in which we work has changed a great deal in recent years. Whilst some people still travel to their place of work each day, others have the option to work from home. This has all become possible since the birth of the internet and smartphones, which enable workers to be in constant contact with their colleagues and clients all over the world. There are both advantages and disadvantages to this new development.

There are definite advantages to people being allowed to work from home. The main advantage is that it gives workers more flexibility in their working lives. This can be particularly useful for parents or people who live far from their workplace. Working from home is also more comfortable – you can take a break whenever you need.

Another advantage is that you have the possibility to work for companies in other countries through the use of the internet. Therefore people can apply for jobs globally as well as locally.

On the other hand, working from home can also have its disadvantages. Travelling to work and working in an office with others can be a very sociable activity which many people enjoy, especially if they live on their own. Without this social interaction many people might feel very lonely. Furthermore, many people may lack sufficient discipline to complete the work they need to do without colleagues around.

In conclusion, therefore, there are clearly advantages and disadvantages to working from home. Perhaps the ideal arrangement would be to spend part of the working week in an office with colleagues, and part of the working week at home, with a certain amount of flexibility and comfort.

LISTENING

1 A limited liability company   B sole trader   C partnership
2 A Correct
   B Incorrect: sole traders may employ other people
   C Incorrect: sole traders must pay tax every year,
      not every month
   D Correct
   E Correct
3 1 borrow money 2 pay debts 3 accounts 4 contracts 5 tax
4 1 personal goods 2 documents … records
   3 income tax 4 sole trader
5 1 the other hand 2 the negative side 3 the same is true
   4 however 5 Similarly
6 1 food, businesses 2 limited (liability)
   3 £10,000, equipment 4 knowledge, experience
   5 three / 3 (motor)bikes / own (motor)bikes
   6 sleeping partner

SPEAKING

1 1 C 2 A 3 D 4 B
3 1 b 2 d 3 a 4 c
4 *Possible answers*

Job	Qualifications / Characteristics needed	Responsibilities	Pay / Salary / Wage	Benefits (e.g. promotion, retirement)
Model	*Tall, good-looking*	*Showing off clothes, having pictures taken*	*Approx $50,000 per year*	*Free clothes, early retirement*
Politician	*Good talker, trustworthy*	*Spending public money, voting on social issues*	*$100,000 per year plus expenses*	*Free apartment and transport*
Reporter	*Good memory, fast typing skills*	*Looking for breaking news stories and reporting on them*	*$500 per story*	*Free camera, easy access to public figures*
Sailor	*Strong stomach, calmness in stormy waters*	*Navigation of the ship, ensuring safety of goods on board*	*$50,000 per year*	*Good travel opportunities*

5 1 e 2 a 3 c 4 d 5 f 6 b
6 *Possible answers*
   1 What kind of person are they?
   2 Who else knows about this person?
   3 When did this person become successful?
   4 Where was this person successful?
   5 How did they become successful?
   6 Why did they succeed where others have failed?
8 *Possible answers*
   1 I once worked as a waiter, which was really hard work.
   2 I've often thought about becoming a singer, which might be very tough.
   3 I've always been an admirer of my father, who is now a successful restaurant owner.
   4 I remember how the music business used to be in the past, when the internet wasn't around.
   5 I would like to work in a museum one day, where I could spend all day in a quiet place.

10 *Possible answers with contraction of modals*
    1 I'd love to be a tour guide.
    2 I wouldn't like to be a vet, as I don't like seeing animals in pain.
    3 I'll apply for a job as a finance manager.
    4 I won't be looking for work as a teacher.
    5 I should've studied harder at school.
    6 If I'd got an 'A' in my exams, I could've gone to Harvard University.

Unit 6   THE NATURAL ENVIRONMENT

READING

1 1 habitat 2 extinction 3 conservation 4 endangered
   5 species 6 threaten 7 poach 8 captivity
2 1 Yes 2 Not Given 3 No 4 Yes
   1 involvement – contribution / make an impact – makes a difference
   3 most people – the majority of [us]
   4 do a great deal – go to great lengths
3 a 4 b 7 c 5 d 3 e 1 f 6 g 2
4 1 Not Given 2 Not Given 3 No 4 Yes
6 1 'Me too.' / 'So do I.' / 'I do, too.'
   2 'I wouldn't.'
   3 'Me too.' / 'So am I.' / 'I am, too.'
   4 'Neither do I.' / 'Me neither.'
7 1 C 2 E 3 A 4 G
8 quickly – 3   animal – 2
10 1 endangered 2 habitats 3 poached 4 conservation
11 1 No 2 Yes 3 Not Given 4 No
    1 E 2 F 3 B 4 J 5 G 6 K

WRITING

3 1 Some people believe … should be fined … do not recycle …
      what extent … agree … disagree
   2 It is not only recycling which … educate themselves about
      environmental issues and then take action.
      Governments could do more … in general.
   3 The writer decided to write about the topic instead of the actual
      question in the task.
      The writer needed more ideas to complete at least 250 words.
      The writer did not start with a plan and forgot to keep the answer
      relevant.
   4 Check the words in the task carefully, make a good plan,
      and ensure it is relevant and you follow it.
4 1 Environmental problems are getting worse every day.
   2 We might not be able to see all the pollution in our environment,
      but it certainly exists.
   3 If this continues, our families will struggle in the future.
   4 There are many things teenagers and families can do to prevent
      pollution, for example, hand-washing clothes or riding a bike to
      school or work instead of using the car.
   5 There could be a solution to helping our environment if we educate
      others and help them to understand how serious the problem is.
5 1 planet's 2 these ideas 3 increase in population 4 it 5 it
   6 it 7 They 8 it 9 issue

6 *Sample answer*

It is certainly true that environmental problems should be taken seriously in order to prevent disaster in the future. Unfortunately, however, most people do not take this threat seriously enough and this is for a number of reasons. The following essay will outline why the majority of people do not care enough about the environment.

Perhaps the main reason people do not give the environment much thought is because at the moment it does not affect their daily life. This is because, generally, they cannot see how global warming or pollution is destroying the environment. It is only when a crisis occurs, such as flooding, that people start to consider the reasons behind it. However, these are soon forgotten and the situation is once again ignored.

Another reason environmental issues are ignored is that people do not know enough about them. Although it is generally understood that recycling helps to save resources, this is perhaps the only step people take to help the situation. Most people have heard of global warming and pollution, but do not fully understand the implications of them. If they did, I am sure they would use their car less and try at all costs to save resources more.

Many people also believe that these environmental problems will not impact society for another 50 to 100 years. Consequently, people feel these problems can be dealt with then by future generations.

Overall, therefore, whilst there may be some people who are fully aware of the environmental problems facing the planet, the majority of the population still do not give them the attention they deserve.

LISTENING

1 **Renewable sources:** wave power, solar power
Non-renewable sources: fracking, petroleum

2 A 2   B 4   C 1   D 3

3 1 You should look at the whole diagram to get a general idea of the topic, but your main focus should be on the missing words and on thinking about what they might be.

2 You do not need to understand all the words. Your main focus should be on the missing words. The exam will not test your knowledge of difficult words which might appear in the diagram. In this diagram, it is clear which part is above ground and which part is below ground, so you can get a good idea that a word you don't know refers to something below ground. However, you don't need to worry about this as your focus should be on the missing words.

3 The large circle shows you some important information in more detail and focuses your attention on an important part of the process. The colours in the large circle help you understand how the process works as it progresses – in particular, how certain liquids flow in and out.

4 It starts at the well where certain materials go down into the ground and then turn to go along through one of the layers. Then something else comes out and goes back up to the well at the top.

5 The first and second words clearly refer to the layers. The third word clearly refers to something happening in the ground. The fourth word clearly refers to something that comes out of the ground. When you look at the diagram, focus on these words and listen for the sections where these parts of the process are discussed. Don't worry about other words that you might not understand.

4 2 shale   3 fissures   4 gas

5 1 Few   2 much   3 All   4 Some   5 a lot of

6 1 a lot of   2 few   3 some   4 more   5 a little   6 fewer

7 **Used only with countable nouns:** few, fewer, several, many, every
Used only with uncountable nouns: [a] little, much, less
Used with both countable and uncountable nouns: all, [a] lot [of], more, some

8 **Correct answer:** B … *the economic benefit … more significant … prices will come down … according to supporters of fracking.* The question says 'those who are in favour of fracking', which refers to the supporters of fracking. The correct answer is 'lower energy bills', which is the same as saying prices will come down. The idea of 'main benefit' in the question is reflected by 'more significant' in the script.
Distractors: A is incorrect because although better energy supply is referred to, it is not referred to as the main benefit; C is incorrect because although electricity generation is also referred to, there is nothing to say it involves increased generation.

9 supporters of fracking; economic benefit; energy prices will come down

11 & 12 **Question:** fracking starts
A: local businesses … lose … employees
B: bring in … most … workers
C: more opportunities … businesses
Correct answer: C *the local economy benefits, with increases in services to the fracking company.* The question says 'it creates more opportunities for businesses in the area', which is the same as saying that the local economy benefits.
Distractors: A is incorrect because the script says 'with most new workers recruited from the population in the surrounding area' but it does not mention these people moving from other local businesses. B is incorrect because the script says 'companies often bring their own workers', but there is no reference to this being 'most of the workers'.

13 **Suggested words to underline**
3 **A:** does not … chemicals … harmful
   B: slightly less … coal … oil
   C: much less water … coal … oil burning
4 **A:** less electricity … produced
   B: more water … production … coal … oil
   C: time … environmentally friendly
3 **Correct answer:** A
4 **Correct answer:** C

14 1 **Correct answer:** B *although countries which produce shale gas … will still continue to increase … little or no benefit to the environment*
2 **Correct answer:** A *there's good evidence that house prices fall*
3 **Correct answer:** A *chemicals … can enter the drinking water supply … residents … seeing brown water and mud coming out*
4 **Correct answer:** B *local, regional and national governments … fracking won't start until they're quite sure that it's safe … they'll prevent any activity … enough evidence to assure its safety*

16 1 first (SE)   2 What's more (AD)   3 Secondly (SE)   4 last (SE)
5 Now (T)   6 While (C)   7 earlier (SE)   8 Clearly (AT)
9 to summarise (SU)   10 that (T)

17 1 B   2 B   3 C   4 A   5 C

SPEAKING

2

Natural disasters	Man-made problems
volcanic eruptions	carbon monoxide
tsunamis	acid rain
drought	radiation leaks
thunderstorms	
tornados	

floods, forest fires, landslides and *sinkholes* can go in either column

3 1 carbon monoxide 2 Forest fires 3 oil spills / radiation leaks
4 earthquakes / tsunamis 5 Acid rain 6 floods / landslides / sinkholes

6 1 calen<u>da</u>r 2 foreigner 3 should 4 g<u>ue</u>st 5 autum<u>n</u>
6 <u>h</u>onest 7 li<u>g</u>ht 8 dou<u>b</u>t 9 cas<u>t</u>le 10 yog<u>h</u>urt

8 1 A: 'What makes it beautiful' and 'why this place is famous' require more information.
   B: 'What you remember most' and 'whether you would like to visit the place again' require more information.
2 A: Where that place is – name of place
   What kind of place it is – nouns (e.g. coast, mountain, lake, etc.)
   What makes it beautiful – adjectives (e.g. unusual, breathtaking, etc.)
   Why this place is famous in your country – reasons (e.g. in poems, travel guides, etc.)
   B: When you visited this place – date
   What kind of scenic features the place had – nouns (e.g. mountains, lakes, etc.)
   What you remember most about the place – memory (e.g. sounds, sights, etc.)
   Explain whether you would like to visit the place again – reasons (e.g. show it to someone else)
3 Number of examples required:
   A: What kind of place it is – 1
   What makes it beautiful – 2 or 3
   Why this place is famous – 1 or 2
   B: Scenic features – 2 or 3
   What you remember most about the place – 1 or 2
   Whether you would like to visit again – 1 or 2
4 Tenses required:
   A Where that place is – present
   What kind of place it is – present
   What makes it beautiful – present
   Explain why this place is famous – present
   B When you visited this place – past simple
   What kind of scenic features the place had – past simple / past continuous
   What you remember most about the place – present
   Whether you would like to visit the place again – present conditional

11 The second set of notes would be easiest to write in just 60 seconds.
12 1 predict 2 suggest 3 compare 4 assess 5 explain
13 1 compare 2 explain 3 compare 4 assess 5 explain
6 predict 7 compare 8 suggest 9 assess

14

Certain	Careful
indeed	perhaps
surely	maybe
clearly	unlikely
no doubt	almost
will	might
of course	occasionally
definitely	seemingly

15

Statement	Agree	Disagree
That's true.	✔	
1 That's right.	✔	
2 I'm not sure about that.		✔
3 That's also how I feel about it.	✔	
4 I have to side with you on that one.	✔	
5 Me neither.	✔	
6 That's incorrect.		✔
7 I beg to differ.		✔
8 You might have a point there.	✔	
9 I'm afraid I don't share that point of view.		✔

Unit 7   EDUCATION SYSTEMS

2 **1** lecture   **2** enrol   **3** fund   **4** assignment   **5** campus   **6** faculty
  7 Master's degree   **8** undergraduate   **9** Bachelor's degree
  10 postgraduate

4 **1** how to apply to an Australian university as an international student
  2 choosing a university and enrolling / applying for a student visa /
  booking your flight and accommodation
  3 **1** adverb   **2** noun   **3** noun   **4** adjective

5 **1** directly   **2** admission   **3** funds   **4** new

7 It illustrates a weekly timetable / schedule.

8 **1** Lecture   **2** Private study   **3** Lecture   **4** Football (training)
  5 Tutorial

9 **1** c
  2 a, b
  3 b
  4 **a:** I don't have to attend / I needn't attend   **b:** You don't have to
  have a great deal … / You needn't have a great deal …
  c: You mustn't / You don't have to / You needn't / You shouldn't
  choose
  5 **a:** I had to attend …   **b:** You had to have …
  c: You should have chosen something you would enjoy / you would
  have enjoyed

10 **1** must   **2** don't have to / needn't   **3** should / ought to
  4 must not / mustn't

11 **1** a – expresses a rule and therefore something which is not allowed
  2 b – expresses a rule and therefore something which is not allowed
  3 a – expresses an idea which is optional

13 **1** [University] library   **2** Gym   **3** Careers centre
  4 [Main] reception

14 **1** No, just the last two paragraphs
  2 *main student facilities* (indicating where the information is) and
  prepositions (e.g *in front of, behind*)

15 **2** Lever   **3** Type hammer   **4** Ribbon   **5** Carriage

16 **lever:** footnote
  ribbon: explanation in the text
  carriage return lever: explanation given by surrounding context

17 **a** explanation in the text   **b** explanation in the text
  c explanation given by surrounding context   **d** footnote

18 **1** Hard drive   **2** Input   **3** LCD screens

19 **1** Professional   **2** Honours   **3** Full-time   **4** Doctoral degree

2 For me, To my mind, Personally, I think

3 **Introduction:** 5, 6, 7, 9
  Main body: 2, 3, 4
  Conclusion: 1, 8

4 **1** D   **2** E   **3** A   **4** C   **5** B

5 **Nowadays**, many parents are choosing to home-school~~ing their~~
children rather than sending them to a private or state school.
There **are** perhaps many reasons for this, but I believe the main
reason is that many schools are not seen as safe any more. In some
areas, schools can be very violent and fighting is a common problem.
I do not believe that home~~s~~-schooling is always more beneficial to
the student than state school, but in some cases it can be. In the
following essay, I **will** discuss this idea further.

If you are lucky enough to be able to attend a good school, with only
minor **discipline** problems, then I think attending a state school is
better for you than being educated **at** home. **S**chool is more than just
learning about different subjects, it is also a place **where** you can make
new friends and learn to socialise. School also gives you the
opportunity to join teams and clubs. **S**ubjects are also taught by
people who have been trained in that particular area.

If, however, this is not the case, and you have to attend a school
with poor **discipline** or somewhere you feel very unhappy,
home-schooling could be more beneficial. It is better to learn in a
comfortable **environment**, where you feel safe than in **a** disruptive
one. In order for home-schooling to be **successful**, however, your
teacher needs to be **knowledgeable** and follow a set **curriculum**.
To summarise, therefore, home-schooling is more beneficial if the child
is in a situation which is making them very unhappy.

6 *Sample answer*
The majority of students start their degree in the same year as
finishing school or college. Some students, however, choose to take a
year out before starting university. In my opinion, this is a very good
idea if the time is used wisely in order to gain new skills or knowledge.
In the following essay, I will discuss this idea further.

It is very important that, when a gap year is taken, the time is not
wasted but used productively. It would not look very impressive to a
future employer if the time was simply used to take a break. This does
not mean to say that a gap year should not be enjoyed.

Many people choose to go travelling during their gap year. This can be
very beneficial to the individual as it exposes them to new ideas and
cultures. It can also mean that they are able to learn a new language.

Other students decide to gain work experience during this year. This
can be particularly useful, especially if connected to their chosen
area of study. Often, students who have worked before attending
university appreciate their course more, as they are able to
understand the relevance of what is being taught.

Overall, therefore, as discussed in this essay, there can be several
benefits to taking a gap year. It is very important, however, that this
time is used wisely and not wasted. This means that the year needs to
be planned carefully in advance to get the most from the experience.

LISTENING

1 & 2   **Nursery:** 4, E
    Primary school: 2, F
    Secondary school: 6, D
    Sixth form college: 7, G
    Further education: 1, C
    University: 5, A
    Adult education: 3, B

3 1 Reception 2 Infant 3 Junior 4 Standard Assessment Tests
   5 Teacher Assessments 6 General Certificates of Secondary
   Education 7 Modern Foreign Languages

4 1 Academic 2 Further education / FE 3 University
   4 Employment 5 Apprenticeship

5 1 five 2 statement 3 reference 4 conditional 5 confirm
   6 clearing

6 1 a 2 b 3 a 4 a 5 b

7 1 Postgraduate Certificate 2 Master … Science
   3 research degree 4 company internship 5 graduate fair

SPEAKING

2 1 teachers, discipline 2 tests, grades 3 academic, private tutors
   4 curriculum, essays 5 technical, graduation

6 *Possible answers*

Problem	Cause
a Parents have to spend a lot of money on private education.	1 *Because students are under a lot of pressure to get good grades.*
	2 As our schools do not cover all the subjects in detail.
	3 Because our society is very competitive.
b Students do not have enough free time to socialise.	1 *Due to the fact that they have to study from morning until night.*
	2 Because we have to prepare for our exams.
	3 As our parents force us to use our free time to study.
c Many students have reported that they are unhappy with studying English.	1 *As they have to spend a lot of time memorising lists of vocabulary.*
	2 Because it is considered more important than their native language.
	3 Due to the fact that it is difficult to learn a foreign language quickly.

7 *Possible answers*

Cause	Effect	
a Because students are under a lot of pressure to get good grades	1	*Parents have to spend a lot of money on private education.*
	2	Their teachers are very strict.
	3	They finish studying at 11 pm.
b Due to the fact that they have to study from morning until night	1	*Students do not have enough free time to socialise.*
	2	They spend a lot of time sleeping in lessons.
	3	Many students suffer from poor health.
c As they have to spend a lot of time memorising vocabulary	1	*Many students have reported that they are unhappy with studying English.*
	2	Students struggle to make real conversation in English.
	3	Students feel like they do not make much progress in their studies.

8 *Possible answers*
   1 spend more money on teacher training
   2 get to know their students' learning styles
   3 try some extra-curricular activities
   4 work together
   5 quickly change its education system

12 1 She'd 2 it's 3 I'll

15 *Possible answers*
   1 people with money do better; students think school a waste of time; should limit cost of tutoring
   2 more important now; tutors for three-year-olds
   3 change curriculum to cover all subjects
   4 do things like drawing, reading, listening to music

Unit 8   FESTIVALS AND TRADITIONS

READING

3 1 False 2 True 3 Not Given

4 limit

5 advertising

6 1 Not Given 2 False 3 True 4 Not Given 5 Not Given

7 1 rely 2 order 3 same 4 carefully 5 synonyms

8 1 False 2 False 3 True 4 True 5 Not Given

9 1 b 2 a 3 **a:** first conditional **b:** second conditional
   5 present simple 6 infinitive 7 past simple 8 would

10 1 go, will be 2 had, would / 'd go 3 have, will / 'll
   4 had, would / 'd 5 wears, will / 'll

11 1 False 2 Not Given 3 False 4 False 5 Not Given 6 False
   7 True

WRITING

2 **Good advice:**
  2 a 3 a 4 b 5 a

4 **Introduction:** e
  Main body: d, c, b (in this order)
  Conclusion: a

5 1 too much about spending money → dominated by shops and
    companies … large profits; could be done to change the situation
    → offer some solutions
  2 I will discuss some of the problems … also offer some solutions.
  3 the second, third and fourth paragraphs
  4 No
  5 No
  6 a recommendation

6 1 suggest measures which could be taken to solve this problem
    suggest ways in which these issues might be tackled
    what can be done to minimise the bad effects?
    how could these problems be solved?
  2 issues, negative aspects, bad effects
  3 D, because it asks you to describe the reasons behind the problems

7 1 (will / shall) discuss 2 is given 3 close 4 has passed 5 want
  6 do 7 be ignored

8 *Sample answer*
  Planning a large family event or celebration can be a stressful
  experience. There are lots of things to consider and you need to make
  sure the plan for the event is successfully communicated to everyone.
  In the following essay, I will describe some of the problems you may
  encounter and suggest ways in which these may be solved or
  avoided.

  Planning a large event is perhaps difficult enough when you do not
  know the people attending the celebration. When you do know the
  people coming, however, the task can be even harder. For example,
  when organising an event for your family, your guests might have
  very particular views on how they expect the event to be, what you
  should be eating and how the decorations should be done.

  Secondly, because it is a family event, you will need to provide food
  and entertainment for different age groups. You may have very young
  children attending, together with your elderly grandparents.

  The solution to these problems is careful planning. You need to plan
  early and make sure you have all the information you need to
  organise your event. You will need to know exactly who is coming so
  the dietary requirements of both young and old can be catered for.
  You could also ask for opinions on the event during the planning
  stages, so your guests feel more included.

  In conclusion, organising a large family event can be problematic.
  Nevertheless, if you plan carefully and include relatives during the
  preparation stage, all should go well.

LISTENING

1 **Music festival:** 3
  Arts and crafts festival: 6
  Poetry and literature festival: 5
  Food festival: 2
  Technology fair: 4

2 1 painting and crafts 2 students 3 catering 4 volunteers

3 1 short film 2 poorly / badly attended 3 three / 3 paintings
  4 low(er) / poor(er) standard / quality 5 paid helpers
  6 business support

4 1 Student band 2 Book local band for the last night
  3 Show only clothes 4 Have students' plays and poems
  5 Have digital and non-digital photographs displayed

5 1 families 2 cooking 3 professionals 4 responsibility
  5 prizes

6 1 forms / types / kinds 2 standards 3 high cost 4 development
  5 trust 6 studies / studying / (academic) work / course(s)

SPEAKING

2 *Possible answers*
  Celebrations were important in the past because
  a people were usually all together as a family.
  b celebrations were not always about money.
  Celebrations are important now because
  a we spend a lot of money on them.
  b it is harder for families to get together all the time.
  Celebrations were not important in the past because
  a people had to work longer hours and had less time to celebrate.
  b people had less money to spend on celebrating.
  Celebrations are not important now because
  a some smaller celebrations are no longer celebrated.
  b the focus is only on money and not the meaning of the event.

3 *Possible answers*
  1 Well, on the one hand, we still spend a lot of money every year on
    celebrations – and it seems like we spend more every year! On the
    other hand, it could be that some of the smaller public holidays
    and events are becoming less important as everyone is too
    focused on the bigger ones. I also think that in the past
    celebrations were more important because they were less about
    money and more about the meaning behind the event.
  2 I think celebrations are more important now than they were in the
    past. Because people work longer hours and sometimes live far
    from where they grew up, it is hard for families to get together all
    the time. While celebrations were also important in the past
    because we were all together as a family, I think that they are even
    more meaningful now as we cannot take meeting our loved ones
    for granted.

9 1 I prefer spending time with my family on my **birthday** rather than
    spending time with them at **New Year**.
  2 **This** holiday is much more exciting than **that** holiday.
  3 **These** ideas might be better for a celebration than **those** ideas.
  4 **Some** people don't enjoy public holidays as much as **other** people
    I know.

LISTENING SCRIPTS

Unit 1   THE MAN-MADE ENVIRONMENT

LISTENING

1 & 2 📊 02

1   This is a very nice ground floor two-bedroom flat. It was recently modernised, with a new bathroom and kitchen. The main bedroom is a double bedroom with an en-suite bathroom and toilet, in addition to the main bathroom and toilet. There is a second, smaller bedroom. The living room is spacious and there is a large kitchen, which is big enough to be used as a dining room. The garden is accessible through the living room and the kitchen.

2   This first floor flat is in a very nice area of the town and is well connected to local shops and services, as well as having good transport connections. There are two double bedrooms, one bathroom, a newly fitted kitchen, a living room and a separate dining room, which could be turned into a third bedroom. There are stairs to the garden at the back. The flat needs some modernisation, but it is very well kept and would be an excellent family home.

3   This is a lovely flat, suitable for a family or for people sharing. The flat is on two levels – there's a first floor and a second floor, above a separate ground floor flat. Upstairs, there's a large double bedroom and a smaller double, as well as a third bedroom, which is only a single, but is still a good size. There's a large bathroom upstairs and also a small shower room downstairs. There's a spacious living room and a large kitchen / dining room, with a rear door to steps leading to the garden.

3 📊 03

Estate agent: Morgan's Estate Agents. How can I help you?

Caroline: Hello. I'm calling about a property that you have for sale – in Churchill Road.

Estate agent: Sorry. Did you say Church Mill Road?

Caroline: No. Churchill Road – C-H-U-R-C-H-I-L-L.

Estate agent: Oh, right. We have two for sale in Churchill Road – a three-bedroom property and a two-bedroom one. Can you tell me which one you're calling about?

Caroline: It's the three-bedroom one.

Estate agent: Oh, yes. Would you like to arrange a viewing?

Caroline: Yes, but first of all, I'd like to check some details.

Estate agent: Certainly. What would you like to know?

Caroline: First, how many lounges has it got?

Estate agent: There are two. There's a small one at the front and a larger one at the back, leading to a sun-room.

Caroline: A sun-room? That's nice to know.

Estate agent: Yes. It's perfect to sit in on those chilly or rainy days as it's got its own heating. And you can get to the garden through the sun-room door.

Caroline: Lovely. I've always liked the idea of outdoor space with a lawn. I do a bit of gardening myself. What about the kitchen?

Estate agent: It's fully-fitted – so it includes a cooker and a dishwasher and all the other things you'd expect in a kitchen. You can also get to the outside space through the kitchen door.

Caroline: That sounds great, not having to buy a cooker and dishwasher.

Estate agent: Yes, it would be perfect for you. I should add that there's a garage and a short driveway.

Caroline: Oh, that's very useful. My husband usually drives to work, but I mostly use public transport.

Estate agent: Well, regarding transport, it's only five minutes from Edgely Station and there are regular buses to the town centre, so it's very well connected.

Caroline: That's excellent!

Estate agent: So, would you like to arrange a viewing?

Caroline: I'm free tomorrow morning. Is 11 o'clock OK?

Estate agent: Oh, no, I'm sorry. I'm busy then.

Caroline: How about one o'clock then, or one forty-five?

Estate agent: One o'clock would be best for me.

Caroline: OK, great. Let's meet then. Oh, my name is Caroline Prendergast. My number is 07945 872310.

Estate agent: I'm Peter Eliot.

Caroline: Is that with two 'l's?

Estate agent: No, one: E-L-I-O-T. My number is 07863 905073. That's 07863 905073. I look forward to seeing you then.

Caroline: OK. Goodbye.

Estate agent: Bye.

4 📊 04

Conversation 1

A: How much is that altogether?

B: That's £53.72, please.

A: Sorry, did you say £43.72?

B: No, £53.72.

Conversation 2

A: So how far is it to Paris?

B: I've just checked. It's 472 km.

A: 472 km? That's a long way. Are you sure you want to drive?

Conversation 3

A: Someone left a message for you, Mr Henry. He wants you to call him on 01897 625730.

B: Sorry, I didn't get all that. Did you say 01857 629730?

A: No, it's 01897 625730.

Conversation 4

A: So how big is the football field?

B: It's 110 m by 55 m.

A: 110 m long and 55 m wide? That's quite big.

Conversation 5

A: Can I book a place on the course on Saturday, please?

B: Certainly madam. What's your membership number?

A: It's B1074.

B: Sorry, did you say D1074?

A: No, B1074.

B: Oh, OK, thank you.

5 📊 05

Estate agent: Hello. I'm Peter Eliot. You must be Ms Prendergast.

Caroline: Yes, that's right.

Estate agent: So, this is the property.

Caroline: Oh, I just wanted to check one thing – the price. If I remember rightly, it's £340,000.

Estate agent: Actually, it's £350,000 at the moment, but we can discuss that later if you like it. As you can see, the front garden is very well kept.

Caroline: Yes. The owners have taken very good care of it.

Estate agent: Shall we go in? Follow me. So here's the hall and the front lounge to the left.

Caroline: Hmm, yes. It's very nice. What are the dimensions?

Estate agent: It's 4.3 m by 3.28 m. That's very spacious for a smaller lounge.

Caroline: Hmm, yes. 4.3 m long and 3.28 m wide. Can we go through to the second lounge?

Estate agent: Certainly. If you'd like to follow me. Here we are.

Caroline: Oh, it's lovely. What's the size of this room?

Estate agent: Er, let's see … the second lounge … er … it's 6.5 m x 4.25 m. And you can see the sun-room at the back and the garden.

Caroline: Can we go and have a look?

Estate agent: Of course. Walk this way. As you can see, there's enough room here for some plants and two sofas. You could even put a dining suite here.

Caroline: That would be perfect for cooler days. I love it!

Estate agent: And as you can see, there's a patio and a large lawn with flowers round the edges.

Caroline: What are the dimensions of the garden?

Estate agent: It's 30 m long and 10 m wide.

Caroline: 30 m by 10 m? That's a good size for a family. It would be lovely in summer.

Estate agent: Of course. Would you like to look upstairs?

Caroline: Yes, OK.

Estate agent: Here's the main bedroom. It's 4.91 m x 3.95 m – perfect for a large double bed. Oh, sorry, that's 4.91 m long and 3.95 m wide. And there's an en-suite bathroom here, though it only has a shower unit and not a big bath like the main bathroom.

Caroline: That would come in very useful when we all get up to get ready for school or work.

Estate agent: Yes, that's a real positive. Here's the second bedroom. It's 4.2 m x 3.55 m – ideal for children to share.

Caroline: 4.2 m long and 3.55 m wide? OK, that's good. Yes, it's got plenty of room to play in.

Estate agent: And here's the last bedroom, which is 3.25 m x 2.5 m. It would be ideal for a child.

Caroline: Yes, it would be fine for my older daughter.

Estate agent: The bathroom is just over here. It's got a large bath as well as a shower fitting.

Caroline: Great! It's just what we need.

Estate agent: So, would you like to put in an offer?

Caroline: Yes, please. This is the best property I've seen so far. I don't think I'll find a more suitable one.

Estate agent: Wonderful! If you'd like to come back to the office, I can take your details and arrange everything.

6 & 8 ▥ 06

Estate agent: So, Ms Prendergast, let me take your details. I'll just enter your name. How do you spell it?

Caroline: P-R-E-N-D-E-R-G-A-S-T.

Estate agent: OK, that's it. And what's your present address?

Caroline: 52, Lanchester Road. That's L-A-N-C-H-E-S-T-E-R. It's in the Riverside part of town. The postcode is KE7 8UD.

Estate agent: And your home phone number?

Caroline: 01594 398210.

Estate agent: And I've got your mobile number: 07945 872310.

Caroline: Yes, that's right.

Estate agent: OK. Now the house is on the market for £350,000, but I know that the owners would be happy to accept a close offer as it's been on for a few months. What would your first offer be?

Caroline: I think £340,000 would be fair.

Estate agent: OK. I'll put that offer to them and we'll see what they say. Now, usually buyers have a mortgage arranged with a bank – a loan to buy the house – so that we can quickly complete the sale. Do you have one arranged yet?

Caroline: We've spoken to our bank and they're happy to offer us what we need, up to £300,000. We also have a 15% deposit in our bank account – about £52,000 – so that won't be a problem.

Estate agent: And is anyone buying your house? Will the sellers of this property need to wait for you to sell yours?

Caroline: No. We sold it a couple of months ago and we're staying with relatives, so we're ready to move in as soon as the sale is completed. So, when do you think you can get an answer on the offer?

Estate agent: I should be able to get one tomorrow. Then, if they agree, we can do things quite quickly. Your bank will do the survey – you know, send someone to check the house is in good condition and at the right price – and, if that's OK, we can then prepare the contracts for you and the seller to sign.

Caroline: How long do you think the sale will take after that?

Estate agent: Well, it's difficult to say. If things go well, we should complete it in about two months at the most. Most sales take about two months. However, if there are any problems, it could take longer, but we hope it won't be more than three months. For example, part of the house, like the roof, might be in bad condition and might need some work. Or there might be plans for a new road in the local area. Anything like that can delay the sale, but most of our sales go through quickly.

Caroline: Oh, I hope nothing like that happens! We're really looking forward to moving in soon. It's not easy living a long time with relatives, and my husband has a long journey to get to work, but those aren't the things I'm really worried about. If we can move in before the end of the summer, it'll be much easier for the children to go to their new school. That's why I hope we can complete everything on time.

Estate agent: Don't worry. I don't see any problems with this sale, so I'm quite sure you'll be in the house by then. So, just to go over things again: I'll talk to the sellers tomorrow. If they accept your offer then we can continue. If they don't, you'll need to put in a higher one quickly, but we should be able to agree by the end of the week. Then you ask your bank to send someone to check the house. If that's all OK, the next step is to prepare the contracts for you and the seller to sign, and we should complete the sale soon after that.

Caroline: Wonderful! I'll look forward to your call tomorrow. Bye.

Estate agent: Bye.

7 ▥ 07

Estate agent: And there's an en-suite bathroom here, though it only has a shower unit and not a big bath like the main bathroom.

Caroline: That would come in very useful when we all get up to get ready for school or work.

SPEAKING

2 & 3 ▥ 08

Examiner: Now, in this section of the test, I'd like to ask you some questions about yourself and where you live. Do you live in a house or an apartment at the moment?

Student: Right now, I'm living in a house with two other students. It's a pretty big house with two floors, a garden and a shared bathroom. I moved in during the summer.

Examiner: Where do you live – in the city or the countryside?

Student: Our house is in the city centre, about five minutes' walk from the train station. We're close to all of the shops and restaurants, and our school is about a 20-minute bus ride from my house. There's lots to see and do around there, so I'm pretty happy with the location.

Examiner: Who else lives with you where you live?

Student: Well – as I said – I live with two other students. They both go to the same school as me. One of them is from China and the other is from India. I'm from Romania, so I think we live in a pretty international house!

Examiner: Is there anything you don't like about where you live?

Student: Well, I don't like sharing my bathroom with others and the kitchen is often very busy, but I think that's normal for a shared house. Also, we need to do the gardening regularly or things get out of control. Sometimes the trains can be a little loud as well, especially in the mornings.

Examiner: Now, let's talk about shopping. Where do most people go shopping where you live?

Student: Most people go to the Citygate shopping centre, as it's the biggest and has the most shops and restaurants. There's also a cinema and ice-rink, so people go there not just to shop, but to hang out with their friends as well. It has all of the famous brands and most importantly, it's warm in the winter!

Examiner: When do you usually go shopping?

Student: I usually go at the weekends as I'm too busy with my studies to go in the week. The only problem is that the Citygate gets very full at weekends and you have to wait a long time to get a bus back home, because so many people are trying to catch the bus at the same time as you.

Examiner: Why do lots of young people like to go shopping at big shopping centres?

Student: I think it's because everything is in one place, and they're clean and comfortable and it's safe for young people to meet. Where else can you go that has all of the shops and entertainment under one roof that the big malls have?

Examiner: Would you ever do your shopping at the local market?

Student: I'm not really sure as the local market is more for older people who just want to go and buy some cheaper food or clothes, and the styles and brands on sale at the market are a bit old-fashioned for me, personally. Maybe my parents would be fine with going to the market, but there's really nothing interesting for me there.

11 ▦ 09

1 Right now I'm living in an apartment with my friends.
2 I'm not too happy with my current accommodation – it's too small.
3 The architecture in my home town is fascinating.
4 I get up early as there's a lot of construction going on across the road.
5 My shopping mall has a lot of escalators, as there are ten floors in total.
6 The inhabitants of my home town are pretty easy-going as we live in a place with good weather.
7 The most famous monument in my home town is the Statue of Liberty.
8 Most visitors to my home town go to the museum as it's very famous.
9 The most boring places in my home town are the residential areas, as there are no shops there.
10 My home town has a huge stadium where people go to see the local football team.
11 These days, many people are leaving the city to go to the countryside, where it's cleaner.
12 I'd say that due to the traffic in my home town, the environment there is getting worse.
13 My home town has interesting geography with big mountains and deep valleys.
14 The most interesting thing about where I live is the regional food that you can only get here.
15 On average we get pretty warm temperatures here in my home town.
16 Because I live in the countryside, the scenery here is beautiful – very colourful and bright.

12 ▦ 10

1 A / **part** / ment   2 Ac / com / mo / **da** / tion
3 **Ar** / chi / tec / ture   4 Con / **struc** / tion   5 **Es** / ca / la / tors
6 In / **ha** / bi / tants   7 **Mon** / u / ment   8 Mu / **se** / um
9 Res / i / **den** / tial   10 **Sta** / di / um   11 **Coun** / try / side
12 En / **vi** / ron / ment   13 Ge / **og** / ra / phy
14 **Re** / gion / al   15 **Temp** / er / a / ture   16 **Sce** / ne / ry

Unit 2   LEISURE AND RECREATION

LISTENING

2 ▦ 11

1 Stay in the middle lane so that you can go over the motorway.
2 You'll have to wait on the right till it changes for you to turn.
3 Go round and take the third exit on the right.
4 Slow down here because it goes to the left quite sharply.
5 When you get there, go straight across.
6 When you get to the end of this road, take the left turn.

3 ▦ 12

Jeff: Hi. This is Jeff here. I'm calling you all about the inter-college sports competition at the South Hinton Sports Centre next week. I'm really sorry but there's been a change of plan. We can't have the competition at the centre because of the flooding last week after all the rain. It damaged a lot of our equipment and also the floors in some of the rooms. Luckily, I contacted the North Hinton Sports Centre and they've kindly agreed to let us use their centre and their equipment for the competition, so I'm phoning to give you directions on how to get there and instructions about what to do there to prepare. You'll need to meet the others there next Tuesday at about nine o'clock to get the centre ready.

OK, as I'm not sure if you know how to get to North Hinton, I'll give you directions avoiding the town centre, because it can be quite busy in the morning. First, come out of our sports centre into Lily Road. Turn left and go about two hundred metres and you come to a roundabout. You see a sign to Hinton saying turn left, but that takes you into the centre of town, so don't take that one. Go straight over that roundabout and you come to a crossroads. The left turn here also takes you into the centre, so don't take that one either. Carry on for about a kilometre. The road goes up onto a flyover over the motorway to Longchester. After the flyover, you come to the junction with Bramley Road. This is where you go left, because that takes you round the town to the sports centre. Carry on for about five hundred metres. Then you go left round a bend and just after the bend you see a petrol station on the left. The turning for Hinton is just after that at the traffic lights, so make sure you look out for it. Turn right into West Road and carry on. The sports centre is on Green Lane, which is just past the Woodland Hotel on the right. You can't miss it. There's a car park there so you shouldn't have a problem parking. Please don't be late as we have a lot to do.

4 ▦ 13

1 This game is similar to tennis, but you don't need to have such strong arms to play it. The playing area is smaller and people hit a shuttlecock – a light object with feathers – instead of a ball. You need to think and move quickly.
2 You have to be very strong in your arms and legs but also light and flexible to do this sport because you use your whole body all the time.
3 You don't need to move around a lot in this sport, but you need to think very fast and move your arms quickly and accurately because the playing area is so small and the ball is so light.

4 You have to train hard every day to get very strong arms if you want to be good at this sport. You also need to have very strong legs to support yourself, but you don't move around to do it.

5 People who play this sport are usually very tall, but you also have to be able to run a lot, move quickly and throw very well.

5 ▥ 14

OK, so when you get there, you'll have to start setting up the rooms for the people taking part in the competition. I've been there and looked at the rooms and the equipment they've got is not as good as ours, but it'll be OK. There's a big store room with all the equipment in it. You should be able to get the key from reception – they'll be there waiting for us.

There are three rooms where the competitions are taking place. Remember that two of the rooms have different competitions in the morning and afternoon. So first of all, let me give you the schedule for the morning. The Dean Room is for the badminton competition. There are two courts in there, so you'll have to set up both of them. Then, the Carsley Room is where the gymnastics will be, and there's quite a lot of equipment to bring in for that. We have to get the Forster Room ready for the weightlifting, which is taking place in there all day, so once you set up the room for the weightlifting, you won't have to change anything, but there's a lot of equipment to put in there.

Now, in the afternoon, the table tennis is taking place in the Dean Room, so you'll need to – oh, wait a minute, we had to change that because there are no basketball nets in the Carsley Room, so actually, the basketball will be in the Dean Room, but as the nets are already there, you won't need to set anything up for that. That means the table tennis will be taking place in the Carsley Room in the afternoon, so you'll have to make sure all the equipment is in there, as there will be a lot to do to change the room around.

Exam skills

6 ▥ 15

Now, about the equipment. For the badminton in the Dean Room, there are two nets in the storeroom to set up and you know what to do so it shouldn't take you long. The players will bring their own racquets with them, but there are some spare ones, so take them into the badminton room as well, just in case. There are also a couple of boxes of shuttlecocks if we need them.

For the basketball in the afternoon, you only need to bring in the balls because the nets are always up and ready, so you can do that between the sports events. In the Carsley Room, you'll have to get the gymnastics equipment in place in the morning. That means bringing in the vaulting horse and putting it in the middle. Put one mat in front and another behind the horse, and have some other mats ready for the floor exercises. Then on the side, set up the bars for the gymnastics. There are two sets of bars: one for the men and one for the women. The other equipment, such as the rings and pommel horse, are already in there, so you don't need to worry about those. It's also a good idea to bring in the tables and nets for the table tennis at the same time. There's enough room to leave them folded while the gymnastics is going on, but you'll be able to set them up more quickly later. The players should bring their own bats with them, but there's a box of bats there, so bring those in as well as we might need them.

For the weightlifting, get someone to help you bring in the barbells and the other weights so that you don't try to carry too much. The bench for the bench press should be in there already, so check that it is when you arrive, but you'll need to bring in the stand with the chalk for the lifters to put on their hands. I'll be there at about ten o' clock as I have an appointment first thing, so you should be ready by then. We can check everything together and then get ready to welcome the contestants and the spectators. I hope everything goes well, and I'm sure we can do it! Call me if you need any extra information.

7 ▥ 16

Hi guys, it's Jeff, again. Can you let me know when you've received this message? I've just realised that I probably won't be able to be there at the start of the competition because I have an appointment that I can't cancel, so I'm going to tell you what event I want each of you to organise during the day, just so that you know. I've tried to work it out so that each of you can be in charge of the event you prefer as far as possible. So, first of all, the morning: now, Steve and Amanda, I know that you both like badminton and Amanda, you used to do gymnastics, so I know you'd be happy with either, but I have to make sure of the best arrangement on the day. Amanda, if I remember rightly, you also once did some training in the rules of badminton, so it might be best if you take that on, rather than the gymnastics. It will be useful to have you there to help with judging line calls and so on. That means either you, Steve, or you, Malik, with the gymnastics. Either of you is capable of doing that, but that leaves the weightlifting. Both of you do a lot of the general training in our sports centre, but this is a bit more specialist in terms of getting the weights right for each competitor. OK, for the moment, I'll put Steve in charge of the gymnastics and Malik can take care of the weightlifting in the morning, as I think you have just that bit more experience of dealing with weights, Malik.

For the afternoon, I know Amanda and Malik would both love to do the basketball as you both play it, but Malik, you're already doing the weightlifting, so perhaps Amanda, you can do the basketball. Actually, no, I've just thought. I'm pretty certain I'll be in for the afternoon, so Malik, you won't need to do the weightlifting then. How about you do the basketball, Malik? Then I can take over the weightlifting in the afternoon as I'm particularly keen on that, as you all know, and I'd like a chance to get involved with it. So then, Amanda, you can do the table tennis, but that leaves Steve without anything. No, that's OK, actually, if we leave it at that. Steve, you can be available to help wherever you're needed in the afternoon, and if something happens and I can't make it in the early afternoon, you can take care of the weightlifting till I arrive, though I don't think there'll be any problems. OK, if you need to check on anything, call me on my mobile. Otherwise, see you next week. I think we're going to have a great day!

10 ▥ 17

1 I think that **rowing** is a **great sport** if you want to stay **fit** and **healthy**.

2 I often enjoy **tennis** as it is **very competitive** and I **like** to **beat** my **friends**.

11 ▥ 18

1 Ryan **Giggs** was a **famous player** for Manchester **United**; he played **hundreds** of games.

2 At London **2012**, the United **States** was **top** of the **medals** table, followed by **China**, then Great **Britain** and Northern **Ireland**.

3 Last **weekend**, I **was** going to go to the **gym** but I **decided** not to **bother**.

4 Michael **Jordan** is the **number one all-time points scorer** in the NBA **playoffs**, although Lebron **James** is catching **up**.

5 I **ran** in the **London marathon** last **year**. I thought I was **never** going to make it to the **end**!

13 ▥ 19

1 My favourite sport is hockey. It's amazing!

2 I like swimming, but I wish there were more places to swim where I live.

3 I've always liked fishing but I don't have time to do it any more.

4 I'm really excited about all the new video games that will come out soon. I can't wait!

Unit 3   THE NEWS AND MEDIA

LISTENING

1   20

Discussion 1

A: All I'm saying is that if this government wins the election tomorrow, I think they'll just continue with the same things they've been doing over the last five years and make the economic situation worse in this country. People are already finding it difficult to live with prices going up and salaries staying the same.

B: I don't think they'll win. People have had enough and are ready to vote for a change. I hope they do. If the other party gets in, it'll be like them winning the World Cup!

Discussion 2

A: Yeah, I saw it last night. I think it was really good the way that all the characters were actually well developed and interacted with each other. The danger with that kind of film is that the science fiction aspect just takes over and you get spaceships and battles with aliens who are trying to take over the Earth.

B: I'm going to see it tonight. I listened to the review on the radio this afternoon and the critic really liked it, which is unusual because he doesn't usually recommend big commercial projects which just aim to make as much money as possible.

Discussion 3

A: Did you see that report on the news tonight – the one about the robot football competition?

B: Yeah. It was quite amazing. I mean, it wasn't like real football, but it is amazing what they can get machines to do with the right programming these days. I mean, those robots can detect the ball as it moves around the pitch and pass it to each other. And that winning goal was like Messi scoring!

A: Yeah, I can see it becoming a real money-making business, just like the real thing!

2   21

Topic 1: Modern art

Speaker 1: I don't really have much of an opinion about it. As far as I'm concerned, if it appeals to someone, that's fine. If it doesn't then why should anyone complain about that? Personally, I like some of it, but I'm not really bothered. I can take it or leave it.

Speaker 2: Well, from what I can see, you have a lot of people looking at it and talking nonsense about how good it is. Then you also have people with too much money and too little sense who are prepared to waste their money on this stuff. It's ridiculous! There's no comparison with the great art of the past few centuries.

Speaker 3: Oh, I think not enough people appreciate it. They look at it and think, well, my kid could do that. They think that something from the eighteenth or nineteenth century is true art and they don't understand that art develops and changes over time. These artists today are just as skilled and creative as those in the past and they should be appreciated for what they do.

Topic 2: Combating climate change

Speaker 1: It's so important that we tackle this issue head-on. We can't let it go on any longer without taking action. All the science shows that it's going to get out of control if we fail to act. The government should be supporting renewable forms of energy and we really need to reduce our dependence on oil and gas. I just wish other people could see that!

Speaker 2: There's so much nonsense spoken about it. Really, I can't understand why people get so upset about it. They quote all kinds of studies, but they don't amount to anything real. If you ask me, the climate is getting colder, at least in this country. Look at the amount of snow we had last winter! They just want to scare people for no reason.

Speaker 3: I'm not really convinced either way, actually. I mean, there are arguments on both sides, but I think it's still too early to tell. Yes, we can see that the weather in different parts of the world is becoming more extreme, but if you ask the climate experts, they never say that it's definitely climate change and just say they need more time to be sure. So that's where I am at the moment.

3 & 4   22

Maria: Hello Simon.

Simon: Hi Maria.

Maria: OK. What topic do you think we should choose for the project we're starting next week? I think we need to make sure that it's going to last over the next few months so that we can complete the project.

Simon: Well, there are several possibilities. Have you heard of the Pluto expedition? The spacecraft is about to arrive there and it's going to send back pictures that we've never seen before. It should be really interesting.

Maria: That sounds like a good idea. What do you think, Dr Thornton?

Dr Thornton: Well, I'm not so sure about that one. I mean, it's already been going for ten years and I think we should look at something which is planned for the future but hasn't started yet. It would give you a better chance to study it in depth and do far more analysis for your monthly update reports.

Simon: I don't think that's a problem. There'll be a lot of coverage on the news over the next few weeks.

Maria: Hmm … that's true … but we really need something to last for a few months. On second thoughts, maybe Dr Thornton's right. Perhaps we should look at something which hasn't started yet. Isn't there something I heard about a new Mars expedition? I think there's a group of people out in America somewhere who are preparing for a trip to Mars.

Simon: Yes. It was in the news last week. They've built a sort of camp in the desert in Arizona. There are ten people living there for six months, just like they would be together on the trip to Mars and after they arrive there.

Dr Thornton: That'd be ideal. Six months is just right for you. You could follow their progress and how the project develops. From what I know, the Pluto project is already a success, but with the Mars one you can assess how successful it is as it progresses and you can write it up for your final report.

Maria: Hmm … yeah … that sounds promising.

Simon: OK, but before we decide, I'd just like to mention one more. I heard that the Chinese are planning an expedition to the moon.

Maria: What? Another man or woman on the moon? That's already been done. I don't think the moon's particularly interesting these days.

Dr Thornton: Simon has a point. I mean, the Chinese are coming up now and they've got some new ideas. I don't think they're sending any astronauts. I think it's just an expedition with robots and machines to find the best place to start a colony.

Maria: Yes, but I don't think that's particularly interesting. I mean, no one has ever seen Pluto close up and no one has tried to go to Mars, so I think they'd be more interesting expeditions to do.

Simon: You have a point. Perhaps it would be better to focus on one of the other two.

Dr Thornton: OK, if you ask me, I'd prefer to see how a group of people get along living together in a difficult situation, like they'll be doing in Arizona in preparation for their trip. I think you'd get far more out of that, but the final decision is yours. What do you think?

Maria: I agree. I'd prefer to go for that one.

Simon: So that's agreed then. Good. Let's make a start.

Dr Thornton: Excellent. I'll make a note of that. We'll meet again next Wednesday and you can give me your project outline. I'm looking forward to seeing it.

5 & 6 🎚 23

Conversation 1

A: It looks like the government is going to raise taxes in the budget tomorrow.

B: Seriously? I really don't see how that could be a good idea. It'll reduce spending and affect the economy without a doubt.

Conversation 2

A: They just said on the local news that the bus companies are planning to reduce fares for travel after ten o'clock to get more people to come into town.

B: That certainly sounds like it would work well. It would definitely help shops and businesses, as well as the local attractions.

Conversation 3

A: Oh no, not again! The air traffic controllers are going on strike. That will cause massive delays at the airports and ruin a lot of travel plans.

B: Well, to be honest, I'm not really worried. I'm travelling by train for my holiday.

Conversation 4

A: It says here in today's paper that the government is going to offer free dental checks to people over 60.

B: I'm all for that. Anything that helps people take care of their teeth has to be a good thing.

Conversation 5

A: There's a report in the sports section that says Athletic are going to buy that Brazilian striker Reginaldo for £40 million.

B: That much? I can't seriously believe that! I really don't think he's as good as the experts say he is.

Conversation 6

A: The government is going to bring more doctors and medical staff from abroad to fill vacancies. Maybe they should try to find more here.

B: It's all the same to me. As long as they're qualified and speak good English, it shouldn't matter where they're from.

7 🎚 24

Dr Thornton: That'd be ideal. Six months is just right for you. You could follow their progress and how the project develops. From what I know, the Pluto project is already a success, but with the Mars one you can assess how successful it is as it progresses and you can write it up for your final report.

Maria: Hmm ... yeah ... that sounds promising.

Simon: OK, but before we decide, I'd just like to mention one more. I heard that the Chinese are planning an expedition to the moon.

Maria: What? Another man or woman on the moon? That's already been done. I don't think the moon's particularly interesting these days.

Dr Thornton: Simon has a point. I mean, the Chinese are coming up now and they've got some new ideas. I don't think they're sending any astronauts. I think it's just an expedition with robots and machines to find the best place to start a colony.

Maria: Yes, but I don't think that's particularly interesting. I mean, no one has ever seen Pluto close up and no one has tried to go to Mars, so I think they'd be more interesting expeditions to do.

Simon: You have a point. Perhaps it would be better to focus on one of the other two.

Dr Thornton: OK, if you ask me, I'd prefer to see how a group of people get along living together in a difficult situation, like they'll be doing in Arizona in preparation for their trip. I think you'd get far more out of that, but the final decision is yours. What do you think?

9 🎚 25

Dr Thornton: I assume you've seen the latest update from the Mars project? One of the people has had to leave the project in Arizona, which is a bit of bad news. It only came out last night.

Maria: Oh, really? We missed that. Who is it?

Dr Thornton: Alfonso, the biologist. That means that they won't be able to monitor the plants they've been growing for food. Apparently, his mother was taken ill, so he decided it was more important to be with her than stay with the project.

Simon: His mother's ill? That's a pity. I hope it's nothing serious. Are they planning to bring someone else in, or have they got someone to take over the plant care?

Dr Thornton: Well, as you know, according to the rules of the project, no one else can come in once it's started, so they'll just have to make the best of it. After all, in a real situation, you can't just call up an agency and get someone else.

Maria: I think Carla would be the best person to take over. As chief medical officer, she's had training in biology.

Simon: That might be true, but I'm not sure that means she's the best person for the job.

Maria: Why not? There's nobody else in the project who's got her experience in that area.

Dr Thornton: Maybe, but I personally think the best solution would be to share the work. I'm sure they can all learn how to do it, and what's more, they can make sure that if anything else happens to one of them, the others will have a good idea of what to do.

Simon: Yeah, I agree with Dr Thornton. That would be the best solution. But I'm sure they'll announce their plans later.

Dr Thornton: Right, so now that update is out of the way, let's see what other progress you've made ...

10 🎚 26

Simon: OK, so the latest from the project is that one of the people taking part, Joe, attacked another person on the team, Martin, and hit him. I really can't believe that Joe would do something like that! He's been the quietest up until now.

Maria: Sometimes that's what happens. You think someone is OK, but it turns out that they're not. Why did he do it? Is it anything to do with personality problems, or is it just a disagreement about something?

Simon: Well, there are strong signs that there've been some emotional or psychological problems which result from being isolated for so long.

Maria: Isolation? What, so you're saying that Joe might be suffering some kind of psychological problems? I can see how that can happen in an environment like that, where there's no escape from the situation ...

11 🎚 27

Dr Thornton: Well, as psychology tutor, I find that really interesting. Many types of people participate in projects studying the effects of isolation. We all know that one of the main issues with a project like this is how people will get on when they are locked away together for such a long time. It can produce all kinds of psychological and emotional problems. That's what I'm particularly interested in and one of the reasons why I wanted you to do this particular project.

Simon: Me too. That'll be one of the most important things to come out of this project – how people can control their emotions and feelings over a long time when they can't get away from each other.

Maria: True, but we have to remember that this is a science project and not some soap opera or television series with lots of silly people locked up in a big house or something.

Dr Thornton: I can see what both of you are saying, but there are always going to be problems like these, so it's not surprising when they happen. In fact, this is the first time someone has got really angry in the first three months, so I think that's quite a positive thing.

Maria: So what do you think will happen? Will they make him leave?

Simon: I don't think they can. It's all part of the programme. And anyway, as the environmental engineer, Joe is an essential member of the team. If he left then the whole environment of the building would go wrong, so I think they'll just have to work the situation out. Remember last month, when the ventilation system broke down? They almost lost all their fresh air. He only had a couple of hours to fix it and he managed to do it.

Dr Thornton: I'm sure they'll work it out. So what else have you found out …?

12 📊 28

Dr Thornton: So now that the project has ended, we need to review it and I can help you plan your final assignments.

Maria: Yes. I never thought that of the ten who started only six would finish in the end, and it was really hard for them to get through the whole programme. So, what have we learnt?

Simon: Well, I've got lots of data on the environmental systems and life support, and that's the key focus of my project report, especially considering the events last week, when the whole system came close to failing.

Maria: Right. When the life support system went offline for four hours, they had to really race to fix it. If that happened on a real trip, it'd be a disaster! They could all die.

Simon: I know. It's good that they weren't actually in danger in this project, but I agree, in a real situation people could have been killed. Who would've thought that it'd be on the front page and the first item on the evening bulletin? It shows how much interest there's been in the project. Anyway, I'm hoping to use the data to design a new system if it's not too difficult.

Dr Thornton: That would be challenging but fascinating at the same time. I think you'll do well with that, Simon. Personally, I'd love to focus on the particularly interesting and useful data on the health of the participants. I think it'd be worthwhile writing about the physical effects of the project, you know, how they kept healthy in the long term, even though they became ill sometimes, but also about the psychological effects of living in an enclosed group like that. It'd be interesting to see if any of them will have any long-term health changes. Would either of you like to take that on?

Simon: Well, I'm not sure if I could take that on as well as producing an assessment of the life support issues. I feel that those are more significant in view of the current developments in technology to support this kind of expedition. I've already looked at the latest reports in the popular science magazines, though there are some fascinating articles due in the next *Journal of Space Studies*. Maybe I could beat them to it!

Maria: That'd be a great idea, Simon – to write an article – but for me, the main thing is the efficiency of the crew and how well they managed to perform their duties. I'm focusing specifically on their abilities to work under the stresses of living in an enclosed environment. I'm going to analyse how well they managed to maintain their effectiveness over time.

Dr Thornton: That's interesting. Maybe you could include a section on the psychological effects of long-term isolation. Remember the incident early in the project? It'd be very interesting to follow that up with the latest developments and results. I can give you some of the latest research on the subject from other studies for you to compare. I think it would significantly enhance your research and findings.

Maria: OK. That sounds like a good idea. It shouldn't be too difficult to develop a wider theme to include the psychological studies. I'll work out a structure for next week.

Dr Thornton: That's great, Maria. We can meet again next Wednesday and I can help you structure it. And what about you, Simon? Do you think you have enough?

Simon: Yes, thanks, Dr Thornton. I've got plenty to think about, especially as the study of life support was the main aim of the whole project. I could include some observations about the effects on the physical and mental health of the participants, as it's relevant.

Dr Thornton: That's fine, then. Is there anything else you want to discuss?

Simon: One thing I'm really surprised about is that they managed to complete the project without any extra costs. Everyone was expecting it to go over the original $10 million. I personally thought that it might even go up to something like $12 million.

Dr Thornton: Well, actually, it says here that the final cost was $9.5 million, so they saved half a million in the end.

Simon: They could give that to us to fund our projects! Is there anything about future developments?

Dr Thornton: Well, I heard that they're going to share their research results with government and private organisations. There are a few other organisations planning trips to Mars that would love to study the results. I'm not sure the government is planning anything, but they'd be interested anyway.

Maria: What about a follow-up? Are they planning another project?

Dr Thornton: Well, depending on the results from this one, they're going to decide whether to have another one that will last a year. Obviously, they'll have to find some more participants. Would either of you be interested in taking part?

Maria: It depends. I wouldn't say no, but I'd have to think a long time about it. I don't know if I'd want to be cut off for so long.

Dr Thornton: I think you should bear it in mind. It would be so interesting to see how staying in a situation like that for a year affects physical and mental health. I'd love to follow your progress myself. I might even volunteer! What about you, Simon?

Simon: Oh, you wouldn't catch me inside one of those places! I'll be happy to follow what goes on and see how the whole system works over a year, but definitely from the outside, not the inside … I wouldn't mind working for the company, though. It'd be great to study it and get paid at the same time!

Dr Thornton: Well, thank you, both of you. You've produced excellent results and I'm looking forward to seeing your final submissions.

SPEAKING

5 📊 29

1A When the report came in to say the mission was a success, everyone felt that we'd seen something extraordinary.

1B When the report came in to say the mission was a success, everyone felt that we'd seen something extraordinary.

2A The disaster was a dreadful tragedy with a massive loss of life.

2B The disaster was a dreadful tragedy with a massive loss of life.

3A I'm feeling pretty uncomfortable about the situation. I hope we can find a solution soon.

3B I'm feeling pretty uncomfortable about the situation. I hope we can find a solution soon.

4A The results were stunning, and the team had done a marvellous job.

4B The results were stunning, and the team had done a marvellous job.

5A It was such an impressive sight and the noise that followed it was tremendous.

5B It was such an impressive sight and the noise that followed it was tremendous.

6A This was such a bizarre event, and it's incredible that we haven't been able to find out what caused it.

6B This was such a bizarre event, and it's incredible that we haven't been able to find out what caused it.

Unit 4   TRAVEL AND TRANSPORT

LISTENING

1 & 2 ▦ 30

Conversation 1

A: The next bus should be here soon.

B: No, it won't. I just checked. It's due in twenty minutes.

A: Twenty? I don't believe it! It should be every ten minutes. This service is getting worse and worse!

B: You're right. It was never this bad. The bus company just doesn't care about passengers any more, as long as they get the money.

Conversation 2

A: Excuse me, could you tell me why the 4.50 train to London hasn't arrived yet?

B: I'm afraid there's been an accident on the line at the station before this one.

A: Oh, sorry to hear that. Do you have any idea when it might arrive?

B: Well, at the moment the line's closed but I've just heard that the company is arranging buses to take passengers to London. There should be one here soon.

A: Thanks for letting me know.

Conversation 3

A: What do you think? Should we take the car? It's the quickest way to get to Bristol. It's straight down the motorway. We should be there in two hours.

B: Haven't you heard? There's fog on the motorway and there are massive jams all the way down. There's really no point in driving.

A: Oh, really? Well, shall we take the train? I know it's expensive, but maybe we can get a cheaper fare. I'll have a look at the train website.

B: Good idea. At least we can get there fairly quickly and safely.

Conversation 4

A: OK, darling, I'm off to work.

B: You're not using the car, are you? Remember what the doctor said. You need to get more exercise and lose weight, especially now that your leg is better.

A: I know, but my leg hurts a bit today. I'd prefer to use the car.

B: Yes, but it won't get better if you sit in the car all day. I really think you should do some more exercise. And it's a lovely day for cycling. You can use the car when it rains.

A: OK, OK, I'll cycle today, but I'll need to use the car tomorrow as I've got a lot of things to take to work.

Conversation 5

A: I'm thinking of buying a motorbike now that I've retired. I'll have a lot of time to ride around like I used to.

B: A bike? Are you sure? I really don't think that's a good idea. They're really dangerous.

A: Only if you don't know what you're doing! I used to ride one when I was younger.

B: How long ago was that? It must be at least 30 years ago. Have you been on one since?

A: No, but I'm sure I can remember how to ride one.

B: Well, if you ask me, I think you're making a big mistake. I wouldn't get back on a bike after so much time, but it's your decision.

4 ▦ 31

Sophie: So the main focus of the project is the transport system in the town. We need to look at the problem carefully and then discuss possible solutions. We have to decide which one we could recommend to a transport committee.

Robert: OK, Sophie. I think the problem is not a simple one as there are various causes that we have to discuss. I think the first one is to do with the bus service in the town. In my view, the lack of buses has meant that too many people are using their cars. The service isn't reliable enough.

Sophie: Yes, you have a point there. It would be good if we could have more buses on the road all the time, but I don't think that's the main reason for the heavy traffic and the problem won't go away just by improving bus services.

Robert: You could be right. More buses would be useful, but that's not enough to put things right. We have to remember that many people come into town by rail and the rail company has been talking about reducing staff and services because of financial problems. If that happens then more people will use their cars to come in. We need to take that into consideration when deciding on a solution.

Sophie: Of course. I think the town council can find some extra money to support the train service because, if anything, we want to increase the service to reduce the traffic on the roads. The more people travel by rail, the less they'll use the road. And we would have the added benefit of safer roads, especially at school travel times.

Robert: True, but one good thing is that the road accident rate has been falling recently, partly due to the high volume of traffic on the roads. After all, when there's too much traffic, it moves more slowly and fewer people, especially children, are in danger.

Sophie: I realise that, but that's exactly what we have to deal with: the problem of too many vehicles coming in. I know children are safer, but the air quality is much worse. We don't want to have more medical problems like asthma and bronchitis, especially for children and older people.

Robert: True, and when I think about it, I can see that the heavy traffic means that businesses lose money, people are late for work and drivers get more stressed. So, let's think about how we can deal with that and look at the possible solutions.

5 ▦ 32

Sophie: So where are the worst affected places in town?

Robert: I would say one of the worst is by the Arts Centre.

Sophie: I'm not sure about that. Statistics show that the worst place is by the town hall.

Robert: Well, as most of the traffic comes in from the east of town, that would be the Arts Centre. The town hall is further over.

Sophie: Actually, Robert, that's not quite right. The traffic gets quite bad along East Road, further out of town. It's been getting worse over the last year or so, especially by the Starview Cinema.

Robert: The Starview?

Sophie: Yes, haven't you ever been there?

Robert: No, I haven't. I thought it was by the main roundabout.

Sophie: Well, in actual fact, it's by the junction of East Road and Station Road. That's where the traffic has been getting really bad, especially in the mornings. It's especially bad for the buses coming from the station as they can't turn right into East Road to get to the centre.

Robert: OK. So that's the first bad spot, then.

Sophie: Yes. Sometimes the traffic backs up for almost a kilometre, and in the evening, when everyone is trying to get home, it gets bad all the way back to the main roundabout. It's bad in the morning and the afternoon as the traffic also comes in from the north and the south. Remember, there's Liverton to the north and Scotsfield to the south and a lot of people commute to both places for work.

Robert: That's true. I live a few kilometres down the Scotsfield Road and I have a lot of trouble coming in during the morning rush hour. It's especially bad just by the Arts Centre where the road comes into the roundabout. The buses have a lot of trouble getting through that as well. OK … so those are the two main hotspots, the Starview and the Arts Centre. I've marked them on the map. And that leaves the town hall.

Sophie: Hmm … yes. I mean, the whole area around Central Park is bad, but you're right, the town hall side of Central Park is the worst in the area. It's bad enough right by the shopping centre on the other side of Central Park, but it's particularly bad on the town hall side, with all the heavy lorries coming into the centre from the industrial estate on the west side of town. They usually make their deliveries in the morning rush hour.

Robert: So you're saying that if we stopped them from coming in early to the area by Central Park where the town hall is, that would make the traffic a lot lighter?

Sophie: I'm sure it would. Now that we've established where the worst places are, let's have a look at the proposals.

6 ▥ 33

Sophie: The first proposal is to introduce bus and cycle lanes on the roads coming into each of the trouble spots, but I'm not really sure that that will solve the problem by itself.

Robert: What do you mean? I think it's a really good idea. I think it would help a lot.

Sophie: On the face of it, yes, but in actual fact it can make things worse. There've been a few studies of towns and cities where they've put schemes like that into operation and one serious problem is that car traffic tends to go off into the areas around town where people live, and that causes more traffic in places where there haven't been problems before. Drivers think they can find emptier roads in residential areas and it just sends the problem there instead.

Robert: Hmm … I hadn't thought about that. What about the second one, a park and ride scheme?

Sophie: Well, we build car parks on the edge of town where the main roads come in. When cars come into town from further out, they can park there cheaply and take special buses into the town centre. It's been quite popular in a few other towns around the country.

Robert: In some places, yes, but not in all. I've had a look at some of those schemes. The main problem is lack of take-up. Drivers just don't use them. A lot of these car parks stay empty for a long time and the buses are often less than half-full. It's not always a good use of public money, especially when drivers avoid using the services and prefer to come into town and pay higher parking fees.

Sophie: You've got a point there. We need to bear that in mind. Do you think either of the other proposals would work? I think the pedestrian area is a very interesting proposal. We could turn the whole of the centre, including the shopping areas, into a pedestrian zone and put in a one-way system round it.

Robert: I'm not convinced that would work. You'd move all the traffic further out of the centre and cause more problems. But the biggest problem would actually be with the shops themselves. It's fine to stop traffic around the shopping areas, but there would be huge problems with deliveries. Some shops could go out of business if they have difficulty getting lorries in with their goods.

Sophie: Right. I'll note that as well. The last one is a new tram system. We'll have to lay down a new line through the centre of town and also from north to south. It's quite a popular solution to traffic problems.

Robert: That may be so, but the main problem with that kind of project is the expense. The initial financial requirements would be huge and so would the maintenance expenses. It might well be far more than the council is prepared to spend on a solution.

Sophie: I'll note that as well. Which brings us to the next point, the question of cost …

7 ▥ 34

Sophie: I've got the details on the cost of each of these projects. The tram system comes out as the costliest. It would cost over £20 million just to prepare the route and to lay the lines down, including widening the roads. Then there's the cost of buying the trams themselves and organising the system.

Robert: And what does it all come to?

Sophie: No less than £30 million in the end. At least that's what they need to try to keep the costs down to.

Robert: £30 million? That does seem a lot. I thought it was closer to £25 million, but clearly it isn't. And what about the cheapest?

Sophie: Well, it seems that it'd be either the bus and cycle lanes plan or the park and ride scheme. At the moment, it looks like the bus and cycle lanes might be the least expensive overall. The changes wouldn't be so large. They estimate around £8 million to set up the signs, paint the roads and so on, and at least another £2 million or so to make other changes.

Robert: So you're saying it's around £10 million? That seems quite reasonable. What about the park and ride scheme?

Sophie: Well, there are sites which have been identified for development to build the car parks, and as they're not in the centre, it won't cost too much to buy them, probably around £5 million. Then they'd just need to lay out the car parks and put in bus shelters, which should be around £6 or £7 million and then get the buses. If they rent them, they could keep the costs down to around £3 million.

Robert: So, if I'm right, that comes to around £15 million for the park and ride in total. And then there's the pedestrian and one-way system. How does that work out?

Sophie: That's the second highest. We'd have to re-route all the traffic while the works are done, then change the roads along the routes to make it safer for cyclists, which is around £12 million. Then there are the new signs and so on, which comes to about £5 million and also the road painting and maintenance, at around £8 million.

Robert: So that's around £23 million. We might be able to manage that.

Sophie: Actually, that's £25 million, Robert.

Robert: So it is! My mistake. Maths was never my strong point!

8 ▥ 35

Sophie: So we've discussed the negative aspects and costs of these proposals, but now I'd like to look at the real benefits which we think each proposal will bring.

Robert: Well, I really think that one of the most important benefits is better public transport. The most important thing is to get more people out of their cars and onto public transport.

Sophie: Well, three of the proposals would help with that – park and ride, bus and cycle-only routes and the new tram system. Which do you think would be the best out of those three?

Robert: I think the bus and cycle routes would be great for town centre transport, but they might push car traffic further out and make it more difficult for buses outside the centre. That leads me to think that the tram system would actually improve public transport the most, even though it's the most expensive, as there will be a new form of transport in the centre, without affecting other parts of town.

Sophie: I think you have a good point there. I agree that in the long term it would be the best thing. Do you think that proposal would also increase the amount of visitors in town?

Robert: Well, of course. Any of the solutions would do that, but I'm not sure if the tram system would be the best. What do you think?

Sophie: I think the park and ride would be better than the tram system for that. The trams would help people who are already in town, but a park and ride would bring more of them in from outside.

Robert: So you think the park and ride would bring most visitors in?

Sophie: Actually, I think if people know that they can get around the centre more easily, do their shopping and so on, they would come in more. So perhaps the pedestrian area and one-way system would be best in that respect.

Robert: True. I've seen other town centres become really busy when they've put in pedestrian areas, so that's clearly the best way of bringing visitors in. So we agree on that, then.

Sophie: And I think that people's health will improve as well as they will be walking around the pedestrian area, rather than driving around town.

Robert: Up to a point, yes, but I'm sure you'd agree that encouraging people to do more cycling would help their health far more.

Sophie: Of course. Creating bus and cycle-only routes would be the best way of getting people to exercise. It would also help reduce pollution, so even the people who don't cycle will breathe cleaner air.

Robert: And we agree that producing less pollution is a really important part of this scheme, though I think that the park and ride would be better at doing that than the bus and cycle-only routes.

Sophie: I'm not sure. Lots of people would need to use the park and ride to help reduce pollution. Bus and cycle-only routes keep cars out of the centre.

Robert: Yes, but if people are encouraged to use park and ride more, it would produce the best results. There would be far fewer cars in the centre and the air would be much cleaner.

Sophie: Yes, that's true, but that's a lot of work for the council. OK, we'll agree on a park and ride, then. What about safety? I'd say the bus and cycle routes would be best from that point of view.

Robert: Probably. I think I agree with you on that.

Sophie: OK then, so we agree on safety.

Robert: Actually, no. When I think about it, you have to take pedestrians into account as well. It's safer for cyclists when there are no cars around, but I'm not sure that it's safer for pedestrians. They still have to avoid cyclists, who don't always pay attention to pedestrians, so I really think the pedestrian area and one-way system would be safer for them. Cyclists won't be allowed in the pedestrian areas, so there will only be people walking.

Sophie: Yes, you have a point there. Shall we change that then?

Robert: OK. I'm glad you agree. So, that's all done then. We have all our recommendations!

9 ⠿ 36

1 Actually, Robert, that's not quite right.
2 I think you have a good point there.
3 On the face of it, yes, but in actual fact it can make things worse.
4 What about the second one, a park and ride scheme?
5 Up to a point, yes, but I'm sure you'd agree that encouraging people to do more cycling would help health far more.
6 I'm not sure about that. Statistics show that the worst place is by the town hall.

10 ⠿ 37

Jane: Have you got the results from the survey we did about the changes that've been made to Ashtown in the last 25 years, Bill?

Bill: Yes, Jane, and there've been a lot of changes. Some of them people are happy about and some of them they aren't.

Jane: What, for example?

Bill: Well, for example, the bus system used to be much better and even though the old uncomfortable buses have been replaced with new stylish ones, fewer people use them.

Jane: Why is that?

Bill: A lot of people think it is because fares are higher, but that isn't true. In fact, the cost compared to average salaries is pretty much the same as 25 years ago. The fact is that the buses now just go to the most popular destinations and, as the city centre no longer allows vehicles, there are even fewer places where buses can go.

Jane: Most people must be happy with fewer cars in the town centre though?

Bill: I'm not so sure. Five years ago a bypass was supposed to be built so that people could easily get from one side of the town to the other, without going into the centre, but those plans still haven't happened. The biggest success in my opinion is the building of areas for cyclists. Far more people are travelling by bike and using the facilities than anybody could have imagined.

Jane: That's all very interesting, but how have the jobs that people do in the city changed? That's sure to have had an impact on what the town looks like.

Bill: You're not wrong there. The town used to be a lot more polluted due to all of the products that were made in factories here. Manufacturing is still important of course and services such as accountancy firms and website developers employ a lot of people in the town, but you only have to see the number of universities and colleges that have opened in the town in the last 25 years to see that is where most of the jobs are now.

Jane: OK, now shall we have a look at how some of the buildings have changed?

Bill: I think that first of all we should look at how the railway station has changed. As there are now fewer buses, more people drive to the railway station to take a train. Twenty-five years ago the car park was much smaller and, although it might not look very modern, most of the spaces have only been there for five years.

Jane: Oh yes, didn't the cinema used to be quite near the railway station? I suppose they built more spaces when they knocked it down.

Bill: That's right, the Grand Cinema used to be next to the railway station, but they rebuilt one exactly the same as the old one over in King Street.

Jane: What about the indoor market? My mum says there used to be an outdoor one, but that closed down a long time ago.

Bill: Yes, and when the outdoor market closed down, the indoor market became a lot more popular. Ten years ago it looked like it would close down too, as the building was really old and it had become dangerous. It used to be owned by the council, but a private business bought it and made the changes so that it could stay open.

Jane: It's good to see it's so popular still despite all the new supermarkets in town. I bet the library isn't as popular as it used to be though?

Bill: You'd be surprised. A lot of people still use the library! Most people think that people are less keen on borrowing books than in the past, but the library has adapted to changes. It's true that fewer people go in there to borrow books, but since they made tablets and computers available, more people have started visiting it. It has really fast Wi-Fi too, so people like it because of that.

Jane: Quite a few of the factories have closed down or been sold in the last twenty-five years though, so what happened to all the buildings that used to house them? I suppose they're all shut down now?

Bill: Some of them have been demolished, and some have been converted for other uses, but that isn't surprising. The thing that I found surprising was that, although education has become more important to the economy of the town, there isn't an art college any more. In fact the art college is now used as a doctor's surgery.

Jane: Oh really? Anyway, I think we need to look at how we're going to present these findings to …

SPEAKING

2 ⠿ 38

Now I am going to give you a topic and I'd like you to talk about it for between one and two minutes. You have one minute to think about your answer. Here's a piece of paper and a pencil for you to make some notes if you wish.

All right? Remember you have one to two minutes for this, so don't worry if I stop you. I'll tell you when the time is up. Can you start speaking now, please?

5 ⊪ 39

Student: I remember a trip I took last year, on the 12th of August, I believe. I boarded a plane to Paris, which was rather exciting as I'd never done that before. Since I come from China it took a long time to arrive, but when I got there, the first thing I did was go to the Louvre Museum – you know, where the big triangle is by the entrance – and took some pictures. After that, I boarded a subway train to the Eiffel Tower to take more pictures. Because I was pretty hungry around that time, I went to a restaurant, although I had trouble ordering food because I don't speak any French. Once I had eaten, I then took a tour bus to the Champs Elysées in order to do a bit of shopping, where I went on to buy as much as I could. I even bought a souvenir snowglobe for my friend Julie, as she collects them. However, when I got back on the tour bus and started taking pictures, I dropped my camera over the side, watching it break on the ground. After everything was over, I took the flight back to China. It was a great experience, although next time I think I should study some French before I go!

7 ⊪ 40

1 I boarded a plane to Paris, which was rather exciting as I'd never done that before.
2 Since I come from China, it took a long time to arrive, but when I got there, the first thing I did was go to the Louvre Museum.
3 I had trouble ordering food because I don't speak any French.
4 Once I had eaten, I then took a tour bus to the Champs Elysées in order to do a bit of shopping.
5 When I got back on the tour bus and started taking pictures, I dropped my camera over the side.

9 ⊪ 41

A **Student:** … and it was a great experience. I think I'll always remember going to Tibet.
Examiner: Do you generally enjoy visiting new places?
Student: Yes, I would say I like to try new things … meet new people, so travelling is something that is very important to me.

B **Student:** … and it was a great experience. I think Paris is one of the best places on Earth for culture.
Examiner: Would you like to visit Paris again?
Student: Oh, definitely. Maybe in ten years' time, I'd like to go back and see if anything had changed.
Examiner: Is there anywhere else you would like to visit one day?
Student: Yes, I've always thought about going to Rome. I mean I'm a big fan of the opera and love Italian food, so it's next on my list of destinations.

C **Student:** … and it was a great experience. London was one of the most interesting places I've ever been to.
Examiner: Is there anything you didn't like about your holiday?
Student: Maybe the weather … London isn't exactly famous for being a hot, sunny place to visit, but I didn't think the weather would be quite so bad as it was.
Examiner: Would you recommend London to a friend?
Student: Yes, definitely. But they would have to bring an umbrella! Everything else was wonderful though – I would definitely recommend it.

Unit 5   BUSINESS AND WORK

LISTENING

1 ⊪ 42

Dr Lethbridge: In last week's lecture I talked about employment and aspects related to it, including contracts, income tax and so on. However, people are increasingly looking at other forms of earning a living by working for themselves and being in greater control of their working lives. Today Dr Korpis and I are going to talk about three different ways in which people can work for themselves. They can set up a company, set up a partnership, or they can work as a sole trader. There are important legal and financial matters to take into consideration when choosing one of these structures as a way of doing business in the UK.

Firstly, I just want to outline the main differences between these three types of business structure, which are to do with tax and registration. Regarding registration, those wanting to set up a limited liability company have to legally register the company with Companies House, the government department responsible for businesses. 'Limited liability' means that, if the business fails and the owners owe a lot of money, they only lose the money and goods which are in the business, and not their own personal money and goods. This is because the owners of the company are separate from the company itself. On the other hand, a sole trader doesn't need to set up a company; he or she can simply start working without any legal registration. A partnership can be limited or unlimited. An unlimited partnership is just like a sole trader, but with two or more partners. In this situation, each partner shares expenses and also income. A limited liability partnership, or LLP for short, is like a limited company, because it must be legally registered in the same way. So just to summarise: with limited liability companies and limited liability partnerships, the owners and the company are separate in legal terms, but with simple partnerships and sole traders, the business and the owner are not legally separate.

The other main difference is to do with money – both with finding money to start your business, and with paying tax. For example, it might be difficult to borrow money from the bank if you're a sole trader, but easier if you have a limited company, as banks trust companies more. Regarding tax, limited companies pay corporation tax, which, unlike income tax, is a tax on business profits, not personal earnings. This is more favourable for companies, as corporation tax is usually less than income tax. On the other hand, with sole traders and partnerships, whether simple partnerships or limited liability partnerships, the owners must pay income tax, which may be higher than corporation tax.

2 ⊪ 43

Dr Korpis: Thank you, Dr Lethbridge, for your introduction. I'd now like to move on to the details of each type of business structure and discuss the advantages and disadvantages of each, starting with the sole trader. This is simply a person who runs a business alone. On the practical side, there's no need to register with Companies House, which means the sole trader is not legally the same as a registered company. The trader can simply choose any name and start trading without paying any fees. There's no need to register an office, so the trader can even work from home. There are also no legal requirements to submit financial accounts to Companies House. As a result, this is the simplest and most straightforward way to start out in business and work for yourself. Another benefit of being a sole trader is that you are your own boss. You don't have to answer to anybody else, you make your own decisions and you don't have to share your earnings with a partner. However, it doesn't mean that you have to do everything alone. You can also employ or give contracts to other people to do work for you, though, of course, you need to be aware of regulations regarding employing others.

So these are the desirable aspects of being a sole trader, but there are other matters which need careful consideration. When you're in employment, you are taxed at source, which means your employer takes your tax from your earnings every month and sends it to the tax office, so you don't need to worry about it. However, as a sole trader, you are self-employed, which means you are responsible for what you earn, what you spend and the tax that you must pay. This means you have to complete an annual tax return. This is a document which you send to the tax office once a year showing what you earn from your business and what you spend in running your business. On the positive side, you're only taxed on your earnings after expenses, such as transport, electricity, office equipment and so on. So, if you work from home, you can save tax by declaring some of your use of electricity as necessary for your business. Another consideration is that if you earn over a certain amount, you pay a higher rate of income tax, which is higher than the corporation tax rates that companies pay. You'll also have 'unlimited liability', which means that if you can't pay your business debts, you may lose your house and car to pay for them, as you are your business. Finally, many sole traders find it difficult to take holidays and breaks from the business and find that they spend far more time working than employed people.

The typical traders associated with this type of business structure are skilled manual workers, such as builders, plumbers and electricians, or professions in which people usually work alone, such as photographers and writers. However, increasingly these days, with the reduction in long-term employment and job security, sole traders are coming from other professions, such as computer programming and even teaching, especially tutoring. Certainly, being a sole trader is a very useful way of starting out in business by yourself.

3 ▦ 44

Dr Lethbridge: Thank you, Dr Korpis. The next form of business structure that I would like to discuss is the partnership. There are two kinds of partnership – a simple partnership and a limited liability partnership, or LLP. I'll talk about each of these in turn. Forming a simple partnership is straightforward, like becoming a sole trader, except that you have to agree to work with someone else. A partnership could be between a husband and wife, or two members of the same family or close friends. For example, a couple might run a catering business, or two car mechanics might leave employed work to set up a partnership together repairing cars. One obvious advantage of this is that if one partner is sick or on holiday, the other partner can carry on the business, and another is that it can be easier for a partnership to borrow money from a bank than it can for a sole trader. Of course, partners usually have an informal agreement to work together, but it's always better to have a formal arrangement to avoid disagreements. As with sole traders, each partner must be registered with the tax office as self-employed and must send in a tax return once a year. In addition, as the partnership is unlimited, all members are responsible for debt, so you and your partners may lose your personal possessions to pay debts if the business fails.

The other structure for a partnership is the limited liability partnership, or LLP. This is similar to a simple partnership as the partners share the income and expenses and also have to pay their own taxes to the tax office, but there are important differences. On the one hand, sole traders and simple partnerships don't have to legally register their businesses. On the other hand, LLPs have to be legally registered with Companies House. This means that at least two of the members are legally responsible for the partnership. They have to make sure that they send accounts to Companies House, as well as to the tax office. They also need to send in an annual return, which is a document showing the name, address and members of the partnership and any changes. If they don't do this, they may go to prison, so it's important to understand exactly what setting up an LLP means.

So why should partners enter into a limited liability partnership? Usually, an LLP suits certain types of professionals who provide services, such as accountants, lawyers, consultants and financial service providers. Another reason may be that partners want to do business with larger organisations who would prefer to give contracts to a registered company or partnership. In any event, an LLP offers the flexibility of being in a simple partnership, but also gives the partners protection so that they lose only the money that they have put into the partnership if it fails. However, if the partners earn a lot of money, they will still pay more tax than the owner of a limited liability company.

4 ▦ 45

Dr Korpis: Thank you, Dr Lethbridge. The last form of business I'd like to talk about is the limited liability company. The owners of a limited liability company are called 'members' or 'shareholders' as they own shares in the company. A 'share' is a divided-up unit or part of the company. All businesses run the risk of failing or going bankrupt. If a business goes bankrupt, it has to close because it owes money and is not able to pay the money back. As I mentioned before, setting up a limited liability company, like an LLP, means that if the company fails or goes bankrupt, the business owners lose only what they have put into the business and not their own personal goods and property. This is the idea of liability – how much a business owes in debt if it can no longer operate and has to close. For example, if a sole trader goes bankrupt, he or she may need to sell his or her own house and possessions in order to pay any debts, because the business is not separate from the owner. With LLPs and limited liability companies, the owners and the businesses are separate, so property and goods owned by the business can be sold to pay debts, but not property and goods personally owned by the members or company shareholders.

Just as with LLPs, limited liability companies (or 'limited companies' for short) must be legally registered with Companies House. This means they must have a registered address, where all the company documents and records must be kept. As with LLPs, accounts and annual returns must be submitted every year so that anyone can have a look at the company's finances before doing business with it. The level of administration is higher than with other business structures and you need to have a managing director and at least one shareholder.

In terms of paying tax, the company has to pay corporation tax on its profits, which is far less than income tax on large amounts, especially over around £50,000. However, you also have to pay income tax on any money you take as a salary from your company. As with the other business structures, the company tax assessment must be submitted to the tax office, but for corporation tax rather than income tax. The shareholders also have to submit their own personal tax assessments separately. As we've already mentioned, the company owners must also submit accounts to Companies House. This can all be quite complicated, so it's a good idea to get professional help and advice from an accountant. It's important to remember that running a limited company is more complex than being a sole trader, so it's important to do careful research and consider your situation before deciding which type of business to run. In any case, you could start as a sole trader and, if business is doing well, turn your business into a limited company at a later date.

5 ▦ 46

Dr Lethbridge: So, let me summarise the differences and similarities between each business structure. On the one hand, it's fairly simple and inexpensive to set up as a sole trader. You don't have to worry about lots of administration and financial organisation, and you can keep total control of your business and decision-making. On the other hand, you may end up paying more in tax than you would as a limited company, you are personally responsible for your debts and losses, and it might be more difficult to get valuable contracts if your business does not have limited liability.

With regard to partnerships, there are two kinds: simple partnerships and LLPs. In comparison with sole traders, partnerships have the benefit of more people to plan and make decisions. It's easier to take care of the business when one partner is not able to take an active part, and it can also be easier to borrow money than for a sole trader. On the negative side, liability is shared among the partners and having more than one owner can make things more complicated when there are disagreements, or if the business needs to be brought to a close. One other difference between sole traders and partnerships is that the partners need to trust each other. If a partnership has serious money problems, one partner may leave the other to deal with the debts. Clearly this is not a problem for sole traders. One similarity between partnerships and sole traders, though, is to do with tax. The sole trader must submit a yearly income tax assessment to the tax office. The same is true of partnerships, as members are treated individually for this purpose.

When we compare simple partnerships with LLPs, we find various differences. For example, LLPs are legally required to submit their accounts and annual returns to Companies House. This is not something that is required for simple partnerships. Another difference is to do with debt. In an LLP, the partners' personal possessions and property are protected. In a simple partnership, however, like sole traders, the members are personally responsible for any business debts.

Finally, limited liability companies have two main advantages over simple partnerships and sole traders: this type of structure limits the financial liabilities of the owners to business losses and not personal losses, and it can save money, as corporation tax is generally lower than income tax. On the other hand, there are a lot more administrative and legal requirements. Company accounts and an annual return must be sent to Companies House. Similarly, there is a legal requirement to keep company records at the registered address.

6 🎧 47

Dr Korpis: To conclude this lecture, I'd like to present three case studies to show the different structures in action. I'll present each case, briefly discuss the possibilities and recommend the most suitable structure.

Firstly, there's the case of Sanjay and Tanya, a couple who want to set up a catering service delivering food to businesses. The idea is to take orders from businesses on a daily basis and prepare food for delivery during the business day. They aim to target businesses in their local area to begin with, and then further afield as they expand. Their plans include a website to display their daily international menus and to provide an online service for customers to order and check when the food will be delivered. Clearly, it's not suitable to be sole traders, but they could organise themselves as a partnership or a limited company. It depends partly on how much money they can raise and how many people they intend to employ to prepare and deliver the orders. It might be best for them to start as an LLP, so that they can get funding more easily than if they were a simple partnership. They could start small and build from there. They could hand out contracts to other companies for some of their services, particularly for the website and delivery, if they intend to prepare the food themselves. Alternatively, they could set up a limited liability company if they expect to grow quickly and want to keep every aspect of their business in-house, employing staff directly. However, I would say the LLP model would work better here – giving them more time to focus on growing the business, rather than dealing with a lot of administration from the start.

Melissa and Jane have an idea for a website design service. They both studied software engineering at university and so they are both well skilled in their field. They have both worked as designers for major organisations, so they have a good understanding of what's involved in running such a business. Melissa has also taken a Master's degree in Business Administration, so she's confident about her skills as a businesswoman. They've managed to save over £3,000 to rent office space and £10,000 to buy equipment to run

their business. The best option for them would be to register a limited company and start trading straight away as they have a good level of knowledge and experience which will benefit them. They don't intend to employ anyone immediately, but the option is there if they need to in the future. An alternative would be for them to start as a simple partnership and expand from there, seeing how their work grows and then maybe setting up a limited liability company in the future (or they could make their partnership a limited one). But if they have confidence in themselves, there's nothing to stop them setting up a limited company immediately.

Barry is a motorbike enthusiast with many years of experience riding bikes. He's been working for a courier company delivering letters and parcels for over five years now and thinks that he'd do better if he worked for himself. The courier company provided him with his work bike and took care of maintenance and repairs, so if he works for himself, he'll have to buy his own bike for work and take care of it himself. This isn't a problem for him as he has three bikes for his own use already. He knows that he can build up regular clients from his contacts, but he's not sure if working as a sole trader is the best thing for him, as he's never been self-employed before. Another possibility would be to set up a limited company with a family member. This person wouldn't take an active part in the business – they would be known as a 'sleeping partner'. Finally, he could also choose to work in a partnership with other riders who are thinking of leaving the company, but he's not sure if that arrangement would last. On balance, the best option for him would be to start off as a sole trader with his own work bike and do that for a year or two to see how well it went, and then make a decision about whether to set up a limited company in the future.

SPEAKING

9 🎧 48

1a I would love to work as a computer programmer.
1b I'd love to work as a computer programmer.
2a I would not like to be a pilot as I do not like heights.
2b I wouldn't like to be a pilot as I don't like heights.
3a I will apply for a position as a receptionist.
3b I'll apply for a position as a receptionist.
4a I will not look for a job straight away after graduation.
4b I won't look for a job straight away after graduation.
5a I should have taken a part-time job at university.
5b I should've taken a part-time job at university.
6a If I had studied harder, I could have got the job.
6b If I'd studied harder, I could've got the job.

Unit 6   THE NATURAL ENVIRONMENT

LISTENING

1 🎧 49

Lecturer: This week in environmental studies, we're going to look at the latest developments in the energy industry and how they might affect our lives in the future. As we've already seen, there are basically two types of energy sources – renewable and non-renewable. As you no doubt remember, renewable sources are those which can be used again and again, while non-renewable sources can be used only once and then they're finished. Historically, coal has been the most-used form of non-renewable energy, but it has also been the most polluting. It's widely accepted that we need to use less of it to help protect the environment for the future. The oldest renewable source is wind power, which has been used for centuries to power windmills and other devices, and which has now been developed further, giving us wind turbines which produce electricity. Over the last 200 years or so, petroleum has become the most important non-renewable source, though natural gas is overtaking it as it's far cleaner and less polluting.

Hydroelectric power has been in use for many years as a renewable resource, especially with dams on rivers and lakes, but these are expensive to create and maintain, and can affect the local environment in negative ways. More recently, there've been great developments in two renewable sources: solar power – that is, power produced directly from the sun – and wave power, which comes from the movement of waves at sea, but, of course, these are only effective in areas with a lot of sun or in coastal areas. While there are clear benefits to expanding solar and wave power, one other source has become particularly significant and important, and that is fracking, which is a way of getting natural gas out of the ground. So, the main focus of today's lecture is on fracking and why there's been so much discussion and debate about it in the media.

2 🎧 50

1 You can use this machine to make a hole in something. For example, you use a small one to make a hole in the wall to hang a picture, or a big one to make a hole in the ground.
2 This is a hole in the ground which is dug in order to extract water, oil or gas.
3 This is a kind of rock deep in the ground that isn't very hard and is easy to break.
4 This is a narrow space which appears inside rock when the rock breaks. The space can fill up with water or gas.

4 🎧 51

Lecturer: So, what exactly *is* fracking? It's a way of getting gas out of the ground. Both oil and gas are found deep underground, so to get to them a well must be drilled. Normally, when a well is drilled into ground where there's gas, the natural pressure of the gas pushes it to the surface, where it can easily be taken away and stored. However, a lot of gas is found inside a type of rock called 'shale', where there is no natural pressure to push the gas out. If a well is drilled into shale, the gas will not come out by itself. It needs extra help. This is when fracking is an important way of getting the gas out. The fracking process works in this way: first, a well is drilled into the ground, through the water table (which is the natural level of fresh water). When the drill reaches the shale, which is where the gas is, it turns sideways through 90 degrees and continues horizontally through the shale. So, to put it simply, the drill goes down into the shale, where the gas is, and then turns to the side. Then, a mixture of water, sand and various chemicals are sent down into the well. The mixture creates pressure in the rock and the rock breaks. These small breaks in the rock are known as 'fissures', and these fissures release the gas from the shale. The pressure of the mixture causes the gas to rise to the surface, where it can be collected and stored.

6 🎧 52

Lecturer: One interesting fact is that fracking isn't new. It's been used for many years around the world, mostly to get the last oil from old wells after the pressure's dropped. But the process has become much better known with the move to fracking for gas and the search for new fracking sites.
Take Canada, for example. Fracking has been used there to extract oil for over 50 years and gas for almost 40 years. More recently, a huge amount of shale gas has been found in many areas of the country and drilling companies are trying to get licences to drill in these areas. For example, in the western region of British Columbia, it's estimated that there are over seven trillion cubic metres of gas which can be extracted. However, most regions haven't allowed fracking to take place because of various environmental issues, which I'll talk about later.

In the USA, the production of shale gas now is around six times larger than it was ten years ago, with more and more licences being given to companies to drill. As a result, shale gas now provides around a quarter of all gas used in the US, and the cost of gas is only around a third of the cost in Europe and a fifth of the cost in Japan. However, because the price has fallen so much, companies are reducing their production and exporting more.

As in the USA, production in Australia has grown massively. Although production in Australia was always lower than in the United States, it's over 20 times greater than it was ten years ago and now supplies a quarter of Australia's gas requirement. It's also helped Australia to become a major exporter of gas. Billions of dollars are being invested in gas exploration and Australia may well become the biggest exporter of gas over the next few years.

The situation in the UK, however, is quite different. The amount of shale gas in the UK has been estimated to be as high as 400 trillion cubic metres. Although fracking could well provide over 70,000 jobs and attract over £3 billion in investment, very little has been done to develop the industry in the UK. Some estimates say that gas bills could be 5% lower if shale gas is produced in large quantities. However, the main problem for fracking in the UK is the high level of population. While in the USA there are on average only about 40 people per square kilometre, in the UK there are almost 250 people, so fracking in any area will affect far more people in the UK.

8 & 9 🎧 53

Lecturer: As you've heard, in countries like Australia and the USA, fracking has been increasing because governments see many benefits for energy supply and their economies. I'd like to discuss these benefits now and then talk about the problems which people have raised about fracking. Well, although increased production of shale gas will make sure that there's always enough gas for people's energy needs and the production of electrical energy, the economic benefit to the consumer is usually seen as more significant. As the supply of shale gas grows, energy prices will come down and consumers will save a lot of money, according to supporters of fracking.

11 🎧 54

Lecturer: Another important economic consideration is the increase in economic activity and employment that results from the development of fracking wells. When a new area is developed, the local economy benefits, with increases in services to the fracking company. Furthermore, as with all industrial developments, employment opportunities increase, with most new workers recruited from the population in the surrounding area – although many workers from outside the area are also attracted by the new vacancies. Of course, companies often bring their own workers with them when they start a new well.

13 🎧 55

Lecturer: Apart from the economic benefits of fracking, its supporters claim that there are significant environmental benefits as well. First, although burning gas produces carbon dioxide, which is the main greenhouse gas causing global warming, the quantities that it produces are far less than the quantities produced by burning coal and oil. Some people estimate that it produces up to 50% less than the other fuels. Burning coal and oil also produces sulphur and mercury, which can be very dangerous to health if breathed in. Another benefit of fracking is that it reduces the amount of water needed for gas production. There's evidence that gas production through fracking uses half the water needed for coal, and a tenth of the water needed for oil. One final benefit could be its use as a bridge to carbon-free energy. This means that, although gas produces carbon dioxide, if gas can replace oil and coal, then the production of carbon dioxide will slow down and the development of renewable sources of energy can take longer.

14 & 16 📊 56

Lecturer: Despite the benefits of fracking which its supporters claim, there are clearly various concerns connected with it. Some of these are real, but it's possible that they're not as well founded as opponents of fracking would have us believe. So, what exactly are these concerns? Well, we can divide them into three categories: environmental concerns, health concerns, and economic concerns.

To begin with, let's look at the environmental concerns. The first and possibly most significant environmental concern is that, despite producing lower levels of carbon dioxide, shale gas is still a cause of global warming and so it should not be used. In effect, it simply stops energy producers and governments focusing on the real need to develop renewable sources of energy. What's more, it's likely that, although countries which produce shale gas will use less coal and oil, the use of coal and oil will still continue to increase in other places, so globally there will be little or no benefit to the environment.

Another environmental concern is pollution. If the production site is badly maintained, dangerous chemicals can get into water sources and rivers. While there's some evidence of this happening at existing production sites, it isn't clear whether this problem happens everywhere, so more research is needed.

The last environmental concern connected with drilling is that of earthquakes. We're more familiar with earthquakes happening in certain areas of the world like Japan and China, but there's evidence that drilling can disturb the ground in the local area, causing it to move and shake, which in turn damages buildings. Usually, these movements aren't serious, but they can cause a lot of worry to the local population, so they need to be considered. In fact, very few of these ground movements have definitely been caused by drilling, and it might be that people are worried because of what they hear or read in the media rather than the actual reality of the situation.

Now I'd like to turn to the economic concerns. Opponents of fracking say that the economic benefits are not as great as its supporters claim. While there's clearly an increase in economic activity in the areas where fracking is carried out, as I discussed earlier, there are often negative effects on agriculture and farming in these areas and there's good evidence that house prices fall, because people aren't willing to move into areas where fracking is taking place or has taken place. Another economic concern is that gas production can be very high at the beginning of the fracking process, but it can drop quickly, down to as little as 10% in five years. This can result in more drilling and greater use of water, which increases the cost of getting the gas out of the ground. The other main economic problem is that the estimated amount of gas in the ground may not be anywhere near as high as fracking supporters claim, so investing huge amounts of money in new wells may not benefit the economy at all.

This brings me to the last major concern: health. Fracking can bring with it a pollution problem. If the well isn't deep enough – less than 600 metres – or if there are problems with drilling, the chemicals can leak into the drinking water supply and cause problems for the local population. There've even been reports of residents opening their water taps and seeing brown water and mud coming out. Pollution can also be carried in the air to local towns and affect people with existing medical problems, especially those with breathing difficulties. There've even been reports of more cases of cancer among people living near production sites, as well as among the workers themselves. Clearly, a lot more research needs to be done on the effects of fracking on health.

So to summarise, there are significant environmental, economic and health concerns connected with fracking, but we need to carry out a lot more research to see whether these concerns are real. Whether they're real or not, they're having an effect on the fracking industry right now. In many places around the world, local people have protested angrily when they've found out that fracking is planned in their area. These concerns have also led local, regional and national governments to announce that fracking won't start until they're quite sure that it's safe. This means that they'll prevent any activity connected with fracking until there's enough evidence to assure its safety, especially in areas with higher populations. In fact, in France, they've decided not to allow fracking anywhere in the country. We can see that the future is very uncertain, and that is what I'd now like to discuss.

17 📊 57

Lecturer: While fracking is being used around the world, we've seen that there are serious concerns about it. What's clear is that fracking isn't the answer to the growing worldwide need for energy as countries increase their consumption. Already, the amount of carbon dioxide in the atmosphere has reached 400 parts per million. This may not seem very high, but we have to remember that 200 years ago the level was around 280 parts per million, so it's increased by over a third since then. As a result, it's estimated that global temperatures have already increased by almost one degree Celsius. This increase changes the climate and affects the weather in many parts of the world. Many places, such as north-west Europe, are expected to become warmer and wetter, and we've seen winter storms becoming worse in this region. Other places such as sub-Saharan Africa are expected to become hotter and drier, with deserts growing in area and seriously affecting farmland. Ice in the polar regions will melt and sea levels will rise, which will put coastal cities in greater danger of flooding.

Clearly, we need to reduce, and eventually stop, using non-renewable resources like coal, oil and gas. It may well be true that fracking can slow down global warming for a while and allow us to develop better renewable resources. However, these resources, like wind, wave and solar power, are currently far more expensive to develop than shale gas production. On top of that, they take a long time to develop and start paying for themselves. Consumers have to pay higher bills to help the development of cleaner sources, and energy companies don't want to lose customers by asking them to pay more. Consequently, it's important for international organisations like the United Nations and national governments to support the development of renewable resources. The problem here, of course, is that governments usually think of short-term answers to energy problems and not longer-term ones. They're afraid that if they reduce the production and use of gas and oil, their economies will do worse than other economies, so they don't want to take action to increase the use of renewable sources.

As I mentioned earlier, there are many people in different countries, like Canada, the UK and France, who don't support fracking, especially if it's going to take place near where they live. Environmental groups also oppose fracking, not just because they want to protect people living in areas where fracking is planned, but also because they see fracking as part of the old way of doing things, like burning coal, oil and gas and increasing global warming. They want to see continued action and are trying to persuade governments to develop wind, wave and solar power, as well as other renewable forms of energy, to fight global warming and ensure the supply of energy in the future. Certainly, coal, oil and gas will run out one day, and if we haven't developed other forms of renewable energy, we'll then have serious problems with supplying energy to the growing world population, and the problems of fracking will seem relatively unimportant.

5 ▦ 58

scenic   business

6 ▦ 59

1	calendar	5	autumn	9	castle
2	foreigner	6	honest	10	yoghurt
3	should	7	light		
4	guest	8	doubt		

Unit 7   EDUCATION SYSTEMS

LISTENING

1 & 2 ▦ 60

Conversation 1

A: I'm sorry to hear that you didn't get the grades to get into university. What are you going to do now?

B: I'm not sure. I can take my exams again at the local college, but I'm not sure if I want to do that. Maybe I'll take a vocational course there instead to learn the skills for a particular job, like accountancy or business studies. At least if I pass that, I can go straight into work.

Conversation 2

A: So how's Jenny settling down? It's always difficult when they start school. My son, Timmy, took weeks to get used to being away from me all day.

B: Oh, she's fine. She loves it, especially learning to write. She doesn't miss me at all. I'm the one with the problem. I really miss her being at home all day. But after all, it's the law – she has to go!

Conversation 3

A: I've found this evening course in photography at my local centre. It's two evenings a week and only costs £150 for the term. You've always been interested in photography as a hobby. Why don't you come too?

B: Oh, I did that course last year. It's really good. I'm planning to take a course on setting up a website, so that I can display all my photos. It does seem strange, though, to be learning something new again after so many years!

Conversation 4

A: I think it's really useful for them to start early. I know it can be expensive, but it's worth it because they already know what it's like to be with others in a class when they start school.

B: That's true. In my case, it's not just the benefits of socialising with other children, it also means I can go back to work. It's a pity I can't get a free place for my son – though I don't have to pay very much, thank goodness.

Conversation 5

A: Well, my daughter is off tomorrow to start her degree course – a whole new adventure in a new city. I'm nervous, but she's really thrilled about it. There's a week for the new students – it's called Freshers' Week – when they find out what they need to know, join clubs and get used to being away from home, and then the course starts the week after.

B: Well, don't worry. I'm sure she'll be fine. After all, she's 18 now and they all have to make their own way in the world sometime.

Conversation 6

A: I'm a bit worried about my son. He's not doing very well. The thing is he needs to understand that it's not like his last school, when he did everything in the same class. He has to make sure he knows his timetable and gets to the right classroom on time. He keeps getting to class late and not doing his homework.

B: Don't worry. It often takes time for them to adjust to the idea of having more responsibility. I'm sure he'll do better when he settles down.

Conversation 7

A: My son passed all his GCSE exams and wants to go to university in two years' time. We can't decide whether he should continue at his school or go to that new college near our house. What do you think?

B: Well, the college has taken the best kids from the local schools since it opened two years ago and almost all of them have passed their A levels and gone on to university, so I think it's really good. Also, it makes them feel more grown-up when they go there.

3 ▦ 61

Lecturer: The British education system is not the same everywhere in the UK. Scotland has its own system, and while Northern Ireland has the same basic system as England and Wales, there are some differences. Because of this, I'm going to focus mainly on England and Wales.

The system in England and Wales is divided into three main levels: primary, secondary and tertiary. In the first part of my lecture, I'll talk about the primary and secondary levels up to the age of 16, and in the second part I'll discuss the options between 16 and 18. Then, finally, I'll talk about tertiary, or 'higher' level, education.

As in most similar countries, education at school is compulsory between the ages of five and 16. Pupils can leave school at 16 but they must stay in an approved learning environment until the age of 18. This can be full-time education, a job or volunteering combined with part-time study, or an apprenticeship, sometimes called a 'traineeship'. Before the age of five, children *can* attend nursery, though they don't *have to* attend any educational institution at all before the age of five. However, when they reach the age of four, they usually start school in an early class called 'Reception', which helps them to adjust to regular schooling.

Primary school runs from the ages of five to 11. The first part of primary school, between the ages of five and seven, is traditionally known as 'infant school' and this is where children learn to manipulate numbers, read and write. Traditional infant schools offer an informal education using child-centred techniques. The second part of primary school, from seven to 11, is known as 'junior school'. The education system has undergone various changes in the last 30 years, most notably with the National Curriculum, which was put in place in 1988 to specify a set of core main subjects that all school pupils have to study. These subjects have to be assessed at four key stages up to the age of 16. At certain stages, the children take exams known as 'Standard Assessment Tests', or 'SATS'. These tests are designed to check the pupils' progress against the national standards, as well as to provide teachers and parents with an assessment of their school's performance.

Key Stage 1 assessment comes at the age of seven, when the pupils do their first 'Teacher Assessments'. Key Stage 2 comes at the age of 11, when the pupils are ready to leave primary school. Although teachers assess their pupils' progress throughout primary school, at the end of Key Stage 2, unlike in Key Stage 1, pupils have to take SATS. Key Stage 3 is reached after the first three years in secondary school, when the pupils are 14. However, this time, the students are assessed directly by the teachers and not by sitting national tests. These assessments help teachers, students and parents to decide which subjects the students should choose to prepare for Key Stage 4, when they take exams which will help decide their future career choices. Unlike SATS, these assessments, known as 'General Certificate of Secondary Education' exams, or 'GCSEs', are not primarily designed to assess progress or give schools an official statement of their performance, but to provide students with their own personal qualifications.

The National Curriculum defined a set of compulsory subjects. These are subjects which the law requires all students to study. There are also some subjects which pupils and students have to study at different stages. For example, Modern Foreign Languages start in primary school, and continue up to Key Stage 3, after which they're optional. In secondary school, students take Citizenship from Key Stage 3. When they enter Key Stage 4, pupils are allowed to make more choices. For example, all learners have to take History and Design and Technology up to the age of 14, but then they can choose whether to continue them or not.

4 🔊 62

Lecturer: Now I'd like to turn to educational opportunities between the ages of 16 and 18. There are various choices open to pupils of this age. The first thing to decide is whether to start work or to continue studying full-time. Of course, starting work means going straight into employment, although young people aged between 16 and 18 will still need either to study part-time, as well as doing their job, or to join an apprenticeship or traineeship scheme.

For those who want to continue studying full-time, there are two paths: academic and vocational. Academic qualifications, mainly Advanced level exams, known as 'A levels', are taken by students aiming for university study. Vocational qualifications, such as those offered by the Business and Technology Education Council (or 'BTEC' for short), prepare pupils for a specific profession, such as engineering or computing. Most of those who wish to continue academic studies will go to the sixth form in their school or a specialist sixth form college. Alternatively, they can study A levels at a further education college, also known as an 'FE' college. Either of these routes will take students to university. On the other hand, those who wish to study a vocational qualification will typically go to a FE college and, after qualifying, will be ready for employment.

There are other options for those who want to start work at 16. Since 2015, young people between the ages of 16 and 18 must continue to learn in a specified learning environment, in addition to working for an employer. The first option is to work for an employer and study part-time for a vocational qualification, such as a National Vocational Qualification (or 'NVQ' for short). The second is to apply for an apprenticeship or traineeship. With apprenticeships, young people get to work with experienced staff and gain job-related skills. They earn a wage, although this is typically less than a 'regular' employee, and get to continue studying part-time – usually one day a week. They study towards a qualification related to the job they are doing and their apprenticeship can last anywhere between one and four years. Almost always, they are offered a permanent job by the same employer at the end of their apprenticeship.

5 🔊 63

Mr Green: So, Amanda, you want me to help you with your application. Let's have a look at the UCAS website. Do you know what 'UCAS' stands for, by the way? It's the University and Colleges Admissions Service. Have you set up an account with them yet?

Amanda: Yes. I did it last week, but I haven't completed my application. One thing I need to know is how many universities I can apply to.

Mr Green: Well, first of all, you need to see how many offer the course you want. Remember, you'll want to choose the universities which have the best reputation, but you need to have some kind of back-up in case you don't get into your first choice. What are you studying?

Amanda: I'm doing A levels in Biology, Chemistry and Psychology, so I'm thinking of taking Biochemistry.

Mr Green: OK. Well, there are seven good choices I could give you. Apart from Oxford and Cambridge, Imperial College in London is very good, and York is also a good possibility and easier to get into.

Amanda: OK. I don't think I'll get into Oxford or Cambridge, so I can include York and Imperial College.

Mr Green: OK. I think you should go for those two, plus three others, because the maximum number that you can put on your application is five. How about Durham, Sheffield and Exeter?

Amanda: OK, I'll look at those. Another thing I'm not sure about is how to make a good assessment of myself and my skills and abilities. I've always found that difficult.

Mr Green: You mean your 'personal statement'? Well, just be honest. I can help you phrase it so that it reads well, but you need to note down what you want to include. If you can do that by Friday, we can write it up together.

Amanda: That's great! Thanks.

Mr Green: Well, that's what I'm here for – to give you the advice that you need. After you've completed your application, I can add the reference and your predicted grades before sending it to UCAS.

Amanda: Great! After we send it in, what happens next?

Mr Green: Well, UCAS processes your application and sends it on to each university that you've chosen. Then the universities assess it and decide whether to make you an offer. Remember that your predicted grades are only provisional, which means they are not confirmed until you get your actual results, so you need to pass the exams to actually get those grades. Usually any offer from a university will be a conditional offer. That means they can't give you a definite offer because it depends on your final grades. Then, when your exam results come through, they get sent to the school here and to the universities.

Amanda: Do I have to contact the universities to ask them about my application?

Mr Green: No. They'll contact UCAS about their offer. If you meet the predicted grades, they'll usually confirm the original offer, but if not, they don't tend to renew it or change it.

Amanda: Oh, I hope that doesn't happen. But if it does, what can I do?

Mr Green: Well, if you don't get a place at any of your chosen universities, you can take a year off and try reapplying next year. Alternatively, you can try to get a place through 'clearing'. This is a way universities fill remaining places on their courses and it's a second chance for students to get into another university if they didn't succeed with any of their chosen ones. It's a sort of safety net, but I hope it doesn't come to that.

Amanda: Well, thanks for your help. I'll complete my application and then come and see you on Friday.

Mr Green: Glad to help, Amanda. See you then.

6 🔊 64

Dr Harris: Hi, Terry. Come in. What can I do for you?

Terry: Hi, Dr Harris. Well, I just wanted to check on some information about the course, as it's all new to me.

Dr Harris: Of course. What do you need to know?

Terry: Well, first of all, I'm not sure exactly what a seminar is for. We never had them at school. I know it's to discuss things together, but is it more than that?

Dr Harris: Well, yes, you're right, it is really. You see, at university we typically have lectures, you know, with about 100 or 200 students in the lecture theatre together. It's a one-way form of learning. The lecturer sets out the topic and discusses it and you take notes. Then you need to review your notes following the lecture and also do some extra reading.

Terry: And where does the seminar fit in?

Dr Harris: It could come at any time once you've had some time to think about the lecture. When you attend the seminar, you should have some of your own ideas to discuss with the other students, usually up to ten of you. It allows you to discuss the topic, exchange ideas and prepare for your assignments.

Terry: OK, thanks. And what about tutorials? Are they like seminars?

Dr Harris: Well, usually we try to space them out over the term, so that we can have a chance to check on your progress and how well you're doing with your assignments. It often depends on when your tutor is available, and at times that might mean you have three weeks between tutorials. Normally, every term you should have one at the beginning, then usually another four, spaced out depending on your programme, and one before the holiday. So that works out at about one every two weeks.

Terry: Right. And what about assessment? How many exams do we have to do?

Dr Harris: Well, that varies from course to course, but generally we focus on continuous assessment more than exams, though exams are, of course, very important too. We tend to assess you over the first two years through your assignments, which is over half of your overall assessment, usually 60%, and then most of your exams will come in the final year.

Terry: OK, I'm happy with that. I get really nervous before exams. And talking about assignments, how long should they be?

Dr Harris: On all undergraduate courses, students tend to write about 3,000 words or so, but it varies depending on the question. However, there's a minimum of 2,000, and while there's no upper limit, you should be careful that you don't write too much as a lot of that might not be relevant to the question.

Terry: So I should aim for between two and three thousand as a rule … there's one last thing I wanted to check about assignments, and that's references. How many do we need generally?

Dr Harris: Well, as your course is international finance, you have to use banking, finance and news sources as well as academic sources. Ideally, you should have around ten references for each assignment to show that you've read widely, but we expect a minimum of five sources which are academic journals and books. From the other sources, we'd generally expect three to be used.

Terry: OK, thank you, Dr Harris. That's cleared up a lot of things for me.

Dr Harris: Glad to be of help, Terry. See you next week.

7 ▦ 65

Dr Ross: So, Jessica, congratulations! You got a first class degree. I always knew you could manage it. What are your plans now?

Jessica: Thank you! I couldn't have done it without all your help. Well, I'm not sure. I'm still thinking about the possibilities. I'm not sure if I want to teach or go into research, or even find a position in a company, perhaps.

Dr Ross: Well, anyone with a degree in Chemistry will always be in high demand. Have you thought about teaching?

Jessica: Yes, but don't you need a degree in education to do that?

Dr Ross: Well, many teachers do that, but, of course, you have to be sure that you want to teach before starting your degree course. In your case though, your main route into teaching would be to do a Postgraduate Certificate in Education. That's another year of study, and you'll learn everything you need to know about teaching, while also getting teaching practice in your subject at local schools. You could study that here if you want.

Jessica: That sounds like a good idea. I'll think about it, but I feel I have more studying to do in chemistry before I think about teaching it.

Dr Ross: Then you could always take a Master of Science degree. That will allow you to specialise in a particular area of chemistry, but if you want to teach in secondary schools, you won't need to have such a specialisation. It's up to you.

Jessica: Yes, I see. Actually, I've often thought of doing a research degree.

Dr Ross: That would be a very good idea, but remember that it will take you at least three years to complete that. It would probably be better to do a Master's degree first and then transfer onto a PhD course. It also costs a lot, and you may need to fund yourself while you're studying. Have you thought of going straight into work?

Jessica: Yes, I have, but I'm not sure if that's the best choice for me.

Dr Ross: Well, you could try doing a company internship for a few months. A company internship is a chance to work in a company without actually being an employee, but possibly with some pay. It'll give you a chance to develop your career and also learn more about your subject specialisation in a commercial environment. After that, you may well get a good position in the company. We have some good commercial contacts for internships here.

Jessica: That might be the best option, but I wouldn't earn much to begin with, would I?

Dr Ross: No, you wouldn't. You could try getting a permanent job now if you want. There's a graduate fair here in the city every year, as well as in other cities around the country. You'll have the chance to meet all the leading companies in the sector and discuss opportunities with them.

Jessica: It's worth considering. Well, I have a lot to think about. Can I meet you again next week?

Dr Ross: Of course. Just send me an email and let me know when would be a good time.

SPEAKING

13 ▦ 66

1 I'd suggest going to bed earlier or you won't be able to remember what you've learnt.

2 We mustn't push young people into studying too hard, or they'll drop out of school.

3 That's not the right solution. Instead, we should've banned homework for pupils some time ago.

15 ▦ 67

Examiner: In your opinion, what is the effect of private tutoring on education?

Student: I think we have an education system where those who have lots of money do better than those who haven't, because many students can't afford private tutors. The tutors teach things at a higher level than the school curriculum, so many students see regular school as a waste of time. That's not really fair, so the government should change the law to limit the cost of private tutoring, so that it's more equal for everybody.

Examiner: Is private tutoring more important today than it was in the past?

Student: Well, I think that private tutoring is certainly more important now than in the past. I mean, in the past we only had tutors for English lessons as it was hard to find people who spoke English well enough to teach conversation in schools. But now we have tutors for everything, even tutors who teach three-year-olds how to pass interviews. Perhaps things have gone a bit too far now.

Examiner: What more can governments do to reduce the need for private tutoring?

Student: I think that governments must make changes to the curriculum so that schools cover all the subjects that are usually taught by private tutors, like English conversation, art, music and other things. If we can get these subjects taught more in schools, then students might not need to go to private tutors to learn them.

Examiner: How can we encourage more parents to teach their children at home?

Student: I know that parents are very busy, but they at least have free time at the weekend. This doesn't mean that they should spend their weekends making their children memorise lists of vocabulary, but perhaps if parents make time to do things like drawing pictures, reading, or listening to music, then children will not need to go to private tutors for those sorts of things.

Unit 8   FESTIVAL AND TRADITIONS

LISTENING

1 🎧 68

Speaker 1: So, in conclusion, we can say that, despite the difficulties we had at the beginning, we managed to complete the programme over the three days without any further problems. In total, 10,000 attended the three days and feedback suggests that the events were exciting and produced true champions, especially the athletics events. Next year we'll have more money, so we're going to add new events to increase the competition and participation levels.

Speaker 2: It's clear, then, that the events didn't go as well as originally planned, so we will have to rethink our arrangements for next year. Clearly, a large tent in the college grounds is not ideal for an event of this type if we're hit by bad weather again, as we were with this year's event. This caused a lot of problems with the preparation of the dishes and the display of the produce from different parts of the world. It also meant that visitors couldn't really get a chance to try everything on display. As a result, much of it went to waste, which is something we have to avoid next time.

Speaker 3: One of the main issues that we had with this event was that the main attraction, Paul Simmons, had to cancel at the last minute as he'd been suffering from a serious throat infection for a week and hadn't managed to recover in time. As a result, we had to find another act, and managed to get Nicky Munroe at very short notice. She performed magnificently, the audience loved her and that saved the festival I would say. Everyone agreed that she has an amazing vocal range.

Speaker 4: The most successful aspect of the event was the variety of products that were on offer. It's wonderful to see students being so creative. We saw practical applications that'll make significant developments in education and even business if they go into production, as well as very entertaining ideas, especially the robot football game. I'm pleased to say that our college team won!

Speaker 5: I'm sure you'll all agree when I say that the quality of the talks and performances over the last three days was very high. The talk given by the top novelist, Henry Peters, on effective plotting and characterisation was excellent, and the audience will have learnt a great deal to help them with planning and writing their future works. What's more, the quality of verse produced in the workshops was very high, and we hope to run that again next time with greater overall participation.

Speaker 6: While there were some wonderful and fascinating works on display, I felt that there wasn't enough variety. Unfortunately, this was because of the limited exhibition space we had. This meant that we could only have one room for portraits and another for landscapes. We hope to extend that next year into other forms, such as still life and abstract, but we'll have to see what rooms are available. We also hope to install clay ovens next year to give our students the chance to create their own pottery and display it for the visitors.

2 🎧 69

Dr Saunders: Hello everybody. Welcome to this meeting to review this year's arts festival. As you know, this is the fourth and biggest festival that we've run at the university and it's clear now that it's fast becoming a fixture in the calendar of the city and the county, and attracting attention from the rest of the country, as well as from abroad. First of all, I'd like to review the preparations for the festival, then go on to do an analysis of the festival itself and how well it went. The plan is then for you to work in teams of three, with one tutor and two students in each team, and for you to discuss the festival in more detail so you can come up with suggestions for the organising committee to consider for next year's festival.

Well, as I said, we're in our fourth year and we've added some new events. The first festival focused mainly on music and the performing arts, as it was felt that those would be the best types of event for both students and the public to take part in. More forms of art, in particular short films and photography, were added over the next two years and this year we have extended our offer to include painting and crafts, with a particular focus on the students here producing their own work, both for exhibition and competition. This was largely successful, but I'll discuss that in detail later. We also invited professional artists in some of the fields to perform, and that will be something for you to review for the next event. What was particularly encouraging this year was that we had contributions to the festival from the highest number of students to date, with representatives from every nationality at the university.

As in previous years, we planned to use the spare university accommodation for all the visitors, both students and non-students, but as we expected a greater attendance at this year's festival, we also arranged accommodation at the city college three miles from here and arranged coach transfers between the college and the university campus. Unfortunately, that proved problematic and we won't repeat those arrangements next year. We also arranged the catering both here and at the city college, and one of the new ideas we tried was to experiment with dishes based on different regional themes over the five days. This allowed our international students … well, the keen cooks among them anyway … to create the menus and work with the catering company to produce breakfast, lunch and dinner.

Of course, one of the main aims of this festival, apart from the obvious ones of extending the university's reputation and giving our students the chance to take part in a wonderful event, was to help develop our young people's organisational skills and give them some experience of real work, mostly as volunteers. Of course, we had to pay for professional organisers to make sure the festival ran well, but as our money was limited and we wanted to give as many opportunities to our students as possible, we made sure that they ran all of the events themselves under the direction of the professionals and, of course, alongside the tutors.

3 🎧 70

Dr Saunders: So, now let me turn to the actual event and how it went. As I said, we had the biggest offer of arts events in the four years we've been running the festival. In total, the number of visitors over the whole five days was 12,500, which is a 10% increase on the previous year and just over three times the number in the first year that we held it. This clearly shows that we're going in the right direction by expanding the variety of events on offer. The short film event at the university cinema was the best attended, with entries from a wide variety of nationalities here at the university on a number of fascinating topics. I think we can all agree that the quality was excellent, as was the standard of the photography exhibition and the paintings in the art gallery. Our feedback from students and visitors was very positive.

However, there are three issues that we should address in our discussions. First, Wayne Rogers, our headline music act, had to call off two days before the event due to illness and we didn't have time to find another act. Needless to say, all those who bought tickets for the main concert were disappointed and we had to return their money. We need to discuss suggestions for avoiding this in the future. Also, while we had some good crafts on display, especially the clothes, pottery, sculptures and glass objects, the exhibition was poorly attended, so we have to decide if it needs to be changed or perhaps reduced in some way. The last issue involves the art gallery and, in particular, security. Although we had attendants on duty all the time, three paintings were stolen, much to the disappointment of the artists who painted them. They were valued at around £3,000 in total, and the artists had expected to be able to sell them in the future, so we need to look into this and think about how we can increase security for next year, while also avoiding any unnecessary inconvenience for our visitors.

Regarding the arrangements for accommodation and catering, generally things went well, but there were some issues with the accommodation in the city college. As there were a lot of late bookings, we had to provide more accommodation than we had originally planned to do, with the result that some people ended up in accommodation of a lower standard than they expected. We apologised to them and gave them back part of their payments, but we need to avoid this issue in the future, especially as the festival is growing and we don't want to harm our reputation. Another issue was that, at certain times of the day, there were not enough volunteers on hand to help visitors, so we'll need to make sure that we organise the availability of volunteers better next time. On the other hand, the transport that we organised was excellent and the catering was highly appreciated, in terms of both variety and quality. So, I'd like you to think of more ideas to extend the catering opportunities for next year.

The last thing I want to focus on now is how much we spent. As I said earlier, we had budgeted for £50,000 to organise the event and expected £50,000 in earnings, but the final balance sheet showed that the event made just over £90,000, so we have some money to go into the budget for next year, which is an excellent result. However, I feel there are still some areas where we could cut our spending and perhaps reduce charges for visitors. Many of the volunteers felt that some of the paid helpers that we brought in to supervise the activities were not really worth the expense. They felt that some of them did very little for what we paid them and others didn't really organise some of the events that well, so I would welcome suggestions on improving organisation while saving money. Also, I feel that another good way of raising funds is to get more business support from local companies, who could help the festival grow by sponsoring events and advertising their products and services more around the festival. Now I'd like to turn to …

4 🎚 71

Dr Reynolds: So, first of all, we need to look at the events and see what should be included in next year's festival and what changes should be made. Dr Saunders mentioned that there were issues with the music and crafts. What are your feelings on those two issues? Do you want to start, Sangita?

Sangita: Well, as regards the music, I think we need to have another artist in reserve in case the main act can't perform, like in this year's festival. It doesn't have to be a well-known band. It could be a small act, like a student band. What do you think, Lawrence?

Lawrence: You have a point, but I'm not really sure if any artists would be happy to perform only if the main act lets us down. In any case, how often does that happen? This was the first time, and I don't see it happening again in the future.

Dr Reynolds: I'm not sure we can take that for granted, Lawrence. If you look at what happened, we lost £3,000 as we had to return money to the audience. I don't think anything bad would have happened, but I think we need to bear in mind that our visitors are the most important aspect of the festival and we have to make sure we keep them happy at all costs.

Lawrence: How about we arrange the programme so that on one night there isn't a famous headline act but a good local band, so that we can change the programme to make them the main act if anyone else isn't able to perform. We could put them on the last evening, and tell them that they may be needed on the other evenings, just in case. That way, we're helping good local talent and making sure that our visitors are happy.

Sangita: Yes, I can see that working. Then we could use the student band to play the last night if we have to switch the local band from the last night to an earlier night.

Dr Reynolds: OK … good ideas. I'll make a note so that we can take it back to the organising committee. Now, let's move on to the question of crafts. As we heard, the event didn't go very well and lacked visitors. What do you think we should do, Sangita?

Sangita: Well, I have a personal interest in this. I've been creating my own fashion designs and I had some clothes on display mixing Western and Indian themes. Actually, I spent some time watching the visitors and I thought they liked the clothes a lot. I think we have to be careful to distinguish the clothes from the other crafts.

Lawrence: Yes, I noticed that. I spent the third day in the craft section helping visitors and I noticed that the clothes exhibition was the most appreciated. I think the glass and ceramic section had hardly any visitors when I was there. Perhaps we should just have the clothes on display, maybe even extend that section?

Dr Reynolds: Yes, that could be a good solution. I don't think we should get rid of the glass and pottery altogether, but I certainly think we should promote the clothes section more.

Lawrence: Well, here's a suggestion: we could even think of turning that into a separate fashion show. What do you think of that?

Sangita: Good idea! I was thinking about that anyway. Can we put that to the committee?

Dr Reynolds: Of course. I've made a note of it. Regarding the theatre and poetry, do you think we need to make any changes?

Lawrence: Nothing major, I don't think, but perhaps we should use at least one day to present new plays and poems by our own students. It's wonderful putting on plays by well-known playwrights and readings of well-known poets, but perhaps we should promote our own talent here in the university. It would certainly help the performing arts students to expand their coursework, and we could have a competition for the best new works.

Dr Reynolds: Excellent idea, Lawrence. What do you think, Sangita?

Sangita: Yes, but let's not limit it to just English. We could also have performances from our international students in their languages. I think that would really help promote the festival as an international event.

Dr Reynolds: Fine. We can propose that as well. And as far as the photography and cinema sections are concerned, they'll keep expanding.

Lawrence: Well, personally, I don't think the quality of the photography exhibition was very high. I think there are issues with digital photography being presented as a printed exhibition. You can never really capture the true meaning of the photograph like that. I would suggest just having digital displays, you know, tablets that visitors can use to see the photographer's collection. That way, it'll encourage photographers to develop their ideas and think about their exhibits almost as films with a story. I think that's the way photography is going these days.

Sangita: I don't agree. I think each image should be appreciated in its own way, as the photographer intends. I don't think we should push photographers into one direction. That said, I think the idea of having tablets and digital screens is a good idea if we can afford it. Perhaps we could have two sections – digital displays and non-digital displays.

Dr Reynolds: Sounds good, Sangita. I can certainly put that to the committee and see if they'll consider it. So, if that's all about the events themselves, I'd like to discuss the organisation of the festival …

5 🎚 72

Dr Reynolds: Now, the next thing I think we should discuss is the accommodation situation. It seems clear that the number of visitors is set to grow, so we need to have a suitable plan in place to deal with the increased numbers. We don't want a repeat of this year. What do you think, Lawrence?

Lawrence: Actually, I saw the accommodation that we used at the city college, and it was pretty basic, though it was clean and tidy. There was only a bed and a desk in each room. Another thing the visitors complained about was the lack of Wi-Fi in the rooms, especially as they'd paid for rooms with Wi-Fi. It certainly wasn't ideal.

Dr Reynolds: Do you have anything to add, Sangita?

Sangita: Yeah … I can understand why they weren't happy. I'd have felt the same in their position.

Dr Reynolds: Well, there's that new holiday development at Elm Park, quite close to the university. Perhaps we could use their rooms. After all, it won't be the holiday high season, so there should be plenty of empty rooms that we could use.

Sangita: That's true. How about taking over some of their rooms and advertising them as accommodation specifically for families with children? They're going to have an outdoor and an indoor adventure area for young people. We had quite a few teenagers this year coming with their parents. If we can attract more by offering them the facilities at the holiday park in a special package, they can go there if they get bored with the festival.

Lawrence: Excellent idea! They'll be around 15 or 16 years old and when they come to the festival, they'll get an idea of what it'd be like to study here. I'm sure it'll help our future prospects as a university.

Dr Reynolds: I agree. I'll be happy to present those ideas to the committee. Moving on to the catering, it seems clear that the idea of theme days with different kinds of national and regional dishes went down very well. I'll recommend repeating it next year, but do you have anything else to say about the catering?

Sangita: Not really … one thing is that maybe we could tell the students about the festival earlier in the year and invite them to suggest themes and also to volunteer their own cooking skills to help with it. I think that'll make sure that we vary what we offer from year to year, so that we don't just repeat the same dishes each time.

Lawrence: But we should always have fish and chips on the menu! We can't do without that! Seriously though, I agree.

Dr Reynolds: OK. I'll make a note of that as well. Moving on to the helpers, you were both directly involved in that. Do you think it was a good idea to get professionals for the organising?

Lawrence: In a word, no. I think the ones that I worked with didn't really know what they were doing. We were paying them a lot to do their work, but I don't think they really took it as seriously as they should have. They were thinking it was just a student event. On more than one occasion, some of the volunteers had to take charge and make sure that the events went smoothly.

Sangita: Yes, you're right. That was my experience as well. We ended up paying them a lot of money for poor service. It was one of the reasons why there were too few volunteers at some events – because the organisation was so poor. I think the idea of bringing back former students is a good idea. At least then we can be more certain that they know about the university and they'll probably be more committed to doing a good job.

Dr Reynolds: I think you're both right. I was disappointed and I think former students will be a great improvement, so I'll note that as well. We need to talk about finance, but before that, I just want to mention the issue of security. Thinking about the stolen paintings, what do you think we should do about that?

Lawrence: I'm not really sure. I mean, we had the university security guards on duty the whole time, so I don't think we can really add to that.

Sangita: Well, I noticed on more than one occasion that there were windows open in some rooms which made it easy for people to climb in and steal things. I think the main thing is to remind students and volunteers that it's their personal responsibility to be careful and look out for any security issues. So if one of us sees an open window, we should either check with security why it's open, or simply close it.

Dr Reynolds: You're right, Sangita. I'm sure the committee is aware of this, but I'll note it just to show that we've given it some thought. Now finance – what are your feelings on Dr Saunders' suggestions about sponsorship?

Lawrence: I don't think that will go down too well with most students. I mean, personally, I'm not against it, but I think students generally won't be very keen to have businesses involved in what they see as their arts festival. I'm sure they'll be happy to take part in more events to raise money throughout the year before the festival, but they won't be happy about big businesses taking over and having their names all over the university.

Sangita: Well, I think it's going to happen anyway. Everything is commercial to some extent these days. I don't think it's a bad idea, as long as it's done in good taste. I think any businesses that do want to sponsor us or advertise should be aware that they need to work closely with us and respect the spirit of the festival.

Lawrence: Perhaps we could involve local businesses as well as national ones that don't just put their name on the festival, but can actually sponsor specific events, award prizes, and so on. So, for example, a local cinema could sponsor the short film event and even send along a representative to judge the films, that sort of thing.

Dr Reynolds: Yes, I see what you mean. In that way, they'll be directly involved in the festival, which will encourage them to take an active part and build up their reputations for supporting the arts. Well, thank you both. We have a lot of useful suggestions to take back to the committee.

6 🎧 73

Dr Reynolds: Hello Dr Saunders. I just want to tell you about the suggestions that Lawrence and Sangita made during our discussion and see what you think.

Dr Saunders: Thanks, yes. Please do.

Dr Reynolds: First of all, regarding the music, they think that it might be a good idea to have a good local band who can replace the main act if it has to let us down at the last minute, which is what happened this year. The band could be scheduled for later in the week on the understanding that they might have to play on an earlier night. We could also have one evening with a student band.

Dr Saunders: Well, it sounds good in theory to plan a rearrangement, but I think it would be too complicated to arrange. We would depend too much on all the bands being able to play on any of the nights. I think it's simpler just to give the audience a refund if it happens again. But I'm happy to have one evening supporting local bands and student bands, as that's the main point of the festival – to encourage people to take part.

Dr Reynolds: The next thing is the crafts. They felt that a fashion show would be a good way of expanding the clothes exhibition, and that perhaps we should reduce or even get rid of the glass and pottery exhibition.

Dr Saunders: Well, first of all, I think that the fashion show is a good idea as it can help the international students to get involved in more activities and develop their ideas with clothes. But I'm not keen to get rid of the glass and pottery exhibitions completely, as it's important for the university to be seen to encourage all forms of art and not just the most popular ones, so we should keep that for the time being.

Dr Reynolds: OK … now … regarding theatre and poetry, they felt that it would be good for students to write and perform their own plays and poetry, as well as those by famous playwrights and poets.

Dr Saunders: That sounds like an excellent idea! It'd help a lot to raise standards in writing and performance. I'd love to see that taking place.

Dr Reynolds: Also on that topic, there was a feeling that works in other languages should be encouraged.

Dr Saunders: Most certainly. That would help the international students feel far more at home and valued as part of the university.

Dr Reynolds: There was one other event we discussed, and that was photography. It was felt that we should have both digital and non-digital exhibits.

Dr Saunders: I don't think we could manage that, at least not yet. High-quality tablets and screens would be too expensive, especially with the number we'd have to buy, so it's not an option for next year because of the high cost.

Dr Reynolds: OK ... as for the accommodation and the catering, they felt that we could use the holiday park that's being built nearby, and we should encourage students to take a greater part in cooking and helping with the catering.

Dr Saunders: Well, first, I know for a fact that the new holiday park is not likely to be completed by festival time next year as they've run into trouble with the building, but we could certainly think about it in the future. I do like the idea of the students having a greater role in the catering and cooking, as it will clearly be helpful for their all-round development.

Dr Reynolds: OK. The next thing is the professional organisers. They felt that the standard was quite low and that the volunteers didn't experience good leadership from them. They think it would be better to ask former students to work as organisers, as they'd be more familiar with the university and more committed, too.

Dr Saunders: I appreciate that, but unfortunately that wouldn't work. It'd be too much trouble trying to find them and get them employed. However, I think we should review the organisers that we used this year and have a much better selection system in place for the next festival.

Dr Reynolds: Now the last two points are about security and finance. As far as security goes, they think we should do more to encourage the students to take it seriously.

Dr Saunders: I agree. If we can encourage students to be more aware of security, not just during the festival, it'd really help to increase trust among all our students because they'll be looking out for each other.

Dr Reynolds: As for finance, they thought that, first, we could encourage students to help raise money throughout the year, and, secondly, we could encourage businesses to sponsor the events and advertise more, though it needs to be handled with care.

Dr Saunders: Well, regarding sponsorship and advertising, the committee is already looking at the possibilities as it will encourage more interest in the activities that we do and also help our reputation generally. Unfortunately, I don't think asking the students to raise more money during the year is a good idea as we already have a programme in place for that, and if the students are involved any more, they'll spend less time on their studies and I don't want anything to disrupt those.

SPEAKING

9 🎵 74

1 I prefer spending time with my family on my birthday rather than spending time with them at New Year.
2 This holiday is much more exciting than that holiday.
3 These ideas might be better for a celebration than those ideas.
4 Some people don't enjoy public holidays as much as other people I know.

13 🎵 75

Examiner: What is the difference between how people celebrate special events today compared with the past?

Student: Well, I think that in the past people would spend a long time preparing food or going shopping for presents, but now people tend to eat out and order their presents online. While this might seem more convenient, perhaps making an effort is part of what makes the festivals so important. I think we're losing that now.

Examiner: Should we learn about the special events of other countries in school?

Student: I certainly think we should find out as much as possible about how people in other countries live. However, I'm not sure we need to introduce all international festivals into our calendar, as people might think less of our own important festivals and culture.

Examiner: What will special events be like in the future?

Student: I think as people are getting busier, fewer events will continue to be celebrated, as people just don't have the time to celebrate all of them. On the other hand, we might also see an increase in online-only events, where family members don't travel to their parents' house but instead wish them Happy New Year or something over webchat software. That way, although people might live far away from each other, they can still celebrate over video chat.

Examiner: Do we spend too much money on special events like Valentine's Day or birthdays?

Student: I'm not so sure about that. I think we've always spent lots of money on those things, although obviously some people do like to spend more than others. Anyway, I don't think it's the money, but the thought that counts.

Shaftesbury Road, Cambridge CB2 8EA, United Kingdom

One Liberty Plaza, 20th Floor, New York, NY 10006, USA

477 Williamstown Road, Port Melbourne, VIC 3207, Australia

314–321, 3rd Floor, Plot 3, Splendor Forum, Jasola District Centre, New Delhi – 110025, India

103 Penang Road, #05–06/07, Visioncrest Commercial, Singapore 238467

Cambridge University Press & Assessment is a department of the University of Cambridge.

We share the University's mission to contribute to society through the pursuit of education, learning and research at the highest international levels of excellence.

www.cambridge.org
Information on this title: www.cambridge.org/9781009280303

First published 2023

20 19 18 17 16 15 14 13 12 11 10 9 8 7 6 5 4 3 2 1

Printed in Malaysia by Vivar Printing

A catalogue record for this publication is available from the British Library

ISBN   978-1-009-28030-3   Student's Book with answers

Additional resources for this publication at www.cambridge.org/mindset

The authors and publishers would like to thank the following people for their work on this level of the Student's Book.

Jane Coates, Edward Street, Helen Forrest and Jock Graham for their editing, project management and proof reading.

Design by Blooberry Design.

Audio produced by Leon Chambers at The Soundhouse Studios, London.

The publishers would like to thank the following people for their input and work on the digital materials that accompany this level.

Dr Peter Crosthwaite; Jeremy Day; Natasha de Souza; Amanda French; Hemalini Guttery; Rod Guttery; Marc Loewenthal; Rebecca Marsden; Kate O'Toole; Emina Tuzovic; Andrew Reid; N.M.White.

Cover and text design concept: Juice Creative Ltd

Typesetting: Blooberry Design

Cover illustration: MaryliaDesign/iStock/Getty Images Plus

Acknowledgements

The authors and publishers acknowledge the following sources of copyright material and are grateful for the permissions granted. While every effort has been made, it has not always been possible to identify the sources of all the material used, or to trace all copyright holders. If any omissions are brought to our notice, we will be happy to include the appropriate acknowledgements on reprinting and in the next update to the digital edition, as applicable.

Key: U = Unit.

Photography

All the photos are sourced from Getty Images.

U1: malc54/iStock/Getty Images Plus; Dinodia Photo/The Image Bank Unreleased; Presley Ann/Patrick McMullan; Dmytro Kochetov/500px; vladimir zakharov/Moment; H. Armstrong Roberts/ClassicStock/ Archive Photos; Fond, Magnus/Johner Images; Photo-Biotic/ Photolibrary; **U2:** Caia Image/Collection Mix: Subjects; Focus On Sport/Focus on Sport; BRIAN BAHR/AFP; Clive Brunskill/Getty Images Sport; George Frey/Getty Images Sport; Richard Hartog/ Los Angeles Times; Jonathan Leibson/Getty Images Entertainment; Stock Montage/Archive Photos; AFP; Dimitri Otis/DigitalVision; Ian Horrocks/Getty Images Sport; Henn Photography/Cultura/Getty Images; Deklofenak/iStock/Getty Images Plus; Thomas Barwick/ DigitalVision; lisafx/iStock/Getty Images Plus; Fang Zhou/Cultura/ Getty Images; DragonImages/iStock/Getty Images Plus; Rubberball/ Mike Kemp/Brand X Pictures; Redchopsticks; ADRIAN DENNIS/ AFP; Julian Finney/Getty Images Sport; Pacific Press/LightRocket; WILLIAM WEST/AFP; KIRILL KUDRYAVTSEV/AFP; **U3:** franckreporter/ iStock/Getty Images Plus; svetikd/E+; 10'000 Hours/Stone; UpperCut Images; forplayday/iStock/Getty Images Plus; mediaphotos; Anadolu Agency; Bernard Bialorucki/iStock/Getty Images Plus; **U4:** Christopher Chan/Moment; Bim/E+; ivanfolio/iStock Editorial; Wolfgang Kaehler/LightRocket; prescott09/iStock/Getty Images Plus; studiocasper/iStock/Getty Images Plus; naveen0301/iStock/Getty Images Plus; BJI/Lane Oatey/blue jean images; Joshua Dalsimer/ The Image Bank; EpicStockMedia/iStock/Getty Images Plus; holgs/ iStock Unreleased; **U5:** sciepro/science photo library/Science Photo Library; Bettmann; Underwood Archives/Archive Photos; Ron Galella, Ltd./Ron Galella Collection; Justin Sullivan/Getty Images News; BOB PEARSON/AFP; Luca Teuchmann/WireImage; View Stock; Tim Boyle/Getty Images News; Mint Images/Mint Images RF; Grant Faint/ The Image Bank Unreleased; Oli Scarff/Getty Images News; Tara Moore/Stone; Bloomberg; TommasoT/E+; Hinterhaus Productions/ DigitalVision; Dan Comaniciu/iStock/Getty Images Plus; kali9/ E+; Solskin/DigitalVision; BLOOM image/BLOOMimage; Satawat Khumsongsee/EyeEm; Echo/Cultura; Monty Rakusen/Image Source; Si Leong/EyeEm; VCG/Visual China Group; Joe Raedle/Getty Images News; VCG/Getty Images News; Wavebreakmedia Ltd/Wavebreak Media; Recebin/iStock/Getty Images Plus; William H. Edwards/ Stockbyte; **U6:** Imagevixen/RooM; Monty Rakusen/Image Source; kokoroimages.com; Ed Freeman/Stone; PUNIT PARANJPE/AFP; **U7:** John Greim/LightRocket; SEAN GLADWELL/Moment; The Washington Post; Elyse Lewin/Photographer's Choice; Jose Luis Pelaez Inc/ DigitalVision; mammamaart/E+; Image Source; Caiaimage/Chris Ryan/iStock/Getty Images Plus; Peter Muller/Cultura; Caia Image/ Collection Mix: Subjects; michaeljung; Jonathan Kirn/The Image Bank; urbancow/E+; Vince Talotta/Toronto Star; **U8:** DANNY HU/ Moment; David Ramos/Getty Images News; Merrill Images/The Image Bank Unreleased; LeonU/iStock Unreleased; VCG/Visual China Group; Frans Jo - Imageenation/Moment; Lane Oatey/blue jean images; Izzet Keribar/The Image Bank Unreleased; Eriko Koga/Taxi Japan; Agung Parameswara/Getty Images Entertainment; Rene Johnston/Toronto Star; Simone Joyner/Getty Images Entertainment; Awakening/Getty Images News; NurPhoto; VladyslavDanilin/iStock/Getty Images Plus; Matt Cardy/The Image Bank Unreleased; John Bashian/Getty Images News.

Illustration

Ana Djordjevic (Astound us) pp53, 57, 63, 66, 84; Sam Parij (Eye Candy Illustration) pp21, 24, 39, 40, 74, 76, 78, 116, 131, 133, 170.